HEALTHY SIN FOODS

HEALTHY SIN FOODS

DECADENCE
WITHOUT THE
GUILT

DR. JOEY SHULMAN,
DC, NUTRITIONIST

VIKING
CANADA

VIKING CANADA

Published by the Penguin Group

Penguin Group (Canada), 90 Eglinton Avenue East, Suite 700, Toronto, Ontario, Canada
M4P 2Y3 (a division of Pearson Canada Inc.)

Penguin Group (USA) Inc., 375 Hudson Street, New York, New York 10014, U.S.A.
Penguin Books Ltd, 80 Strand, London WC2R 0RL, England
Penguin Ireland, 25 St Stephen's Green, Dublin 2, Ireland (a division of Penguin Books Ltd)
Penguin Group (Australia), 250 Camberwell Road, Camberwell, Victoria 3124, Australia
(a division of Pearson Australia Group Pty Ltd)
Penguin Books India Pvt Ltd, 11 Community Centre, Panchsheel Park, New Delhi – 110 017, India
Penguin Group (NZ), 67 Apollo Drive, Rosedale, North Shore 0745, Auckland, New Zealand
(a division of Pearson New Zealand Ltd)
Penguin Books (South Africa) (Pty) Ltd, 24 Sturdee Avenue, Rosebank,
Johannesburg 2196, South Africa

Penguin Books Ltd, Registered Offices: 80 Strand, London WC2R 0RL, England

First published 2009

1 2 3 4 5 6 7 8 9 10

Copyright © Dr. Joey Shulman, 2009

Back-cover photos depict recipes on p. 239 (salmon spa cakes),
p. 247 (gourmet egg bake), and p. 367 (frozen lemon berry torte).

Manufactured in the U.S.A.

LIBRARY AND ARCHIVES CANADA CATALOGUING IN PUBLICATION

Shulman, Joey
Healthy sin foods : decadence without the guilt / Joey Shulman.

Includes index.
ISBN 978-0-670-06926-2

1. Nutrition.   2. Cookery.   I. Title.

RM222.2.S489 2009   613.2   C2009-902353-9

Visit the Penguin Group (Canada) website at **www.penguin.ca**

Special and corporate bulk purchase rates available; please see **www.penguin.ca/corporatesales**
or call 1-800-810-3104, ext. 477 or 474

This book is dedicated to my two boys, Randy and Jonah, and to our new beautiful addition—Faith Ella. She's here ... she's finally here!

contents

101 *healthy sin foods* recipes

introduction

When you hear the term *healthy sin foods*, you likely think, "Healthy sin foods ... are they really possible? How can foods that taste so delectable and rich still be good for you?" As you'll soon discover, they can be. There are a variety of foods and recipes that are nutritious, delicious, and can even help you lose weight at the same time. In fact, *Healthy Sin Foods* offers mouth-watering and tasty options ... without the guilt!

Unfortunately, when the term *health food* is mentioned, most people still visualize tasteless, boiled, steamed, or dull food options. However, the notion that a nutritious diet is without appetizing taste, texture, natural sweetness (depending on the dish), and flavour is completely false. From pasta dishes to lower-fat and -calorie desserts, any recipe can be tweaked into a healthier version. Most of the food options and recipes you'll find in *Healthy Sin Foods* are lower in calories and sodium, higher in fibre, free of trans fat, and loaded with antioxidants, vitamins, and minerals.

Identifying the new weight-loss trends

After writing several books and articles on topics ranging from pediatric nutrition to hormonal weight loss, I've gained a much deeper understanding of what's on the minds of North Americans when it comes to health care and disease prevention. Over the years, I've received countless emails from readers detailing their positive health transformations. I've also been privy to the needs and wants that both clients and

1

health care practitioners determine as unfulfilled by the weight-loss industry. By listening to clients and experts alike, I've identified two general trends.

1. People are frustrated with the ups and downs of weight loss and feel overwhelmed by choices. While two-thirds of North Americans need to lose weight, they no longer believe or want the "quick fix" magic bullet approach. In fact, the majority who have been on the physical and emotional weight-loss roller coaster are seeking permanent—not temporary—change. The general trend is toward wellness and a balanced lifestyle that promotes permanent change for health and disease prevention.

2. Nobody (and I mean nobody!) wants to give up their favourite foods completely. People are fed up with using deprivation to lose weight, whether it be eliminating all carbs or drinking only protein shakes. Most have also come to the conclusion that these temporary, overly restrictive approaches do not create long-lasting behavioural changes. You need an approach that allows for life events (special occasions such as seasonal holidays, birthdays, weddings, even the Super Bowl) while maintaining positive health changes. Instead of undergoing constant deprivation, you need to be able to "cheat" within reason and then get back on the health wagon. If you feel that you're in a constant state of food denial, you'll eventually succumb to your old eating behaviours. Willpower gradually wanes and a "Forget this bland eating—life is too short!" attitude kicks in. Then you're at risk of breaking your diet or having a full-on food binge that is emotionally and physically based. I've observed clients gain back 10 pounds in a week!

To address these trends, I knew *Healthy Sin Foods* would have to provide an easy-to-follow program with delicious recipes. The goal was to share with you all the need-to-know information on nutrition that can positively affect your health, energy, mood, and weight without boring you with all the biochemistry of nutrition. Given today's hectic pace—whether you're a working mother of three or a CEO of a corporation—I've presented this essential nutritional information in a clear, easily accessible, and quick-reading format. Consider this book your nutritional guide for life. If you do fall off the health wagon during a business trip or at a wedding or birthday celebration, for example, *Healthy Sin Foods* will help you get back on that wagon fast. You'll be able to easily understand how to use foods to regulate your hormones, which will help to balance cravings; control blood sugar, mood, and body weight; and boost energy. I've outlined foods that help prevent disease and foods that cleanse the system, along with a detailed list of the top 50 superfoods for health and weight loss that are must-haves in your dietary rotation.

Healthy Sin Foods also provides delicious, healthy, and easy-to-make recipes, including versions of some of your old favourites—once considered "no-no" foods. From healthier cookies and chicken wings to über-nutritious salads, shakes, chicken, fish, and pasta, these dishes will put the simple and the satisfying back into your food repertoire so that you'll never feel deprived. As a result, you'll no longer be prone to bingeing, and as your relationship to food shifts, you'll be better able to enact long-lasting behavioural changes.

curing "excusitis"

How each of us looks after our health is extremely personal, and dietary approaches are no exception. I know from my clinical experience that until someone is ready to change, behavioural modifications won't last. You can't force a smoker to quit smoking, nor can you force someone with high blood pressure or excess weight to eat healthier. It must come from an inner desire to take charge.

I often find that when I recommend a healthier approach, people come up with a plethora of excuses for why it will be too difficult for them—a syndrome I like to think of as "excusitis." Some say they feel nervous about changing their diet or that they doubt they'll have the strength to give up their old favourites. Others feel they don't have the time, energy, or money.

In my clinical practice, I meet with hundreds of clients each year, and I feel fortunate to hear the stories of such a variety of people. When I first met with Stacy (one of my dearest clients, who has lost all her excess weight, kept it off, and brought her cholesterol levels down to normal range), she said, "I hope you're not telling me to give up my latte with chocolate sprinkles, because I'm not going to do it!" I hadn't even opened my mouth to speak and already she was dishing out a reason why she couldn't succeed. As it turns out, Stacy did me a favour. By defining her nutritional boundaries from the get-go, she and I were able to work around them to build a healthy eating plan. Soon after, she was able to boost her energy and lose more than 30 pounds.

Some of the most common excuses I hear in practice are

- I don't have enough time.
- I don't have enough money.
- I don't know how to cook.
- Healthy eating isn't really my thing.
- I don't like bland food.
- I've tried everything before!
- I'm extremely picky.
- I have uncontrollable cravings.
- I'm an emotional eater.

Do any of these sound familiar? These excuses are merely roadblocks preventing you from becoming the healthiest you yet. Healthy eating doesn't have to be tasteless, more expensive, more time-consuming, or overly difficult ... you simply need to know how to begin. Furthermore, if you do struggle with your weight or experience extreme food cravings, the *Healthy Sin Foods* method of eating and recipes will help you become free of cravings and shed excess weight.

my personal weight-loss journey

Although I've been a nutritional clinician, writer, and speaker for almost a decade, I've also experienced my own struggles with nutrition and weight loss. While pregnant with my first child, I fell off the health wagon for many months and gained 70 pounds! How did this happen? Just like it happens to everyone else—my portion size was off, I didn't exercise regularly, and my cravings for sugar were totally out of whack, which caused the weight to pack on unnecessarily. I was consuming way too many high glycemic index foods and had irregular meal patterns. In a nutshell, I started to oversecrete the fat storage hormone called insulin (explained in greater detail in Chapter 2) and gained a lot more weight than I should have. Uncomfortable, self-conscious, and lethargic, I simply did not feel like "me" anymore. I knew I had to turn this state around immediately.

Having never been overweight in my life and always a healthy eater, I look back at this time and am actually grateful for the experience. Why? Simply put, the lack of energy, mood changes, and aches and pains I felt from eating all the wrong foods were astounding. It affected virtually every area of my life. With a book tour around the corner that included a lot of television appearances, I knew I had to lose the weight in a quick and sensible manner (no pressure!). I also knew that depriving myself by eating only bland vegetables, tasteless cubed tofu, and egg whites wouldn't work for me. Instead, I implemented hormonal nutritional strategies to keep myself healthy, fit, strong, lean, and energized. All these key nutritional strategies are outlined for you in the next section, Back to the Basics, as well as the big-three macronutrients—low glycemic index carbohydrates, lean proteins, and essential fats. Remember, people who know better tend to do better, and health and nutrition are no exception.

On my weight-loss journey, in addition to following hormonally balanced, nutritional strategies, my husband and I began to create unique and easy-to-make recipes that are low in fat, sodium, and calories but big on taste. Our goal was twofold:

1. to create recipes loaded with fibre, antioxidants, lean protein, vitamins, minerals, and essential fats
2. to ensure that the recipes were so incredibly delicious and decadent that you'd want to create them over and over again—for your family, yourself, or your next dinner party. The dishes are so delectable that they do taste sinful!

taking charge of your health, your body, your corporation

You are the CEO of your future health, vitality, and vigour, and it's up to you to take charge of your own personal healthy corporation. We all come equipped with different genetic wiring, but the food choices we make, our activity level, and our methods of handling stress have major impacts on the prevention (or onset) of a variety of ailments. After learning all the strategies in *Healthy Sin Foods*—from information and recipes to shopping lists and more—it's up to you to make the difference. I already have great confidence in you. The very fact that you're reading this passage means you're motivated to learn about health, wellness, nutrition, and making a positive change.

Nutritional pioneer Adele David once said, "We are indeed much more than we eat, but what we eat can help us to become much more than who we are." I could not agree more. Of course you are much more than the sandwich you had for lunch or the high glycemic index muffin you grabbed for a snack, but the food choices you make will influence your mood, body, and energy. I'm always in awe of the transformations I'm lucky enough to witness when clients take charge of their health. They walk a little taller, smile a little wider, and have extra pep in their step. It's as if they take off a heavily weighted mask and their real self emerges.

I applaud you for taking charge, being informed, and enjoying decadent, healthy sin foods … guilt-free! Wishing you the best health,

Dr. Joey Shulman, DC, Registered Nutritionist

need-to-know nutrition

one
back to the basics

Okinawa, a small village in the southernmost part of Japan, stands as one of the most ideal models of health and longevity in the world. In addition to having the longest-living people on the planet, Okinawa boasts some of the lowest rates of coronary heart disease and breast, colon, and prostate cancer. Of a population of 1 million, there are 900 centenarians (people aged 100 or older) enjoying active living and a disease-free state. This percentage is more than four times higher than the population of the United Kingdom and the United States. In Okinawa, it is not unusual for men and women in their nineties and beyond to be tending their gardens, making a homemade meal, or going for a long walk.

Okinawans believe in the principle of *nusci gushci*, which means "food should nourish life … this is the best medicine." Unfortunately, somewhere along the way North Americans lost touch with this sentiment and the true essence of health. The good news is, with the current surge in natural health care and integrative medicine, the importance of diet, exercise, and lifestyle is now being discussed in doctors' offices across North America. Today, we are seeing more money than ever before being poured into double-blind research studies dedicated to integrative health care and the role it plays in prevention of disease and extension of lifespan. From understanding the effects of omega-3 essential fats on brain function to recognizing the antioxidant and disease-preventing effects of fruits and vegetables, we've certainly come a long way.

And yet, when we consider the top "killers" of the twenty-first century—including heart disease, high cholesterol, type 2 diabetes, and even cancer—many are intimately linked with the way we eat and live. In other words, while information on how to keep ourselves healthy is readily available, the "implementation factor" hasn't yet been perfected. One of my main goals in writing *Healthy Sin Foods* is to put a little Okinawan lifestyle into the North American way. If you combine the fresh, tasty, easy-to-make recipes with all the need-to-know nutritional information and the top 50 must-have superfoods, you'll live a healthier, more vibrant life.

an ounce of prevention ...

Everyone is born with his or her own genetic map. Most view their genetic map, or family health history, as a predictor of what their future health will hold. If your dad suffered from heart disease, you may think that that's your health destiny as well. In fact, research has determined that a certain degree of genetics can be quite malleable. While your genetic map can play a role in your future health, it's not necessarily the absolute predictor of what lies ahead. The level of your health and wellness can be influenced by several nutritional, environmental, and lifestyle factors. Of course, there are certain unexplainable and heart-wrenching situations that take our breath away, such as when a young child is diagnosed with a tumour or an apparently healthy, fit 20-year-old is diagnosed with terminal cancer. While these cases are beyond sad and make us question why, they thankfully make up a much smaller part of our health care system. For the most part, lifestyle changes can be made and risk factors can be reduced dramatically.

In 2004, Harvard researchers investigated the risk factors that increase the chances of developing cancer. (A variety of cancers were studied, such as breast, ovarian, skin, stomach, pancreatic, uterine, prostate, and colon cancer.) What they determined was truly fascinating. More than one-third of the 7 million cancer deaths worldwide were linked to nine "modifiable risk factors":

1. tobacco use (smoking was by far the biggest risk to mortality at 21 percent)
2. excess alcohol intake (5 percent of all deaths)
3. low fruit and vegetable intake (5 percent of all deaths)
4. physical inactivity
5. overweight/obesity
6. unsafe sex

7. urban air pollution
8. indoor smoke from household fuels
9. contaminated injections in health care settings

This study's main goal was to focus on prevention and recommend activities that could reduce cancer risk from an early age. As you can see, simply not smoking, limiting alcohol, maintaining a healthy body weight, eating fruits and vegetables, and working out significantly reduces the risk of cancer. So why are cancer rates still at an all-time high? While we may be making new advances daily in detection and treatment processes, the root of prevention through lifestyle needs far greater emphasis, research, and follow-through.

According to the U.S. Centers for Disease Control and Prevention, the leading killers for men and women in North America (unintentional injuries aside) can all be linked to significant modifiable risk factors. Keep in mind that this is good news. Why? Because, just like the Harvard cancer study, there are considerable steps we can all take to prolong our healthy lives.

heart disease

Heart disease is the leading killer of men and women. Men typically develop heart disease 10 to 15 years prior to women. In fact, as much as one-fourth of all heart disease deaths in men occur between the ages of 35 and 65. In women, the condition is responsible for approximately 29 percent of deaths. To reduce the risk of heart disease dramatically, exercise, eat colourful fruits and vegetables, practise stress management, maintain a healthy body weight, and don't smoke. Certain supplements such as omega-3 distilled fish oils and coenzyme Q10 can also be very beneficial for blood flow and the heart muscle.

> Omega-3 fatty acids, a type of polyunsaturated fat, may decrease your risk of heart attack, protect against irregular heartbeat, and lower blood pressure.

cancer

While breast cancer is the most common cancer in women, lung cancer is the leading cause of death for men and women (90 percent caused by cigarette smoking). Prostate cancer and colorectal cancer are the second and third leading causes of death in men. Similar to heart disease, preventable measures include maintaining a healthy body weight, eating high-fibre foods and colourful fruits and vegetables, avoiding cigarette smoke and other carcinogenic substances, and exercising 30 minutes a day. Consuming high-antioxidant foods (see Top 50 Superfoods) and opting for certified organic food choices are also good preventable steps to take.

A study published in the *New England Journal of Medicine* found an increased risk of all types of cancer (to varying degrees) in those with excess weight and a body mass index above the healthy range (>25).

stroke

Strokes affect men and women equally, yet men have a better chance of surviving a stroke than women. To prevent the onset of a stroke, eliminate saturated fats and trans fatty acids from your diet (see Chapter 4). In addition, supplement your diet with foods rich in omega-3 fats (fortified foods, oily fish, fish oils, nuts, and seeds) and fruits and vegetables, and manage stress, maintain a healthy body weight, and exercise regularly.

leading causes of death for men (2003)

RANK	CAUSE	PERCENTAGE OF MALE DEATHS
1	Heart disease	28.0
2	Cancer	24.0
3	Unintentional injuries	5.9
4	Stroke	5.1

leading causes of death for men (2003) *(continued)*

5	Chronic obstructive pulmonary disease (COPD)	5.1
6	Diabetes	2.9
7	Influenza and pneumonia	2.4
8	Suicide	2.1
9	Kidney disease	1.7
10	Alzheimer's disease	1.5

Source: U.S. Centers for Disease Control and Prevention

leading causes of death for women (2004)

RANK	CAUSE	PERCENTAGE OF FEMALE DEATHS
1	Heart disease	27.2
2	Cancer	22.0
3	Stroke	7.5
4	Chronic lower respiratory diseases	5.2
5	Alzheimer's disease	3.9
6	Unintentional injuries	3.3
7	Diabetes	3.1
8	Influenza and pneumonia	2.7
9	Kidney disease	1.8
10	Septicemia	1.5

Source: U.S. Centers for Disease Control and Prevention

body talk: the seven principles of health

By reviewing the disease processes and the preventable steps that can be taken, it is clear that our bodies respond positively once we've implemented the right approach. Keep in mind that at all times your body is trying to be perfectly healthy by using its innate self-healing and self-regulating ability, called homeostatic balance. For example, the body knows precisely what temperature to maintain to preserve life, how to fight off the countless micro-organisms we face every day such as bacteria, viruses, and allergens, and how to eliminate a toxic substance that may enter the body through a food source (e.g., food poisoning). It is only when we "get in the way of ourselves" with faulty nutritional choices, stress, lack of activity, and smoking that we weaken immune system function and allow symptoms and even disease to proliferate.

In order to stay healthy, it is prudent to be aware of the seven principles that help the body thrive. By simply knowing these principles and allowing them to become part of your daily habits, you will change your life and health dramatically.

1. your body has a voice ... listen to it!

While your body cannot literally say to you, "Hey ... cut that out! I don't want to eat any more packaged or processed foods!" it does communicate with you quite effectively in another manner: symptoms. When you have knocked yourself off balance due to a variety of circumstances, your body's first response will be to send you a red flag, an indication that it's working to take care of the problem. Symptoms can be as small and simple as a runny nose, a headache, or some reflux after a meal.

If you tend to ignore your symptoms or quiet them with medication (e.g., take an antacid to dull the reflux pain or an anti-inflammatory for your inflamed shoulder), your body over time will typically send you another symptom. This isn't to say there isn't a time and a place for medication; indeed, there is. However, if you don't take care of the underlying problem and continue with the abusive behaviour—be it smoking, eating poorly, or high stress—the symptoms will get louder and more serious, such as heart palpitations, dizziness, or extreme abdominal discomfort. After a period of time, the body will desperately try to maintain balance and restore functions that may have damaging effects (e.g., high blood pressure, high cholesterol, or an inflamed colon). It does not matter if you are young or old, pre- or post-menopausal: You need to put the body back into a state of balance—hormonally, calorie-wise, and lifestyle-wise. The information in *Healthy Sin Foods* will help you to do exactly that.

2. your body thrives on routine.

Your body responds beautifully to a routine—whether it's sleep, nutrition, exercise, or stress management. I often see the struggles of clients who work shifts (e.g., nurses) and have irregular sleeping patterns. Symptoms such as fatigue, irritability, headaches, and excess weight gain are common. Because of the back-and-forth change in schedule, the body is never allowed to settle into a flow and starts sending out red flags in the form of symptoms. If you are in this situation (and of course cannot change your work schedule), it is important to "stay sharp" in other areas such as eating fresh live foods, avoiding all refined flours and sugars, working out regularly, supplementing your diet with high-quality multivitamins, and drinking plenty of fresh clean water and high-antioxidant tea (green or white tea). These steps will help to keep your immune system strong even under the stress of an ever-changing sleep pattern.

A nutrition routine is equally important. Skipping meals (e.g., breakfast) or eating erratically will promote excess weight gain and a decrease in insulin sensitivity (see Chapter 2). When excess insulin is secreted, excess fat will be stored, especially around the abdominal region. Simple routine steps such as eating three meals and two snacks a day, stopping eating by 7 p.m. (or a minimum of three hours prior to going to sleep), and slowing down while you eat can change health and weight in a very short time.

> You need a healthy sleep routine to lose weight! Several research studies show that individuals who were sleep deprived had an increase in the hunger hormone ghrelin. In addition to having difficulty losing weight, sleep-deprived individuals experienced more cravings and greater degrees of hunger throughout the day.

3. your body responds to nutrient-dense foods quickly.

I always say you need to "eat live to feel live." Consider how you feel when you eat a meal of refined flours, sugars, and high-fat dairy products. If you order in a pepperoni pizza, have a large pop, and perhaps a doughnut or cookie a little while later, do you feel like jumping off the couch and going to the gym for a terrific workout? Of course not! You're probably lying on the couch, surfing channels, and nodding off because of the food fog you've just put yourself in.

On the flipside, if you did have a meal of nutrient-dense foods such as vegetables, fruits, fish, poultry, high-quality dairy products, eggs, nuts, seeds, and/or whole grains, your energy would not dip at all. You'd still have your "get up and go" to continue on with your day as a full participant (not a sleepy couch potato). While it is expected that you may eat yourself into a food fog once in a blue moon (seasonal holidays, your birthday, weddings), I encourage you to watch and monitor your energy fluctuations in relation to the food you're consuming. While it is normal after a long day to feel tired and plop into bed for a restful and restorative sleep, it is not normal or healthy to continually experience energy fluctuations, intense hunger, and sugar cravings throughout your day. If you do, this is another symptom you can treat by introducing nutrient-dense choices into your diet.

> If you experience the "3 p.m. slump," take a moment to examine the last thing you ate. Was it a sugary or starchy processed muffin, cookie, or white flour item? If so, chances are your energy has taken a dive due to hypoglycemia (low blood sugar) because of what you've eaten.

4. one of your body's key systems is the digestive system.

The body is made up of several systems, such as cardiovascular, lymphatic, respiratory, nervous, and so on. While all the systems are equally important and overlap to be "one orchestra of health," one of the master systems is the digestive system. The digestive system begins with the mouth (chewing) and ends with elimination (you must do so daily!). When this system is compromised due to stress, inflammation, faulty food choices, and/or lack of water, the body is in a dire situation and cannot perform to its top ability. In other words, the body cannot break down and absorb all the nutrients and eliminate all waste required for health on a daily basis. Common symptoms that indicate a compromised digestive system include:

- constipation
- diarrhea
- bloating
- belching and excessive gas

- dark circles under the eyes (often referred to as allergic shiners)
- skin breakouts (e.g., eczema or acne)
- fatigue
- inability to lose weight

More serious conditions include:

- a bowel blockage
- diverticulosis: a condition marked by small sacs or pouches (diverticula) in the walls of an organ such as the stomach or colon
- irritable bowel syndrome
- inflammatory bowel disease (e.g., colitis or Crohn's)

A healthy digestive system will eliminate a minimum of once a day without strain. Without getting too detailed, an ideal bowel movement should be S- or C-shaped (reflecting the shape of your sigmoid colon) and should float.

If your digestive system is not responding properly and you do experience some of these symptoms, the following simple tips may help:

- Be sure to include both insoluble and soluble fibre in your diet (many foods contain both). *Insoluble fibre* promotes regular bowel movement, prevents constipation, and reduces toxic waste from building up in the intestinal tract. Examples include dark leafy greens (such as spinach), fruit skins, whole grain products, tomatoes, nuts, and seeds. *Soluble fibre* will partially dissolve in water and is different from insoluble fibre. It helps to reduce cholesterol and slows entry of sugars into the bloodstream (ideal for diabetics). Soluble fibre sources include strawberries, blueberries, oranges, apples, sweet potatoes, oatmeal, and quinoa. Ground flaxseed contains a combination of both soluble and insoluble fibre and promotes regularity. One tablespoon (15 mL) a day is recommended.
- Ensure you are well hydrated. Drink a minimum of 8 cups (2 L) of water a day to flush the system properly. Watch beverages that cause water loss, such as coffee, tea, and sugary juice or pop. Include mint tea and/or warm water with lemon into your daily routine as they both help to soothe the bowel and promote elimination.

- Exercise often. Cardiovascular exercise will help to stimulate daily elimination.
- Supplement with fish oils and probiotics (the friendly bacteria) daily. A high-quality fish oil supplement is anti-inflammatory and will help to soften the stool naturally. Mixed-strain probiotics will help to normalize a healthy digestive microflora that is critical to healthy elimination and absorption of nutrients.
- Add chlorophyll to your daily water intake. Chlorophyll is the substance responsible for the green colour in plants and may be useful for a number of bowel disorders. In a preliminary trial, chlorophyll supplementation eased chronic constipation in elderly people. Chlorophyll can be found in most health food stores and is available in mint flavour.

If your condition does not improve, or if you are experiencing an intense flare-up, speak to your primary health care practitioner.

5. your body prefers an alkaline environment to an acidic one.

An alkaline environment is believed to be one of the major deterrents to tissue damage, aging, and the growth of disease organisms. Virtually all degenerative diseases— including cancer, heart disease, arthritis, osteoporosis, kidney and gall stones, and tooth decay—are associated with excess acidity in the body. To measure if your body is alkaline or acidic, a scale called the potential of hydrogen, or pH, is used. A pH test involves dipping pH paper into a sample of your saliva or urine to determine your body's pH. If the pH paper turns bluish-green, your pH is more basic and ideal for health and digestion. If it turns greenish-yellow, your pH is more acidic and is not ideal for health. A healthy salivary pH would be anywhere from 6.75 to 7.2, whereas a healthy urine pH would have a slightly higher pH of 7.5. On average, the pH of the typical Western diet is about 5.5 to 6.0. This may not seem too much lower; however, it is important to remember that the pH scale is logarithmic, which means each step is 10 times the previous (e.g., 4.5 is 10 times more acidic than 5.5, which is 100 times more acidic than 6.5, and so on).

When testing your pH, for accuracy's sake, it is recommended that you test two to three times a day to get the average reading. If testing with saliva, it is best not to eat one to two hours prior to testing. Rinse your mouth out by swallowing a few times (not with water, with your own saliva).

If your pH does indicate a strong acidic reading, it is possible to shift this to an alkaline state with diet. All foods consumed possess a pH rating of extremely acidic, mildly acidic, extremely alkaline, or mildly alkaline. Foods that are "strongly" acidic are red meats, cheeses, fish, and eggs. This is not to say all fish and eggs must be removed from the diet, as they provide wonderful lean protein, essential fats, and so on. However, to maintain a proper pH balance, the diet should be composed of approximately 70 percent alkaline-forming foods and 30 percent acid-forming foods.

alkaline foods

VEGETABLES

Artichokes	Courgette	Lettuce
Asparagus	Cucumber	Onion
Beetroot	Garlic	Peas
Broccoli	Grasses (wheat, straw,	Radish
Brussels sprouts	barley, dog, kamut,	Red cabbage
Cabbage	etc.)	Spinach
Carrot	Green beans	Swede
Cauliflower	Kale	Turnip
Celery	Lamb's lettuce	Watercress
Chives	Leeks	

FATS & OILS

Avocado	Hemp	Olive
Borage	Oil blends (such as	
Evening primrose	Udo's Choice)	
Flax		

FRUITS

Avocado	Lime	Tomato
Grapefruit	Rhubarb	Watermelon (is neutral)
Lemon		

DRINKS

Almond milk	Lemon water (pure water +	Pure water (distilled,
Fresh vegetable juice	fresh lemon or lime)	reverse osmosis, ionized)
"Green drinks"	Non-sweetened soy milk	Vegetable broth
Herbal tea		

alkaline foods *(continued)*

SEEDS, NUTS, & GRAINS

Almonds	Flax	Spelt
Any sprouted seed	Lentils	Sunflower
Buckwheat groats	Pumpkin	
Cumin seeds	Sesame	

OTHERS

Aminos (soy sauce alternative)	Hummus	Tahini
Bragg Liquid	Sprouts (soy, alfalfa, mung bean, wheat, little radish, chickpea, broccoli, etc.)	

acid foods

MEATS

Beef	Other seafood (apart from occasional oily fish such as salmon)	Pork
Chicken		Turkey
Crustaceans		
Lamb		

OTHERS

Artificial sweeteners	Honey	White bread
Biscuits	Soy sauce	White pasta
Condiments (tomato sauce, mayonnaise, etc.)	Tamari	Whole meal bread
	Vinegar	

CONVENIENCE FOODS

Chocolate	Microwaveable meals	Tinned foods
Fast food	Powdered soups	
Instant meals	Sweets	

FRUITS

All fruits except for those listed in the alkaline column

DAIRY PRODUCTS

Cheese	Eggs	Milk
Cream	Ice cream	Yogurt

acid foods *(continued)*		
DRINKS		
Beer	Fizzy drinks	Spirits
Coffee	Fruit juice	Tea
Dairy smoothies	Milk	Traditional tea
FATS & OILS		
Corn oil	Saturated fats	Vegetable oil
Hydrogenated oils	Sunflower oil	
Margarine (worse than butter)		
SEEDS & NUTS		
Cashews	Peanuts	Pistachios

6. your body needs movement.

From reducing cancer risk to improving mood and digestion, exercise is a must-do. For optimal health benefits, it is ideal to engage in your favourite form of physical activity four times a week or more. Your joints, muscles, spinal alignment, and discs thrive on motion and mobility. Whether it is going for a walk, getting up earlier to hop on your treadmill or elliptical, or investing in free weights, you will feel an instant surge in energy, mood, and vitality along with a decrease in body weight when on a routine exercise schedule. As a bonus, you will sleep better in the evening and will enter a disease-prevention mode.

7. your body needs sufficient fuel.

In North America, we tend to gobble up our food very quickly in order to make our next meeting, drop the kids off at school, or run to our next big event. Unfortunately, this fast eating pace creates the tendency to consume excess calories without realizing it. Considering it takes the brain 20 minutes to register a full signal once eating commences, it is common practice in North America to eat until we are stuffed and our pants actually feel too tight!

To avoid this tendency, it is recommended you eat like you were living in Okinawa. Take your time, use your utensils, chew your foods, and be conscious of when you are hungry versus mindless eating. In Okinawa, the elders are in tune with their satiety cues and tend to stop eating when they are about 80 percent full. Sounds hard to do at first? It is not so much a difficult practice as it is a mind shift toward awareness eating. Follow these tips to focus on your true hunger cues.

- Wait until you hear your stomach grumbling a little to begin eating. Don't eat according to the clock.
- Put an ink dot on the outside of your thumb. When you're eating, look at the dot as a reminder to slow down, chew your food, and enjoy.
- Chew your food! For optimal digestion and to slow down your meals, chew your food completely until it is small enough and dissolved enough to be swallowed with ease.
- Talk to your loved ones at the table about their day when there isn't food in your mouth. This will force you to take breaks between bites.
- If eating alone, practise awareness eating and chewing. Do not eat in front of the television or computer screen.
- When you feel comfortably full, stop eating. Do not force yourself to clean your plate.

your personal health journey

Now that you're aware of the seven principles of health, you're on your way to improving overall health, vitality, and wellness. Keep in mind, health is an extremely personal topic and has different meanings for different people. For some, the word *health* may simply refer to the absence of a symptom or a disease process. For a growing number of people, the word *health* refers to being at the top of your game—hitting your target weight, feeling vibrant and energetic day in and day out, sleeping well, exercising, not smoking, drinking in moderation, and feeling balanced in life and work.

Before moving on to the next chapter, take a moment to reflect on your definition of health and what steps you could take to be at the top of your health game.

My definition of optimal health is:

_____

_____

_____

_____

Five ways I could improve my health are (exercise more, drink more water, etc.):

_____

_____

_____

_____

In writing this book, one of my goals was to ensure that *Healthy Sin Foods* wasn't just a "Jacuzzi experience" for readers. What do I mean? When you're in a Jacuzzi, you feel bubbly, warm, content, and have the best intentions to take on any new change. After reading this book, you may become extremely motivated and dedicated to change your health, wellness, and day-to-day vitality. However, as life comes back into the picture and you're focusing on carpool and work, by next Thursday you've forgotten all about your plan to implement new health habits and have unconsciously gone back to your old ways.

My sincere objective is to help you make easy, long-term changes—whether weight loss or otherwise—that can prolong life, increase your sense of daily wellness, and put you into a disease-prevention mode. And let's not forget one key aspect of *Healthy Sin Foods*—this all has to be done in a delicious and non-depriving manner (and it can be).

You will find that whatever your health changes, the body has an incredibly forgiving nature. When given the proper environment, it always gravitates toward a state of health. It is truly an incredible experience to watch your well-being respond in a positive way simply by implementing a few baby steps toward health, such as eating more fruits and vegetables, drinking more water, and exercising regularly. Are you ready to learn all the need-to-know nutritional information to keep you at your very best? Let's read on!

two
crazy for carbs

Recently Dina visited my office, seeking some weight-loss answers. Like many of my clients, Dina had tried every diet on the market and was still on the "wrong" side of the scale. After taking her health history, I weighed and measured her. She was 5-foot-4, 167 pounds, with a waist circumference of 34 inches (86 cm), which is far too big for a woman her age (47) and weight. Seeing the upset in her face and her eyes welling up with tears, I started to ask her about her current nutritional habits. By the time we started to discuss her typical daily intake, she said to me point-blank, "I'm a lost cause … I'm completely addicted to carbs!"

Situations such as Dina's are not unusual and can keep the roller-coaster cycle of weight loss and weight gain going and going. Think about it: Have you ever noticed that if you succumb to your cravings, they'll only intensify? When you do "food binge" and eat sugary, refined carbohydrates or white bread, pasta, or cereal, you tend to want to eat more and more. This is not an indication that you are weak or have little willpower when it comes to eating carbohydrates. It is, however, an indication that you are biochemically "off" because you're eating too many of the wrong types of carbohydrates. Once you understand how carbohydrates are processed in the bloodstream and their direct interaction and influence on your insulin levels, you will gain back control permanently. When this occurs and blood sugar levels are once again balanced, you can eat bread, certain types of pastas, and even fall off the health wagon and indulge without suffering any of the bulge or cravings. To begin, it is critical to understand the interplay between specific foods and hormonal balance in your body.

what are carbohydrates?

Carbohydrates are considered macronutrients, which are foods that need to be eaten in reasonably large quantities in order to sustain life. The macronutrient category of food includes three big guys: carbohydrates, proteins, and fats. Nearly all foods (except for oils) contain a mixture of carbohydrates, proteins, and fats. A food is classified as a carbohydrate, protein, or fat according to the percentage of the macronutrient that is highest in that specific food (e.g., if a piece of bread is 85 percent carbohydrate, 5 percent fat, and 10 percent protein, it is classified as a carbohydrate). Unlike macronutrients, micronutrients such as minerals or vitamins only need to be consumed in small quantities for optimal health and wellness to flourish.

Carbohydrates are the primary and preferred source of fuel for the body. Similar to a car needing constant fuel, after eating a meal or snack that contains carbohydrates, the body breaks down carbohydrates into glucose (sugar), the main source of fuel that keeps the body's energy running smoothly. Carbohydrates can be classified into two categories: simple and complex.

simple carbohydrates

Simple carbohydrates are one sugar molecule (e.g., monosaccharide) or two sugar molecules (e.g., disaccharides) linked together. Simple carbohydrates such as white sugar have a higher glycemic index rating and tend to cause blood sugar spikes. This can be problematic when it comes to weight gain, blood sugar control, and pre-existing conditions such as type 2 diabetes.

Examples of simple carbohydrates include:

- white "table" sugar (sucrose)
- honey
- molasses
- candy
- regular soda
- many processed snack foods

As you will discover later in this chapter, sugar is snuck into many different food sources for taste and is considered empty calories. All of the above foods contain one or more of the various forms of sugar (including sucrose, high fructose corn syrup, maltose, and glucose/dextrose). They are absorbed into the bloodstream very quickly, causing a spike in insulin levels and increased fat storage (among other negative health effects). With the exception of fruits and low-fat dairy products such as milk, yogurt, and cottage cheese, simple carbohydrates should be kept to a minimum in the diet, especially if you are trying to reduce body fat.

complex carbohydrates

Complex carbohydrates are composed of several sugar (glucose) molecules. They are a more complicated and larger structure, and therefore the body does not metabolize them as quickly as simple carbohydrates (with the exception of fructose). The chemical name for complex carbohydrates is polysaccharides, meaning "many sugars." Complex carbohydrates such as vegetables, fruits, legumes, and whole grain items such as bread, pasta, rice, or cereals raise blood sugar levels slower than a monosaccharide (simple) sugar.

Optimal complex carbohydrate choices (fruits, vegetables, whole grains, and legumes) are also rich in minerals, vitamins, antioxidants, fibre, and phytonutrients (plant-based chemicals that ward off and can prevent disease).

what is an oligosaccharide?

Recently you may have discovered food packaging that contains the words *prebiotics* or the ingredient *inulin* fibre. These items refer to the oligosaccharide content in the food. Oligosaccharides are carbohydrates that have 3 to 10 simple sugars linked together. They fall in between monosaccharides (one sugar molecule) and polysaccharides (several hundred sugar molecules).

Oligosaccharides are derived mostly from plant sources such as the chicory root, from which most commercial inulin is extracted. They can also be found in onions, legumes, wheat, and asparagus. Recent research demonstrates that in addition to adding a naturally sweet taste to food, oligosaccharides have a beneficial prebiotic effect. Oligosaccharides support the growth of the good bacteria in the colon. Unlike other carbohydrates, oligosaccharides such as inulin are non-digestible and pass through the small intestine to ferment in the large intestine. Through the fermentation process, the inulin becomes healthy intestinal micro flora (bifidobacterium). The bacteria that feed on the oligosaccharides produce several beneficial substances, such as a variety of B vitamins and short-chain fatty acids (SCFAs), and may even promote the absorption of a variety of minerals such as calcium and magnesium. Other possible health benefits of oligosaccharides may include:

- lowering cholesterol
- reducing triglyceride levels
- improving insulin resistance and glucose metabolism (extremely important for individuals who are overweight or type 2 diabetic)
- boosting immune system function

the glycemic index and the glycemic load

In recent years, the glycemic index has become the benchmark as a rating system for carbohydrate metabolism. The glycemic index measures the speed of entry of a carbohydrate into the bloodstream. The categories of the glycemic index are:

- low (up to 55)
- medium (56 to 70)
- high (over 70)

Individual foods with a high glycemic index rating, such as simple sugars (refined flours and sugars), enter the bloodstream at a rushing speed and cause a dramatic rise in blood sugar levels. Because the body always attempts to maintain balance in all areas, blood sugar must be kept within a certain range. In order to compensate for this sudden rise in sugar, the pancreas is triggered to secrete the hormone insulin, which "mops up" excess blood sugar and disperses it to other parts of the body. This sounds like a fairly efficient system, doesn't it? Unfortunately, when we consume too many high glycemic index carbohydrates, the pancreatic duct tends to overreact and secretes too much of the hormone insulin. There are a few major health issues that can occur with the oversecretion of insulin.

1. What goes up must come down, and blood sugar levels are no exception to the rule. When excess insulin is secreted in response to too many high glycemic index carbohydrates in the diet, the blood sugar levels go from being too high (hyperglycemia) to being too low (hypoglycemia). Symptoms of low blood sugar include fatigue, mental fogginess, and cravings to bring blood sugar back up again. Unfortunately, we don't crave broccoli or salmon to bring up blood sugar, we crave sweets and starches. This is our body's attempt to normalize blood sugar levels. By grabbing another cookie, sugary latte, or muffin, we are only bouncing around blood sugar even more and causing the vicious cycle to occur repeatedly.
2. Excess insulin facilitates the excess storage of fat—especially around the midsection (abdominal region). Not only does this take us further away from our ideal body weight and weight-loss goals, but an excess storage of fat around the abdominal region is a risk factor for type 2 diabetes, high blood pressure, and heart disease.
3. Excess insulin secretion will eventually lead to insulin resistance. This state (where the body does not "feel" its own insulin any longer) is correlated with glucose intolerance and type 2 diabetes.

Insulin is responsible for:
- controlling blood sugar
- balancing blood lipids
- monitoring excess nutrients (from glucose and calories) and converting them to fat
- building muscle and storing protein
- regulating magnesium and calcium levels

Although the glycemic index is a useful tool, it can also reflect inaccuracies due to its standard of measurement. The glycemic index uses a standard amount of carbohydrates (50 g) to measure the effect a specific food has on blood sugar. Because the glycemic index takes into account only a small percentage of carbohydrate content, it may not be as relevant as a complementary scale called the glycemic load. The glycemic load takes into account portion size and carbohydrate content. To calculate glycemic load:

Glycemic load (GL) = Glycemic index (GI)/100 × Net Carbs
(Net carbs are equal to the total carbohydrates minus dietary fibre)

For ranking purposes, the glycemic load categories are:

- 1–10 = low
- 11–19 = medium
- > 20 = high

For example, a watermelon has a high glycemic index rating of 72. However, an average slice of watermelon only contains 5 g of carbohydrates because it is mostly water. If we calculate the GL of watermelon, it would be $72/100 \times 5 = 3.6$, a low glycemic load rating. While the GI and GL are usually fairly in line with each other, there are indeed exceptions to the rule.

> For optimal health and wellness, choose low GI carbohydrates that cause only small fluctuations in blood glucose and insulin levels. By doing so, you will reduce your risk of heart disease and diabetes and will be able to sustain a healthy body weight.

I've identified the glycemic index and the glycemic load of relevant individual foods listed in Top 50 Superfoods. That said, it is not always realistic to count the GI and GL of every food you eat. In order to eat carbohydrates wisely and prevent fluctuations of blood sugar levels and excess storage of fat, stick to vegetables, fruits, whole grains, low-fat dairy products, and lean proteins. When eating breads or pastas, opt for whole grains and substitute brown rice for white rice. Instead of white potatoes, choose sweet potatoes. When choosing vegetables, opt for dark leafy greens and orange vegetables such as sweet potatoes and carrots. In terms of fruits, select an assortment of berries and apples as your first two selections.

As mentioned, the GI and GL of certain foods can reflect inaccuracies. Fibre, protein, and fat slow the entry of a food into the bloodstream and therefore lower GI and GL levels. If you look at a comprehensive glycemic index listing, you will discover that peanut M&Ms are ranked as low at 46 GI. This is not to suggest that peanut M&Ms are healthy and should be eaten in abundance. However, their GI is lower due to the fat in the peanut.

factors affecting glycemic index	
Fibre	Fibre, especially soluble fibre, slows down the digestion of starch, resulting in a lower glycemic index. This is the reason that whole grains have a lower GI than refined grains.
Fats and proteins	Fat and protein slow down foods from leaving the stomach; therefore, foods containing fat and protein such as beans and milk have lower glycemic index values.
Acid content	Lemon juice or vinegar can also lower the glycemic index.
Ripeness	Unripened fruits (e.g., bananas) have a lower glycemic index than ripened fruits.

An apple-shaped body type has a greater fat deposition around the abdomen, whereas a pear-shaped body type has greater fat deposition around the hips. Apple shape is linked with a high secretion of insulin from the pancreas. Women with a waist circumference greater than 35 inches (89 cm) and men with a waist circumference greater than 40 inches (102 cm) are at a higher risk for type 2 diabetes, high blood pressure, and heart disease.

refined foods and hidden sugars

Another way to categorize carbohydrates is by the amount of processing they have undergone by food manufacturers. As would be expected, the more processed a carbohydrate is, the less healthy it is for you. Consider some of the facts when it comes to processed foods.

- Refined flours and sugars tend to be higher on the glycemic index and cause blood sugar spikes.
- Refined flours and sugars will cause an oversecretion of insulin, which will result in weight gain.
- Refined flours and sugars are key contributors to the development of type 2 diabetes.

- Refined flours and sugars lose precious minerals and vitamins during the refining process. Even if a grain, cereal, and so on is fortified (minerals or vitamins are added back by the food manufacturer to attempt to top up what has been stripped away), it is impossible to make the food as nutritious as it was when whole.
- Certain fruit juices and pops contain an abundant amount of white sugar—as much as 9 to 11 tsp (36 to 44 g) of sugar per can of pop!
- One-third of ketchup is sugar.

Nowadays, refined sugars are snuck into many processed food products to enhance flavour and mask the lack of fat in the food product. Strolling through the grocery aisles, you're likely to pick up a food item labelled "real fruit" or "low fat." This sounds pretty healthy, doesn't it? On closer inspection, the food in question may contain as much as 3 tsp (12 g) of sugar—yikes! For example, if a product is labelled "low fat" (dairy products being the exception), check the amount of sugar on the Nutrition Facts panel. Often-times a lack of fat equals a lack of taste, and sugar is added to the food to compensate.

> To determine how much sugar is in a food item, it is important to know that there are 4 g in 1 tsp of refined sugar. If a product contains 16 g of sugar, that translates into about 4 tsp of sugar per serving.

According to recommendations by the World Health Organization, added sugars should not account for more than 10 percent (200 calories) of an individual's daily caloric intake (see Maximum Daily Sugar Intake). This does not include naturally occurring sugars found in fruits (fructose), vegetables, and dairy products (lactose). The typical North American diet consumes far more than this.

refined sugar consumption, select years from 1976 to 2002

YEAR	KILOGRAMS PER PERSON
1976	41.29
1981	37.10
1986	41.32

1991	36.35
1996	38.02
1998	37.27
1999	37.86
2000	39.07
2001	40.94
2002	44.89

Source: Adapted from Canada Food Statistics, Table 4: Food Disappearance, by Commodity, 2002, vol. 2, no. 1

maximum daily sugar intake

DAILY CALORIE INTAKE	GRAMS	TEASPOONS
1200	30	7.5
1500	36	9
1800	44	11
2100	52	13
2400	60	15
2700	68	17

How can you determine whether a food product contains sugar? This process can be quite confusing to figure out. Sugars listed on Nutrition Facts panels are all lumped together—naturally occurring and added. This explains why 1 cup (250 mL) of milk contains almost 3 tsp (12 g) of sugar even though it doesn't have any sugar "added" to it.

The first clue is to check the ingredients list and look for the following words:

- sucrose
- fructose
- maple syrup
- molasses
- dextrose or dextrin
- turbinado

- amazake
- carob powder
- high fructose corn syrup
- corn sweetener
- corn syrup, or corn syrup solids
- dehydrated cane juice
- fruit juice concentrate
- glucose
- honey
- invert sugar
- lactose
- maltodextrin
- molasses
- raw sugar
- sorghum or sorghum syrup

When determining how much sugar is in a food product, keep in mind that ingredients are listed according to quantity: The largest ingredient is listed first and the smallest quantity is listed last.

You may also find sugars such as maltitol, sorbitol, isomalt, and xylitol on your ingredients list. These are sugar alcohols (also called polyols) and differ in nature from sugar. Sugar alcohols are mostly manufactured from sugars or starches and have less impact than sugar because they are not fully absorbed by the body. The upside of sugar alcohols is that they contain fewer calories and do not appear to cause tooth decay. The downside is that because they are not completely absorbed by the body, they ferment in the gut and can cause bloating, stomach upset, gas, or diarrhea.

According to the U.S. Department of Agriculture (USDA), foods that tend to contain the most added sugars are:

- regular soft drinks
- candies
- cakes
- cookies
- pies

- fruit drinks (not 100 percent fruit juice)
- milk-based desserts and products (e.g., ice cream cakes, sweetened yogurt)
- grain products such as sweet rolls, sweetened cereals, and cinnamon toast

Helpful tips to reduce sugar intake include:

- Avoid soft drinks and fruit punches or "ades"—they can contain up to 12 tsp (48 g) of sugar.
- Eat a cereal with less than 1 to 2 tsp (4 to 8 g) of sugar per serving.
- Eliminate snacks or other foods with sugar as the first or second ingredient.
- Try to add no more than 1 tsp (4 g) of added sugar to your tea or coffee.
- If you enjoy flavoured yogurt, substitute in one-half portion of plain yogurt to reduce your sugar intake.

nature's goodness: whole grains

Working in the weight-loss industry for years, I have observed the many mistakes that clients make when trying to take off weight and keep it off. Even with all the fad diets, there are certain situations that never cease to amaze me. Recently, I had a new client, Anna, who was in a complete metabolic rut because of several years of yo-yo dieting. Anna's latest effort was a restricted carbohydrate diet with high protein and no bread or fruit. After four to six weeks on this diet, not only did Anna's hair begin to fall out in clumps, but she was very distressed when she failed her life insurance policy due to elevated liver enzymes. Because Anna did not present with any other conditions, it was assumed she had a drinking problem because of her elevated liver enzymes. As it turns out, Anna had an allergy to alcohol and had not had a drink in more than 10 years. What was the cause of the elevated liver enzymes? In an attempt to slim down, Anna had been on and off a hard-core high-protein diet for many years and it was finally taking a major toll on her physically. In addition to eventually burning out her metabolic engine (she could no longer budge her weight), she was constipated, tired, and looking for a new life insurance policy!

I have seen far too many people cut out carbohydrates altogether in an attempt to slim down fast. While you will lose weight quickly, the gains are short-term. The body does *not* want to run on protein as its primary source of fuel, and it will soon rebel and give you red flags in the form of symptoms. It is not necessary to cut out carbohydrates to lose weight. It is necessary, however, to eat the right type of carbohydrates to slim down, feel energetic, and provide the body with the perfect source of fuel. Instead of eliminating grains altogether, what is the answer? Enter nature's goodness: whole grain carbohydrates.

A whole grain contains a tremendous amount of nutritional goodness in each of its three parts.

1. The **bran** is the outer shell of the grain and is rich in fibre, B vitamins, and trace minerals.
2. The **germ** is the inner part of the grain and is rich in B vitamins, vitamin E, unsaturated fat, and phytonutrients (plant chemicals that prevent disease).
3. The **endosperm** contains carbohydrates, some protein, and B vitamins.

Unfortunately, when whole grains are processed to create white flour, the bran and germ are stripped down, leaving just the endosperm. The processing of grains into white flour, rice, or pasta eliminates a majority of the nutrition initially offered in the whole grain. In Canada, manufacturers are required to enrich white processed flour with vitamins and iron through a process called fortification. However, it is nearly impossible to make a refined grain whole once again. Fortified grains still lack some precious nutrients and fibre that are an essential part of optimal health and development. In addition, the overconsumption of white flour has been linked to type 2 diabetes, obesity, and blood sugar fluctuations. The body does not discriminate between a refined white piece of bread and white sugar. High glycemic index food products are all processed the same way—with a dramatic insulin response.

There are numerous significant health benefits that have been linked to eating whole grains on a regular basis, such as:

- a reduction in cholesterol and of overall risk for heart disease
- a reduction of the risk of several types of cancers, such as colorectal cancer
- an improvement of bowel health and promotion of healthy bacteria and regularity
- a lower body weight and lower blood pressure
- a reduction of inflammatory diseases

When looking to buy whole grain products, do not go by the colour of the bread. Oftentimes, refined flours that are white have had blackstrap molasses or other colouring added to make the bread appear brown. Tricky, isn't it? A few simple rules to ensure that you are buying the right type of bread include:

- In Canada, whole wheat bread is made with whole wheat flour, which may have had much of the germ removed. Thus, the bread may not be whole grain. In order to ensure that you are consuming whole grain bread, look for the words *whole grain* on the label and in the ingredients list.
- If bread is labelled *multigrain, stone ground, seven grain,* or *organic,* it does not necessarily mean it is whole grain. Again, look for the words *whole grain.*
- If there is a phone number or website on the bread's packaging, contact the company to see if they have the glycemic index rating of the bread in question.

> After you eat bread, notice if you feel tired soon after. Food items that are higher on the glycemic index often leave you in a hypoglycemic (low blood sugar) state, resulting in symptoms of fogginess and fatigue.

It is recommended that individuals consume a minimum of three servings of whole grain products a day. A serving is equal to:

- a 50 g slice of 100 percent whole grain bread or toast
- 30 g of cold whole grain cereal (that's about 3/4 cup to 1 cup/175 mL to 250 mL of most cereals)
- 1/2 cup (125 mL) cooked brown rice or whole grain pasta
- 1 small whole grain pancake or waffle (about 4 inches/10 cm in diameter)
- 1 small whole grain muffin
- 1/2 cup (125 mL) cooked, old-fashioned-style oatmeal

Examples of whole grains include:

- barley
- brown rice

- bulgur
- oatmeal
- popcorn
- whole oats
- whole rye
- wild rice

---

less common types of whole grains:
- amaranth
- kamut
- millet
- quinoa
- sorghum
- spelt
- triticale

In addition to whole grain breads, opt for whole grain pasta, cookies, crackers, and wraps, and brown rice instead of white. For a weight-loss tip, cook your pasta al dente (undercook slightly) to lower the glycemic index value.

what is sprouted grain?

You may have seen the words *sprouted grains* on bread or wrap packaging in the grocery store. When a whole wheat kernel is sprouted for a certain period of time (e.g., 12 to 48 hours), the grain is allowed to turn itself into a plant that sprouts a mini green shoot. The advantage to the sprouting process is that it predigests some of the starch in the grain and lowers the glycemic index of the bread. This is ideal for weight loss and controlling blood sugar fluctuation.

make your plate a rainbow of colour

When it comes to fruits and vegetables, the more, the merrier! In addition to being loaded with minerals, vitamins, and fibre, fruits and vegetables have a unique combination of phytonutrients that prevent and can even reverse a variety of disease processes, ranging from cancer to heart disease to lowering blood pressure and helping with urinary tract infections. Scientists are only beginning to grasp the profound effect these plant nutrients play on health and have discovered approximately 9000 phytonutrients so far. Research also suggests that along with reducing the risk of disease, phytonutrients may help to prevent the aging process and help you to look your very best from the inside out.

As a general rule, the more colourful the fruit or vegetable, the better it is for you. The vibrant colour, or the pigment, reflects the density of nutrients found in the specific food. This is why filling your diet with blue, red, green, orange, and yellow produce is of the utmost importance. Examples include blueberries, raspberries, blackberries, strawberries, goji berries, red grapefruit, watermelon, tangerines, oranges, mango, papaya, kale, spinach, broccoli, Swiss chard, squash, tomatoes, brussels sprouts, carrots, and sweet potato.

examples of specific phytonutrients in fruits and vegetables:

RED: lycopene, found in tomatoes, watermelon, and pink grapefruit
ORANGE: beta-carotene, found in carrots, mangoes, and cantaloupe
YELLOW: beta-cryptothanxin, found in pineapple, oranges, and peaches
GREEN: indoles, found in broccoli, cabbage, and kale
PURPLE: anthocyanins, found in blueberries, grapes, and eggplant
WHITE: allicin, found in garlic, onions, and chives

Unfortunately, certain fruits and vegetables are heavily sprayed with herbicides, pesticides, and fungicides. In addition to increasing your toxic load, these chemicals are meant to "kill" pests, so surely when eaten on a regular basis they will have some effect on the body. Research indicates that several of the hundreds of chemicals used to spray crops are indeed carcinogenic (cancer-causing). In order to avoid this risk, I am a huge advocate of buying organic. Because demand for organic goods has grown enormously, they are now widely available and the cost has come down considerably. When purchasing organic goods, look for the "certified organic stamp" to ensure that you are purchasing foods that are indeed 100 percent organic. If you cannot make your entire grocery shop organic, there are certain fruits and vegetables that are more heavily sprayed than others. According to the Consumers Union and the Environmental Working Group, the top fruits and vegetables to buy organic because of potential pesticide residue are:

- apples
- cantaloupe
- grapes
- green beans
- peaches
- pears
- raspberries
- spinach
- strawberries
- tomatoes

Other ways to start eating certified organic include:

- finding out where your local farmers' market is located to shop for your fruits and vegetables
- joining a food co-op or program that has an organic box delivered to your home
- buying organic produce in-season and freezing/preserving
- growing your own fruits and vegetables

common carbohydrate questions

A lack of knowledge about carbohydrates can create many unwanted effects in the body, such as weight gain, fatigue, constipation, and so on. In order to understand how to use carbohydrates to your health advantage, I have answered the most common questions I am frequently asked about carbohydrates.

will bananas and carrots make me fat?

In all my years of working in the weight-loss industry, I have never encountered one client that is overweight or obese from eating too many carrots or bananas. However, since bananas are starchier than other fruits, and carrots have a higher sugar content, certain strict low-carb diets recommend their elimination. On closer inspection, it is clear that bananas and carrots don't have to be removed from the diet altogether as they both contain an abundant amount of vitamins, minerals, and phytonutrients. Consider the typical grams of carbohydrates in a variety of carbohydrate food items.

- 1 serving of fruit (1/2 cup/125 mL, 1/2 banana, or 1 small fruit) = 10 g of carbohydrates
- 1 cup (250 mL) of vegetables = 5 g of carbohydrates
- 1/2 cup (125 mL) of beans = 20 to 25 g of carbohydrates
- 1 whole wheat tortilla = 12 g of carbohydrates
- 2 pieces of crisp Wasa bread = 15 g of carbohydrates
- 1 slice of bread (whole wheat) = 15 g of carbohydrates

When considering carrots, it is important to keep the glycemic load in mind. While carrots may have a higher glycemic index reading, the amount of carbohydrates you would actually consume in a normal serving is low (6.2 g). Therefore, the glycemic load of carrots is low at 2.

Pinpointing one or two food items as the obstacle that stands in the way of you reaching your goal weight is not wise. The main culprits that are contributing to today's epidemic of obesity are much more grandiose than one or two foods and include:

1. Portion distortion. From the size of our plates to "2 for 1" deals, North Americans are consuming more food than ever before. When comparing portion sizes in the United States to France, it was discovered that the average candy bar in Philadelphia was 41 percent larger than the same candy bar in Paris; an average soft drink was 53 percent larger; and an average hot dog was 63 percent larger!

2. Refined flours and refined sugary products. From coffee shops to grocery stores, refined flours and sugars are everywhere in the North American food industry—in sugary cookies and muffins, white bread, pasta, pop, candy, and juice.
3. Lack of activity.
4. Fast food dining.

are beans a protein or a carbohydrate?

While beans do contain a rich source of protein (about 25 percent of their total calories), they are classified as carbohydrates. The highest-protein bean is the soybean at about 34 percent protein. Beans are generally low in fat, low on the glycemic index, high in fibre, and rich in nutrients, making them a wonderful addition to the diet. In fact, beans contain about 25 g of fibre in 1 cup (250 mL). Canned beans can be quite high in sodium. Select dried beans and soak overnight or thoroughly rinse canned beans prior to use.

amount of carbs in bean varieties

COOKED BEANS (100g/4oz)	CARBS
Aduki beans	22 g
Baked in tomato sauce	15 g
Black-eyed beans	20 g
Black kidney beans	25 g
Red kidney beans	7 g
Borlotti beans	28 g
Broad/Fava beans (1 cup/250 mL)	33 g
Chickpeas/Garbanzo beans (1 cup/250 mL)	55 g
Great Northern beans (1 cup/250 mL)	37 g
Lima beans (1 cup/250 mL)	40 g

what is the difference between brown sugar and white sugar? what about sugar substitutes?

The difference between white sugar and brown sugar is … colour! I wish I could tell you that brown sugar is head and shoulders above white sugar in terms of nutrition, but alas, it is not. Most brown sugars on the market are sucrose (white refined table sugar) with the presence of molasses to make the sugar appear brown. If you are searching for a "healthier" brown sugar, choose one that is unrefined, such as demerara or muscovado. Demerara is a traditional unrefined sugar with a sparkling appearance and is an excellent sweetener in coffee or tea. When storing brown sugar, store in a glass jar or plastic bag in a dry, cool environment.

Other natural sweeteners that contain more minerals and vitamins include:

- apple sauce
- barley malt
- dates (*Note:* extremely high on the glycemic index—ranked at 103)
- pure maple syrup
- rice syrup
- ripe bananas mashed for baking
- Sucanat (granulated cane juice)

Another natural sweetener available in many health food stores is stevia, derived from a herb found in Paraguay. While some people use stevia as a natural sweetener in baking, others find it has a licorice aftertaste.

> If brown sugar, such as muscovado, becomes solid, add a slice of apple to the container for a couple of days to restore the moisture balance.

what is high fructose corn syrup?

High fructose corn syrup (HFCS) is a very popular and inexpensive sweetener and preservative found in processed foods, fruit-flavoured drinks, and sodas. Cheaper and sweeter than sugar, HFCS also extends the shelf life of a product, which holds a great deal of value for food manufacturers. HFCS is made by changing the sugar (glucose) in cornstarch to fructose. The end product is a combination of fructose and glucose.

The problem with HFCS is multifaceted. For starters, researchers have reason to believe that HFCS is linked with the development of type 2 diabetes and obesity. Additional studies have found that appetite, which normally decreases after eating, decreased less after drinking fructose-sweetened beverages—and that it caused triglycerides to increase, an indicator of risk for cardiovascular disease. Lastly, food items that contain HFCS are devoid of nutrition and tend to be high in calories and oftentimes contain food colouring. As a general rule, it is best to eliminate HFCS from the diet completely.

The average Canadian drank more than 21 gallons (95 L) of soft drinks in 2007, according to Statistics Canada—that's more than any other beverage except coffee.

what is the difference between soluble and insoluble fibre?

Fibre is a necessary part of every diet and has been shown to protect against several conditions, including colon cancer, high cholesterol, heart disease, constipation, and diverticulosis. Fibre can also be very beneficial when it comes to weight loss because it fills you up and tends to have a lower glycemic index rating. It is recommended that adults consume 20 to 35 g every day of soluble and insoluble fibre combined. Most plant foods contain both sorts of fibre, although proportions vary. Insoluble fibre largely passes through the intestinal tract undigested and helps to bulk up stool and remove toxic waste from the colon. Insoluble fibre also appears to prevent colon cancer by keeping the pH (acidity) of the bowel optimal, which thereby prevents microbes from developing into potentially cancerous cells. Examples of insoluble fibre include green beans, dark leafy greens such as spinach and kale, fruit with skin on, tomatoes, whole wheat products, wheat oat and corn bran, nuts, and seeds.

Soluble fibre binds with fatty acids and forms a gel. Soluble fibre prolongs stomach emptying and therefore sugar is released more slowly. Thus, soluble fibre is ideal for type 2 diabetics and has also been shown to lower cholesterol levels. Examples of soluble fibre are oats and oat bran, dried beans and peas, nuts, barley, flaxseed, oranges, apples, and vegetables such as carrots.

To boost fibre and omega-3 values daily, add 1 tbsp (15 mL) of ground seed to your morning breakfast or salad daily. Keep ground flaxseed in the refrigerator for eight to 10 weeks.

what is gluten? what are the gluten-free grains?

Gluten is a protein found in wheat, rye, barley, and possibly oats. Certain people may be "sensitive" to gluten while others who suffer from a disease called celiac disease (CD) may have to eliminate gluten from the diet altogether. According to the U.S. Department of Health and Human Services, "Celiac disease (CD) is a digestive disease that damages the small intestine and interferes with the absorption of nutrients from food. People who have CD cannot tolerate the protein called gluten. When people with CD eat foods containing gluten, their immune system responds by damaging the small intestine. Specifically, tiny, finger-like protrusions, called villi, on the lining of the small intestine are lost. Nutrients from food are absorbed into the bloodstream through these villi. Without villi, a person becomes malnourished—regardless of the amount of food eaten."

green light grains for celiac disease

- amaranth
- basmati rice
- beans
- brown rice and brown rice flour
- buckwheat (kasha)
- lentils
- millet

- potato flour
- quinoa
- sweet potatoes
- wild rice

Now that you have a thorough understanding of carbohydrates and their effect on the body, let's move on to the second big guy of the three macronutrients: powerful proteins!

three
powerful proteins

Have you ever noticed after eating cereal, a bagel, or an English muffin for breakfast that you're starving by 10 a.m. and already thinking about lunch? Your unrelenting hunger is *not* because of your insatiable appetite. Your breakfast simply lacked one very important element: protein.

Every cell in your body contains protein, and it's a major part of your skin, muscles, organs, and glands. It's also found in all body fluids, except for bile and urine. Protein is responsible for several critical functions, including cellular repair and growth and development during childhood, adolescence, and pregnancy. Unlike fat and glucose, our body has little capacity to store protein. If we were to stop eating protein, our body would start to break down muscle for its needs within a short time. But if protein is so important for health and wellness, why is this precious macronutrient still so misunderstood? With so many protein powders on the market and so many popular high-protein diets to choose from, there seems to be confusion about the amount and type of protein that should be in our daily diet.

what are proteins?

Proteins are found in a variety of foods such as lean meats, chicken, fish, tofu, eggs, soy, nuts, and grains. The "building blocks" of protein are called amino acids, which are composed of carbon, hydrogen, nitrogen, and oxygen. There are 22 kinds of amino acids, divided into two categories: essential (meaning the body cannot make them and they must be found in the diet) and non-essential (meaning the body can make them).

The amount of protein we should consume daily is a hotly debated topic and differs from source to source. According to the U.S. Recommended Daily Allowance (RDA), you should consume 0.36 g of protein for every pound of your normal body weight. So, if you weigh 150 pounds, multiply your weight by 0.36 to find out your daily protein intake: 54 g.

Some experts recommend that protein should make up about 15 percent of your total caloric intake. I've found that for weight maintenance and for those who are metabolically sluggish (e.g., post-menopausal women), a slightly higher amount of protein is optimal (20 to 25 percent of total daily calories). This protein should be derived from foods lower in saturated fats, such as fish, lean chicken and turkey, low-fat dairy products, and soy. Protein should never exceed more than 30 percent of your total caloric intake.

Like carbohydrates, proteins contain 4 calories in each gram.

Proteins are compounds composed of carbon, hydrogen, nitrogen, and oxygen. These elements combine to form strings of amino acids.

essential and non-essential amino acids

ESSENTIAL AMINO ACIDS (MUST COME FROM THE DIET)	NON-ESSENTIAL AMINO ACIDS (PRODUCED BY THE BODY)
Isoleucine	Alanine
Leucine	Arginine
Lysine	Asparagine
Methionine	Aspartic acid
Phenylalanine	Cysteine
Threonine	Glutamic acid
Tryptophan	Glutamine
Valine	Glycine
	Histidine
	Proline
	Serine
	Tyrosine

In my clinical practice, I've observed two categories of protein consumption. In the first category, clients tend to eat too little protein, which can contribute to carbohydrate cravings, fatigue, intense hunger, and weight gain. In the second, clients tend to eat too much protein, relying on it as their primary source of fuel. Out of fear of gaining weight, some clients are afraid of eating any carbohydrate. Mistakenly, they rely on protein options high in saturated fat, which can cause serious health consequences such as inflammation, clogging of arteries, and high blood pressure. I've witnessed far too many people make critical errors in this area of health care and weight loss. For example, Melanie first came to see me last year for poor digestion and weight maintenance. Desperately trying to keep her weight down, she was visiting fast food restaurants, ordering a double-patty burger, eating the patties, and throwing out the bun. Yikes! No wonder her digestion was sluggish and she had severe halitosis (bad breath), poor energy, and lack of focus throughout the day. Melanie was attempting to run her body on next to no sugar (glucose) from carbohydrates. As we now know, the body's preferred source of fuel is glucose. If it doesn't receive enough glucose, eventually it will rebel with myriad symptoms.

hormonal balance, weight loss, and proteins

Unlike insulin, which is a fat-storage hormone, protein triggers the secretion of glucagon, a fat-burning hormone. Think about glucagon as insulin's enemy. When one is up, the other is down.

Glucagon has several roles, but one of its most important functions is to shift your metabolism into a "high-gear burning mode," which is optimal for weight loss.

Here's how glucagon works:

- In response to adequate protein from meals, the pancreas stimulates glucagon.
- Glucagon raises low blood sugar and maintains stable blood sugar (glucose) levels in the body.
- Glucagon shifts metabolism into burning mode.
- Glucagon mobilizes the release of stored body fat from the adipose tissue directly into the bloodstream, allowing muscles to burn fat instead of glucose for energy.

- Glucagon converts dietary fats to ketones and sends them to the tissues for energy.
- Glucagon releases fat from fat cells into the bloodstream for use by tissues as energy.

For example, when you eat a piece of white bread, your blood sugar (glucose) levels increase and your pancreas starts to secrete insulin. If you follow the bread with 3 oz (75 g) of protein (chicken, fish, soy, etc.), glucagon is secreted. Glucagon will oppose insulin and thereby help to balance blood sugar levels. To make the best choice for health and weight loss, choose low glycemic index carbohydrates (vegetables, fruits, and whole grains) and have a protein selection at every meal to ensure that you aren't oversecreting insulin. Keep in mind, an oversecretion of insulin is linked to type 2 diabetes, energy fluctuations, and excess weight.

examples of protein-rich foods

HIGH-PROTEIN FOOD SOURCES	PROTEIN (g)	CARBOHYDRATES (g)
Eggs (1 medium)	6	0
Milk (1 pint/500 mL)	19	24
Milk (8 oz/250 mL)	6.3	8
Soy milk	6	8
Tofu (100 g)	8	0.8
Low-fat yogurt, plain (50 g)	8	10
Low-fat fruit yogurt (150 g)	6	27
Fish (3.5 oz)	21	0
Cheddar cheese (3.5 oz)	25	0.1
Roast beef (3.5 oz)	28	0
Roast chicken (3.5 oz)	25	0

what's so bad about high-protein diets?

Although your body needs a certain amount of protein, too much can be harmful and wreak havoc. A good motto to follow is "Everything in moderation, nothing in excess." Excessive protein consumption (especially animal protein) can result in a variety of health issues such as heart disease, stroke, osteoporosis, and kidney stones. Many people who follow an overly high-protein diet also experience an increase in their bad cholesterol, or low-density lipoprotein (LDL), if they remain on the diet too long.

Part of the reason that high-protein diets make the numbers on the scale drop so rapidly is water loss. When you greatly increase the amount of protein you're consuming (especially from animal products), your levels of uric acid and urea are elevated. Uric acid is a toxic by-product of protein breakdown and metabolism. In order for your body to get rid of this uric acid, it must pump a lot of water into the kidneys and the urinary tract to flush out the system. Unfortunately, this massive "water flush," or diuretic effect, also results in excess mineral loss, especially calcium. Thus, the prolonged intake of a high-protein diet can overleach calcium from the bones, putting you at risk for osteoporosis.

Another risk with high-protein diets is that some of the protein you consume on a daily basis tends to be higher in fat (e.g., red meat, full-fat cheeses). The high fat content puts you at risk for developing high blood pressure, clogging arteries, raising cholesterol, and causing systemic inflammation throughout the body. Saturated fat consumption has also been linked to an increase in cancer risk.

Lastly, high-protein diets are generally low in fibre. Fibre is necessary for lowering cholesterol and forcing the excretion of waste from the body. An excess amount of protein long term can overtax the digestive system, which can lead to constipation, bloating, and gas.

You may lose weight in the short term on a high-protein diet, but you're putting your heart and health at risk if you follow it for the long term. When you do consume protein, make sure it's from selections that are lower in saturated fat, such as fish or seafood (not breaded or fried), chicken or turkey (remove the skin), egg whites, low-fat dairy products, soybeans, and lean cuts of beef on occasion.

the 5 pros of protein

It's crucial that you strike a balance between eating enough protein for muscular and cellular repair and metabolic boosting and not eating an excess amount that can have negative health consequences. To ensure that you're getting enough protein, play the "protein game." Be able to name your protein source at each meal (don't be concerned about snacks). On average, women need to consume 4 to 6 oz (115 to 170 g) of protein with each meal, whereas men who are more muscular can consume about 5 to 7 oz (140 to 200 g). To visualize, 3 oz (75 g) of protein is the same size as a deck of cards or the palm of your hands without fingers or thumb. There are five main advantages to eating an adequate amount of protein.

1. proteins are thermogenic and are necessary for weight loss.

The term *thermogenic* applies to food sources and/or supplements used to stimulate the body's burning of fat. Thermogenesis is the process in which the body generates heat to burn food, increasing the metabolic rate above normal. Exercise and exposure to cold can also initiate a thermogenic effect.

All foods have a thermogenic effect because all foods require energy to be burned and digested. Compared to carbohydrates or fats, proteins have a significantly higher rate of thermogenesis and are therefore better at boosting metabolism and keeping weight down. Thus, if two people eat 2000 calories a day, the person with a higher protein intake will have a higher metabolism.

Examples of thermogenic protein selections are:

- almost all types of fish
- bison, buffalo
- chicken breast
- egg whites (limit the yolks)
- game meats (venison, elk, etc.)
- shellfish and other seafood
- turkey breast
- very lean red meat, such as top round and lean sirloin (grass-fed is especially nutritious)

Other food sources that have a thermogenic effect include green tea, apple cider vinegar, and hot spices such as cayenne pepper, chili pepper, mustard, ginger, and bitter orange.

> Research shows higher-protein, lower-fat diets have great success with weight loss short term (six months). These diets also tend to include low glycemic index carbohydrates such as vegetables, whole grains, and fruits. Portion size and exercise are also critical to weight maintenance.

2. proteins suppress appetite.

When you consume a solely carbohydrate-dense meal, such as a bowl of white rice for dinner, a bagel and butter for lunch, or a bowl of cereal for breakfast, you'll likely be hungry one to two hours later. Why? Because your body has just burned through the carbohydrates you've consumed for fuel and your blood sugar has dipped too low. This hunger will get worse if the carbohydrates you've eaten are refined flours and sugars or processed foods.

Oftentimes, people feel in control of their food choices at home but panic a little when dining out. I am frequently asked "What can I eat?" prior to weddings, birthday parties, seasonal celebrations, and so on. One of the best pieces of advice I can offer to keep your hunger and cravings at bay at these special events is to consume 3 oz (75 g) of protein prior to your party. Selections can include an egg, a piece of chicken, a few turkey slices, or one of the *Healthy Sin Foods* protein shakes described in "Morning Starters" on page 209. You'll balance out your blood sugar and ensure that you aren't hungry for a sustained period of time. In addition, I always explain the 80-20 rule of eating to keep things realistic, which encourages healthy eating 80 percent of the time and allows for indulgences 20 percent of the time. We must keep in mind that food is one of our many pleasures and part of celebrations, festivities, and special functions. If on occasion you fall off the health wagon, don't panic. I actually encourage this! Life is all about balance, with food being no exception. If you do overeat, don't go into a state of food guilt or overanalysis. Simply move on! I have seen far too many clients self-sabotage by the thinking, "Oh … I just blew it! I'm going to throw in the towel and eat more!"

3. proteins are low on the glycemic index.

As explained in Chapter 2, the glycemic index (GI) is a tool that measures the speed of entry of a carbohydrate into the bloodstream. The faster the entry (triggered by refined flours and sugars), the more insulin is secreted in response, the more fat is stored. There are three factors that can slow the entry of carbohydrates into the bloodstream:

- protein
- fat
- fibre

This is one reason why fruits, vegetables, and whole grains have a lower GI than refined flours and sugars that have been stripped of their fibre. This is also why avocados, nuts, and seeds don't have a GI ranking because they are higher in fat and don't fluctuate blood sugar levels. Protein also has a very low GI rating and slows entry of food into the stomach. In fact, most proteins don't even have a ranking on the glycemic index because they would simply register too low a value. Those few that do have a GI rating include:

FOOD	GLYCEMIC INDEX	GLYCEMIC LOAD	RANKING FOR GI & GL
Milk, full fat	39	3	low
Milk, skim	37	4	low
Yogurt	36	3	low
Soy milk	34	4	low
Soybeans	16	1	low
Lentils	32	5	low
Kidney beans	24	4	low

Dairy products contain lactose (milk sugar) and beans contain carbohydrates, which is why GI testing can be done on them. Chicken, fish, eggs, and so on don't contain carbohydrates (or contain very little) and therefore will have no effect on blood sugar level.

4. proteins won't cause cravings.

If you suffer from "sweet toothitis," simply boost your protein intake. Remember, cravings are not an indication that you're weak or lack willpower. They're telling you that you're biochemically unbalanced. Having protein snacks and protein-rich meals, drinking a lot of water, adding spices to your foods such as cinnamon, cloves, and bay leaves, and avoiding refined flours, sugars, and artificial sweeteners will help you kill your cravings.

5. proteins aid in musculature repair post workout.

One of the many roles protein plays is as a repair agent. Your body uses protein to build, repair, and maintain almost all the tissue in your body, including muscle. When you weight train (e.g., lift free weights), you're actually "tearing" your muscle fibres under stress and breaking them down. While lifting weights is necessary to strengthen bones and muscles and to boost metabolism, the body perceives the muscular tears as a "trauma" that needs to be fixed. No macronutrient is more important than protein for building and maintaining muscles after a workout. Maintenance, repair, and growth of body tissue and musculature are accomplished by the digestion of protein into subunits called amino acids. In this form, these amino acids can enter cells, where, following direction from DNA, they can be synthesized into new proteins as needed. Without the proper support of protein after a workout, strength training and repair of muscles will be compromised.

> Approximately 75 percent of your muscle is made of water; 20 percent is protein; and 5 percent is carbohydrates (glycogen), fats, vitamins, and minerals.

common protein questions

A lack of knowledge about proteins can create many unwanted consequences in the body, such as fatigue, intense hunger, inflammation, clogging of arteries, and high blood pressure. In order to understand how to use proteins to your health advantage, I've answered the most common questions I'm frequently asked about proteins.

what is ketosis and/or a ketogenic diet?

The state of ketosis or a ketogenic diet refers to a diet in which more than 30 percent of your total caloric intake is derived from proteins. When this occurs, an excessive amount of ketones are produced, which triggers the kidneys to flush themselves free of toxins. As explained in Chapter 2, the body normally uses glucose from carbohydrates as fuel. When there is not enough glucose in the bloodstream (because of an overly high protein diet), fats have to be used as the primary source of fuel. When fats are used excessively as fuel, they are converted to ketones. The health risk with using ketones as fuel is that they aren't as efficient as glucose and are overly acidic. High levels of ketones in turn make the blood abnormally acidic. Ketone levels will show abnormally high in starvation diets, diets that are overly high in protein, and untreated diabetes. In addition to being overtaxing and dangerous to the kidneys, ketosis can result in some not-so-pleasant side effects, such as constipation and bad breath.

- insulin = fat storage hormone
- glugacon = metabolism-boosting hormone that helps break down fat
- glycogen = stored glucose (in liver and muscles) needed for quick energy

what are pulses?

Pulses are peas, beans, and lentils and are relatively energy dense. The average protein level in pulses is about 27 percent. Many vegetarians have to seek alternative sources of protein. Vegans have the most restricted protein variety (they do not eat fish, eggs, milk, or any food that is an animal by-product), while lacto-ovo vegetarians (who consume milk and eggs) and pesco vegetarians (who consume fish) have greater options. For vegetarians of all kinds, the option of pulses as protein is quite good.

are there any grains that are high in protein?

Quinoa (pronounced keen-wa) is known as the "Mother of all Grains." It has a very high protein content (12 to 18 percent)—about twice that of rice—and is a complete protein, which means it contains the eight essential amino acids your body can't make on its own (see table on page 48). Quinoa may be an especially good choice for vegetarians and vegans because it has particularly high levels of the essential amino acids lysine, cysteine, and methionine, which are typically lacking in most grains. Quinoa is also a very good source of manganese, magnesium, iron, copper, and phosphorus. It is gluten free, easy to digest, and one of the least allergenic grains.

For more information, please see Quinoa on page 176 in Top 50 Superfoods.

are protein powders a good idea?

Absolutely! Proteins are not as easy to grab as carbohydrates and take some thought and preparation. I always encourage clients to pre-cook extra chicken breasts, hardboiled eggs, or fish fillets and to have nitrate-free turkey slices, low-fat cottage cheese, or plain yogurt in their fridge for grab-and-go protein options.

High-quality protein powders are also a handy and quick way to give you a protein boost at any meal or after a workout. Most protein powders are sold in two forms: a concentrate powder or an isolate powder. Isolate powder has a higher protein content (>90 percent) than concentrate powder and has even been shown to boost immune system function. I highly recommend investing in a whey protein isolate powder. Whey protein is derived from milk and is typically lower in carbohydrates and well absorbed by the muscles. Opt for a powder that is free of artificial sweeteners and added sugars. A variety of delicious flavours are available. Please see the Product Resource Guide for recommendations.

what is the difference between dark meat and white meat? is one better?

What makes one cut of turkey or poultry darker than the other depends on what type of muscle it contains. Dark meat contains higher levels of myoglobin—a compound that is required to transport oxygen needed for fuel and activity (this is why turkey and chicken legs are darker meat).

Although many people think that white meat is healthier, the differences between white and dark meat are minimal. According to the U.S. Department of Agriculture, 1 oz (25 g) of boneless, skinless turkey breast contains about 46 calories and 1 g of fat. A skinless thigh (dark meat, 1 oz) contains 50 calories and 2 g of fat. Dark meat contains more iron, zinc, riboflavin, thiamin, and vitamins B6 and B12 than white meat. Both white and dark contain significantly less saturated fat than red meat and are a much healthier choice.

Now that you have a complete understanding of how to balance your proteins to your healthy weight advantage, let's move on to the third big macronutrient—fabulous fats!

four
fabulous fats

Of the three macronutrients—carbohydrates, proteins, and fats—none has received such an undeserving bad rap as poor little fats. As you'll soon discover, the issue is not how much fat you consume, but how much of the *good* fat you consume and how much of the *bad* fat you consume. And all fats are not created equal. Without the right type of fats, so critical to overall health, normal functioning of the human body would cease.

Gram for gram, fats are the most efficient source of food energy. While a gram of carbohydrates or protein provides 4 calories of energy, each gram of fat provides 9 calories of energy. All fats are made up of a combination of saturated, monounsaturated, and polyunsaturated fatty acids, but one type will generally predominate.

the role of fats in the body

Fats, also called fatty acids, are crucial to your health. They are the basis for every hormone, brain, and nervous system function. Good fats are a vital part of every outer cellular membrane, which is the outer barrier that allows for the transport of nutrients and the entry of glucose (sugar) and protects the cell from toxic exposure. Without a healthy cellular membrane, each cell could not function. In addition to being critical to overall cellular health, fats serve many other functions.

fats help build healthy brains.

By providing structure to the brain's myelin sheath, which surrounds and insulates each nerve fibre, omega-3 fats help nerve signals travel more efficiently. The main type of fat in the brain is DHA (docosahexaenoic acid), which is a derivative of the omega-3 fat ALA (alpha-linolenic acid) found in flaxseed, chia seeds, walnuts, and green leafy vegetables. DHA can also be found in coldwater fish and fish oils. Loss in DHA concentrations in brain cell membranes leads to a decline in structural and functional integrity of this tissue. It should come as no surprise that researchers have found that a deficiency of essential fatty acids correlates with depression, Alzheimer's disease, and attention deficit hyperactivity disorder (ADHD). Essential fatty acids are also integral to fetal brain and eye development.

Eating too many processed fats, such as trans fatty acids (TFAs), can also have a deleterious effect on brain function because essential fats (such as DHA) and TFAs (such as partially hydrogenated fats found in margarine and deep-fried and processed foods) have an inverse relationship. When one is up, the other is down. Studies have shown that eating too many TFAs drives down the levels of omega 3 in the brain. This will "harden" cellular membranes, making nerve communication difficult. This occurrence only gets worse with aging. All the more reason to eat your fish, nuts, seeds, and foods fortified with omega 3 (or DHA) and … supplement with fish oils!

> Myelin, the protective sheath that covers communicating neurons in the brain, is composed of 30 percent protein and 70 percent fat. One of the most common fatty acids in myelin is oleic acid, which is the main component of olive oil and is also available in almonds, pecans, macadamia nuts, and avocados.

fats keep arterial walls flexible.

No discussion about brain function would be complete without addressing the importance of blood flow in the brain. The brain contains 400 miles (640 km) of capillaries responsible for absorption of nutrients, delivery of oxygen, and elimination of toxins.

Essential fats such as DHA support the flexibility of blood vessels to ensure fluid transport, whereas chemical fats such as trans fatty acids harden arterial walls and can cause blockages in all areas of the body.

fats are involved in hormone production.

Fats are structural components of some of the most important substances in the body, including prostaglandins, hormone-like substances that regulate many of the body's functions. Fats regulate the production of sex hormones, which explains why some teenage girls who are too lean experience delayed pubertal development and/or loss of menstruation.

fats help the body use vitamins.

Vitamins A, D, E, and K are fat-soluble vitamins, meaning that the fat in foods helps the intestines absorb these vitamins into the body. A good rule of thumb: always take your multivitamin with food to encourage greater absorption.

fats are excellent for anti-aging and healthy, beautiful skin.

Your skin is the largest organ in your body and is often a reflection of what's going on internally. In my career, I've witnessed hundreds of individuals transform their skin as they improve their diet and clean up their nutritional act.

One of the classic signs of an essential fatty acid deficiency is dry, flaky skin. Research has shown that the essential fatty acid EPA (eicosapentaenoic acid, also a derivative of omega-3 fats) has a positive anti-inflammatory effect on skin, reducing the signs of aging (fine lines) and protecting against UV damage. EPA also helps improve conditions such as acne, psoriasis, and eczema. Supplementing your diet with a high-quality fish oil and eating omega-3-rich foods keeps skin moist, strong, and younger looking.

A 2001 study showed that vegetables, legumes, olive oil, and fish were protective against wrinkles, while butter, meat, and dairy were found to contribute to them due to the oxidative stress they cause.

fat forms a protective cushion for your organs.

Many of the vital organs, especially the kidneys, heart, and intestines, are cushioned by fat that helps protect them from injury and hold them in place. Consistent with our body's constant innate ability to protect us, the protective fat surrounding our internal organs is always the last to be drawn upon when the body's energy reserves are being tapped.

fats are satiating and give food a wonderful "mouth-feel."

Fats make food taste good and offer a satiating "mouth-feel," or texture, when consumed. When food manufacturers remove fat from an item to make a label more appealing (i.e., "low fat"), they often add sugar to enhance taste. Instead of consuming sugary, "low-fat" options, add some natural fats to your diet such as nuts, seeds, and healthy oils. If you are hungry midday, eat a few (10 to 15) raw almonds or walnuts and watch your hunger disappear and your energy soar.

debunking the top four fat myths

Prior to delving into what type of fats should make up the mainstay of your dietary intake, let's break down the top four fat myths that still persist in the health and weight-loss world.

myth #1: avoid all nuts—they are fattening!

If you were to avoid all nuts for fear of eating excess fat or calories, you would be missing out on myriad health advantages. Loaded with fibre, phytonutrients, antioxidants, vitamin E, selenium, and protein, nuts offer a powerful nutritional punch. Most importantly, they are high in monounsaturated "heart-healthy fats" and omega-3 essential fatty acids.

Researchers have found that men and women who consume nuts on a regular basis have a lower risk of developing heart disease. Nuts also help to lower cholesterol, stabilize blood sugar abnormalities (e.g., type 2 diabetes or metabolic syndrome), and are part of a well-balanced weight-loss plan.

In 2003, the U.S. Food and Drug Administration stated, "Scientific evidence suggests but does not prove that eating 1.5 oz a day of most nuts as part of a diet low in saturated fat and cholesterol may reduce the risk of heart disease." The statement included raw almonds, hazelnuts, peanuts, pecans, pine nuts, pistachios, and walnuts (all of which contain less than 4 g of saturated fat per 50 g). It is recommended to consume 1 to 2 oz (25 to 50 g) of raw nuts a day, which is equivalent to a small handful of nuts.

The two "superstar" nuts are walnuts and almonds. Tasty and satiating, walnuts have been shown to lower LDL cholesterol (the "bad" cholesterol) and prevent free radical damage in cells. Walnuts also contain more omega-3 essential fatty acids than any other nut. Almonds contain vitamin E, which offers antioxidant and anti-aging effects. They are also rich in magnesium, fibre, and protein. Almonds offer an abundant amount of heart-healthy monounsaturated fat. For a detailed breakdown of the nutrient value and health benefits of walnuts and almonds, please see pages 197 and 94 in Top 50 Superfoods.

> Adding a daily ration of almonds to a low-calorie diet enhances weight loss and significantly reduces risk of heart disease. Researchers cited almonds' heart-healthy monounsaturated fat as being very satiating, helping satisfy the appetite and prevent patients from overeating.

Because nuts are so high in fat (albeit the "good" fat), they are very high in calories. For example, 15 cashews contains 180 calories. (And these are raw nuts. Unless you are having the occasional treat, avoid nuts coated in sugar, salt, or candy.) Trust me, it is far too easy to overconsume nuts if they are left out in a bowl on your counter or in a large bag. Portion them out in advance by putting 10 to 15 nuts in a small container or plastic bag. This way, you'll reap all the health benefits without the risk of overeating.

Don't forget to also enjoy some heart-healthy seeds in your daily diet, such as flaxseed, pumpkin seeds, and sunflower seeds—all are rich in omega-3 essential fatty acids.

One-quarter of a cup (50 mL) of walnuts provides 90 percent of the recommended daily intake of omega 3.

the amount of fat in nuts

	TOTAL FAT (% OF TOTAL WEIGHT)	SATURATED FATS (% OF TOTAL FAT)	MONO-UNSATURATED (% OF TOTAL FAT)	POLY-UNSATURATED (% OF TOTAL FAT)
Almonds*	52	10	68	22
Brazil nuts	66	26	36	38
Cashews	46	20	62	18
Hazelnuts*	63	8	82	10
Macadamia nuts*	74	16	82	2
Peanuts	49	15	51	34
Pecans	68	8	66	26
Pine nuts	61	15	40	45
Pistachios	48	13	72	15
Walnuts**	62	10	24	66

 * Almonds, hazelnuts, and macadamia nuts are highest in monounsaturated heart-healthy fat.
** Walnuts are highest in omega-3 essential fatty acids.

myth #2: avoid seafood and eggs—they raise cholesterol.

Do you remember in the 1980s when we were told to minimize shrimp and eggs in our diet to keep cholesterol levels at bay? As it turned out, this statement was simply not true and therefore qualifies as a myth. Cholesterol in eggs, seafood, and other meats has little to no effect on cholesterol levels in the body. In fact, it is estimated that 80 percent of total cholesterol comes from the body, with a remaining 20 percent being derived from the diet. What *does* have the greatest impact on your cholesterol levels is your dietary intake of saturated fat and trans fatty acids. While seafood does contain cholesterol, it is also low in saturated fat, making it a wonderful protein option. Eggs contain a substance called lecithin, which actually helps to decrease cholesterol in the body.

myth #3: fats lead to heart disease and cancer.

If you're referring to trans fatty acids (TFAs) and saturated fats, then yes, this myth does contain some truth. Saturated fats and TFAs are pro-inflammatory and linked to high cholesterol, heart disease, obesity, and a variety of cancers.

If you're referring to the good fats—the monounsaturated and essential fatty acids—then this myth is still firmly a myth. Foods such as olive oil, raw nuts and seeds, coldwater fish, fish oils, flaxseed, avocados, and natural nut butters have been shown to be heart healthy, possess anti-cancer effects, and are actually beneficial for lowering cholesterol and helping with the battle of the bulge.

myth #4: fat-free and lower-fat foods are the solution to obesity.

Ah, if this were only true, the onslaught of "low-fat diets" and "low-fat foods" would show a dent, not a rise, in the soaring current obesity statistics. Fats make food taste delicious, and without them, sugar is typically added back into the product to compensate for taste. We have all seen the red licorice at the checkout of our local movie theatre or grocery store that claims "no fat!" While this is indeed true, it does not state that the licorice has a high glycemic index that will trigger excess secretion of insulin. Excess insulin = excess fat. In order to get the "skinny" on food labels and health, it's important to put the nutritional puzzle pieces together!

the "good" fats and what they do

Now that we've debunked the prevalent fat myths, let's focus on the types of fats that are necessary for optimal physical and mental well-being and can even help with weight loss. Because fats make foods taste so good, you'll find the fats discussed here (a.k.a. the "good" types of fats to eat) are also listed in Top 50 Superfoods and included in the 101 *Healthy Sin Foods* Recipes.

When discussing fats that are beneficial for health, there are two main categories: monounsaturated fats and essential fatty acids.

monounsaturated fats

Monounsaturated fats are usually liquid at room temperature but can turn solid in the refrigerator. Examples include olive oil, canola oil, peanut oil, sesame oil, macadamia nuts, avocados, and almonds. These fats have been highly researched to determine their status as heart-healthy fat options that can also lower bad cholesterol (called low-density lipoprotein, or LDL).

Of all the monounsaturated fats, the most popular and highly researched is olive oil, which is made up of about 75 percent monounsaturated fat. Numerous studies have shown olive oil to have enormous health benefits, such as:

- reducing blood pressure
- reducing bad cholesterol (LDL)
- inhibiting the growth of some cancers
- assisting with blood sugar control in diabetics
- reducing the severity of asthma and arthritis
- helping to maintain a lower body weight

When selecting an olive oil, choose one in a dark bottle labelled "extra virgin," which means it came from the first pressing of the olive. The less pulverized the olive (i.e., the less processing), the greater the antioxidant and nutrient benefits in the oil.

essential fatty acids

Essential fatty acids are classified as polyunsaturated fats, but they are unique in that they can't be made by the body and therefore must come from the diet. There are two main categories of essential fatty acids: omega 3 (alpha-linolenic acid, or ALA) and omega 6 (linoleic acid, or LA).

omega-3 essential fatty acids

Omega-3 essential fatty acids (also called n-3 fats) have received a lot of media attention because of their enormous health benefits. There are two groups of n-3 fats:

1. Eicosapentaenoic acid (EPA) and docosahexaenoic acid (DHA), which are derived mainly from fish and fish oils and are highly absorbed by the body.
2. Alpha-linolenic acid (ALA), which is found in flaxseed oil, nuts (especially walnuts), leafy green vegetables (broccoli, spinach), canola oil, and wheat germ.

ALA is converted into DHA and EPA by the body. However, research has demonstrated that most people aren't that efficient at this conversion, so it's important to incorporate fish and distilled fish oils into your diet to reach your ideal levels of DHA and EPA. The best fish are oily and low in toxicity, including wild salmon or herring, sardines, rainbow trout, kippers, and mackerel.

Unfortunately, most North Americans tend to be deficient in omega-3 fats, which can result in myriad symptoms and disorders. Many scientists think an omega-3 deficiency is linked to several Western degenerative diseases on the rise, such as heart disease, cancer, allergies, asthma, arthritis, and even certain brain function disorders such as ADHD and depression. My feeling is that these diseases and disorders are increasing because of a combination of lack of exercise, poor diet, overconsumption of processed and packaged food, a decline in fresh live food, an increase in environmental toxicity, and, most definitely, a deficiency of omega-3 essential fats.

On average, an ideal omega-3:omega-6 ratio is 1:2. Most North Americans are critically low in their omega-3 intake and have an omega-3:omega-6 ratio of about 1:20. Why is omega 3 so critically low in the Western diet? First, our consumption of bad fats (saturated fats, trans fatty acids, and omega-6 refined oils such as safflower, sunflower, and corn oil) is way too high. Too many of the bad fats drive omega-3 levels down. Second, food manufacturers shy away from using essential fatty acids because they are so fragile. The average shelf life of an omega-3 fat is very short and thus doesn't suggest as high a profit margin when the product becomes rancid within a short time. However, some incredible new research on omega-3 fats has caused food manufacturers to take a second, closer look. There are a variety of "functional foods" now available in grocery stores that have been fortified with DHA and EPA—from omega-3 bread and bagels to soy milk, yogurt, infant formula, and orange juice. I would encourage you to include these omega-3 fortified foods in your diet wherever possible.

Possible signs and symptoms of omega-3 deficiency include:

- skin problems, including acne, psoriasis, eczema, dry skin, poor wound healing, and premature aging
- poor fertility
- inflammatory conditions such as arthritis
- high cholesterol and impaired glucose tolerance
- obesity
- hormonal fluctuations and premenstrual syndrome (which can exacerbate disrupted sleep patterns, hot flashes, etc.)
- allergies
- asthma
- learning disorders such as ADHD and ADD
- depression
- Alzheimer's

Because your brain is composed of more than 60 percent fat and is very rich in omega-3 derivatives such as DHA, it's important to boost your diet daily with omega-3-rich foods (especially those from marine sources). Some simple tips to boost your omega-3 daily intake include:

- Add a distilled high-quality fish oil into your daily supplement regime.
- Sprinkle crushed walnuts on your salad or steamed vegetables.
- Eat high-quality fish sources such as wild salmon two to three times a week.
- Buy omega-3-fortified eggs, orange juice, yogurt, or bread.
- Add 1 tsp (5 mL) of flaxseed oil to your protein smoothie.
- Use ground flaxseed in muffins or sprinkle on top of yogurt.
- To avoid the 3 p.m. slump, choose walnuts or almonds as your healthy snack.

omega-6 essential fatty acids

Omega-6 essential fatty acids are consumed in much higher amounts in the Western diet and are found abundantly in refined soy oil, safflower and corn oil, sunflower seeds, pumpkin and sesame seeds, nuts, and borage and primrose oil. The typical North American diet contains too much linoleic acid (LA), or omega-6 fats, in comparison to alpha-linolenic acid (ALA), or omega-3 fats. While a certain amount of high-quality omega 6 is necessary in the diet, an overingestion of refined vegetable oils (corn, safflower, sunflower) found in processed foods such as crackers, cookies, margarine, and so on can cause inflammatory reactions in the body and drive down omega-3 levels.

Although polyunsaturated fats do lower the levels of bad cholesterol (LDL), they are also believed to lower the levels of good cholesterol (high-density lipoprotein, or HDL). As a general rule, avoid the refined vegetable oils in clear plastic bottles on the grocery store shelves such as safflower, corn, and sunflower oil. Not only are these oils highly refined and contribute to inflammation, but they can oxidize very quickly, which puts them at risk for becoming rancid. The best type of omega-6 oils in the diet are found in raw nuts, seeds, legumes, borage oil, grapeseed oil, and primrose oil in dark bottles. Similar to olive oil, store these oils in a dark, cool environment.

the "bad" fats and what they do

saturated fats

Saturated fats are typically solid at room temperature and are found in animal sources such as meat, poultry, butter, and cheese. Saturated fats are also found in tropical oils such as coconut, palm, and palm kernel oils.

Eating an excess amount of saturated fat can contribute to the development of high cholesterol, high blood pressure, heart disease, and inflammation. Thus, the American Heart Association recommends limiting the amount of saturated fats you eat to less than 7 percent of total daily calories. For example, if you need about 2000 calories a day, no more than 140 of them should come from saturated fats. That's about a 1/2 oz (16 g) of saturated fats a day.

When it comes to some of your old favourites like hamburgers and ice cream, there are ways to still enjoy the close "cousins" of your favourite foods without eating all that saturated fat. Instead of a hamburger, why not switch to a salmon or veggie burger? Loaded with all the toppings of mustard, relish, onions, tomatoes, and more, you won't even notice the difference! Look at the fat grams you'll be saving:

- typical hamburger = 4 to 7 g of saturated fat
- extra-lean ground beef burger (90 percent lean) = 3 to 5 g of saturated fat
- chicken, turkey, or salmon burgers = 2 to 3 g of saturated fat
- average veggie burger = 0 to 1 g of saturated fat

what about cheese?

North Americans love cheese. Our cheese consumption has hit the roof, with the U.S. Department of Agriculture estimating that Americans eat 30 pounds (14 kg) of cheese a year! That compares to only 11 pounds (5 kg) in 1970. Must we eliminate cheese altogether from the diet to keep our hearts healthy and our cholesterol low? The answer is absolutely not. Cheese can be consumed in moderation, but it should be treated as a flavouring ingredient, not as a main element of your meal. For example, use Parmesan shavings in a salad, sprinkle some goat cheese into an egg white omelette, or grate some organic sharp mozzarella over your warm chili. As far as quantity goes, 1 to 2 oz (25 to 50 g) of full-fat cheese 2 to 3 times a week is plenty (the size and thickness of your thumb is about 1 oz/25 g of cheese).

Try drinking skim milk and fortified orange juice and eating low-fat plain yogurt, low-fat cottage cheese, and dark green leafy vegetables as wonderful calcium sources.

the amount of saturated fat in cheese

CHEESE (1 OZ/25 g)	SATURATED FAT (g)	TOTAL FAT (g)
Blue cheese	5.3	8
Brie	4.9	8
Cheddar cheese	6	9.5
Cottage cheese (2% fat)	2.8	4
Edam cheese	5	8
Feta cheese	4.2	6
Goat cheese	7	10
Gouda cheese	5	8

Did you know that 2 tbsp (25 mL) of regular cream cheese contains a whopping 10 g of fat with two-thirds of the fat being saturated? You can cut the fat in half by opting for light cream cheese, which contains about 5 g of total fat for 2 tbsp (25 mL) with 2 to 3 g being saturated fat.

In order to determine the type of fat you may be consuming, check the Nutrition Facts panel on food labels. The panel also lists the amount of saturated fats and trans fatty acids per serving. Remember, it's important to check the serving size to ensure that you're not eating two times the value listed on the Nutrition Facts panel!

trans fatty acids (TFAs)

A small amount of trans fatty acids occurs naturally in meat and milk, but the majority of TFAs are found in packaged and processed foods. TFAs are created by flooding vegetable oil with hydrogen atoms, which changes the oil's slightly curved chain molecule to a straight chain molecule. The straight chain molecules withstand better in food production, and thus TFAs are added to processed foods to generate a longer shelf life—the advantage every food manufacturer is looking for. Unfortunately, the disadvantage to our health is great. TFAs are the worst type of bad fat, with a long list of damaging side effects, including:

- raising the risk of coronary heart disease—the number-one killer of men and women
- raising cholesterol
- promoting the development of inflammation
- promoting the development of Alzheimer's disease
- possibly raising the risk of certain types of cancers such as breast and prostate cancer
- increasing the risk of type 2 diabetes
- increasing the risk of obesity
- possibly promoting the incidence of infertility

The U.S. Food and Drug Administration (FDA) Food Advisory Committee recommends that daily trans fatty acid intake be reduced to less than 1 percent of energy (i.e., 2 g per 2000 kcal diet). Thankfully, it is now much easier to identify trans fatty acids in food sources. As of January 1, 2006, all packaged food products in North America must list trans fat content on the Nutrition Facts panel. The amount of trans fat per serving of food appears under Total Fat. The FDA requires that the amount of trans fat in a serving be listed on a separate line under saturated fat on the Nutrition Facts panel. However, when the Nutrition Facts panel says the food contains 0 g of trans fat, it means the food contains less than 0.5 g of trans fat per serving. So if you eat more than one serving, you could easily and quickly reach your daily limit of trans fat. You can also check your ingredients list. If you see the words *partially hydrogenated*, the food item contains trans fatty acids.

what is cholesterol?

Cholesterol is a waxy, fat-like substance found in all cells. Your body needs cholesterol to make hormones and vitamin D, to maintain healthy cell walls, and to make bile acids that aid in fat digestion. While cholesterol is found in certain foods naturally (eggs, cheese, red meat, shrimp, etc.), a majority of the cholesterol in your body is produced by your liver.

Cholesterol travels in the bloodstream in mini-packages called lipoproteins. These small packages are made from lipids (fats) on the inside and proteins on the outside. There are two main lipoproteins that carry cholesterol in the blood:

1. Low-density lipoprotein (LDL) is considered the bad cholesterol, as it's more likely to clog up arteries. LDL carries the cholesterol away from the liver into the bloodstream (where it runs the risk of sticking to vessels). The buildup of cholesterol along arterial walls is plaque buildup, called atherosclerosis (hardening of the arteries). If over time there is a blockage in the brain, it is called a stroke. If there is a blockage in one of the arteries travelling toward the heart, it can lead to a heart attack.
2. High-density lipoprotein (HDL) is considered the good cholesterol. HDL carries the cholesterol back to the liver where it can be broken down.

While a certain degree of genetics does play into cholesterol levels, from a dietary and exercise standpoint, there's a lot that can be done. For example:

- Limit saturated fats as much as possible and avoid trans fatty acids.
- Eat high-fibre foods (both soluble and insoluble).
- Exercise on a regular basis (a minimum of five times a week).
- Maintain a normal body weight, body mass index, and waist circumference measurement. The body mass index is a calculation that uses your height and weight to estimate how much body fat you have. The equation is a person's weight in kilograms (kg) divided by height in metres (m) squared. A BMI > 25 is considered overweight, whereas a BMI > 30 is considered to be obese. To calculate your own body mass index quickly, visit www.nhlbisupport.com/bmi.
- Make all your sandwiches with whole grain bread (see the Product Resource Guide).
- Use extra virgin olive oil in your salad dressing to help lower LDL levels.
- When you have an alcoholic beverage, opt for red wine. Research has shown it to be beneficial in boosting HDL levels. Red wine contains a plant compound called saponins that is believed to be responsible for this positive effect.
- Spice it up with cinnamon! A study conducted in Pakistan found that about 1 tsp (6 g) of cinnamon a day reduced LDL cholesterol in type 2 diabetics and reduced cholesterol overall by 26 percent.

> There aren't any signs or symptoms of high blood cholesterol. In fact, many people don't know their cholesterol level is too high. High cholesterol is diagnosed by a blood test that checks cholesterol levels.

how much fat do we need daily?

According to the World Health Organization (WHO), we should restrict our dietary fat intake to 30 percent of our calories. Of that, a maximum of 10 percent should come from saturated fats. Certain heart associations typically recommend less fat, at about 20 to 25 percent of total daily calories, with only 7 percent being derived from saturated fat. If you follow the WHO guidelines, on a 2000 daily caloric intake, your maximum fat grams would be equivalent to:

$$30\% / 2000 \text{ calories} = 600 \text{ calories from fat}$$
$$600 \text{ calories} / 9 = 66 \text{ g of total fat}$$

Whether you eat 25 or 30 percent of your total daily calories from fat, the "take home" point on fats is to remember the statement in the first paragraph of this chapter: The issue is not how much fat you consume, but how much of the *good* fat you consume and how much of the *bad* fat you consume. In order to tally up how much fat you are consuming daily, check food labels and refer to "Fats and Food Labels," below, for the meaning behind fat claims.

Fats and Food Labels

THE FOLLOWING CLAIMS ARE DEFINED FOR ONE SERVING:

Fat-free	Less than 0.5 g fat
Low fat	3 g or less fat
Reduced or less fat	At least 25% less fat*
Light	One-third fewer calories and/or 50% less fat*

* As compared with a standard serving size of the traditional food.

Tips to skim unwanted fat in the diet include:

- Instead of bacon bits in your salad, sprinkle sesame seeds or pumpkin seeds for an extra crunch.
- Replace whole milk with skim or low-fat milk in puddings, soups, and baked products.
- Choose lean cuts of meat, and trim any visible fat from meat before and after cooking. Remove skin from poultry before or after cooking.
- Choose cuts of red meat and pork labelled "loin" and "round"; they usually have the least fat.

- Change your method of cooking. Broil, bake, steam, or poach rather than fry.
- When purchasing cheese, pick low-fat varieties. Use cheese as a flavouring ingredient instead of a main part of your meal.
- Do you love pepperoni pizza? If so, opt for vegetarian pepperoni made from soy. Once the sauce and low-fat cheese are loaded on top with vegetables, you won't even notice the difference!
- Avoid flavoured milk, such as vanilla, chocolate, or strawberry. It usually has added sugars, fat, and calories.
- When purchasing eggs, opt for omega-3 eggs, which contain about 300 to 400 mg of omega-3 essential fats per egg.

Now that you have all the need-to-know information on carbohydrates, proteins, and fats, let's find out how to stock your kitchen for optimal health and decadence!

five
the complete kitchen

You've learned how to manage and combine the big-three macronutrients—carbohydrates, proteins, and fats—to get the most out of your dietary strategy. Now it's time to discover the rest of the nutritional equation necessary for healthy eating and living. In addition to stocking your kitchen with oils, nuts, seeds, lean proteins, fruits, vegetables, and high-quality dairy products, it's critical to have the proper information and tools to make smart and delicious eating second nature. In this chapter, I've provided simple methods to stock your kitchen, compiled the ideal *Healthy Sin Foods* grocery list, and advised on how to interpret food labels. The Top 10 *Healthy Sin Foods* Rules to jumpstart your health are also included. Implement these 10 simple rules and you'll reward yourself with a natural surge in energy and mood. Best of all, your body will automatically gravitate toward a healthy and stable body weight.

must-have kitchen basics

There are certain kitchen utensils and tools that make food preparation and healthy eating more efficient and practical. While it may be a small investment upfront, a well-stocked kitchen will ensure that you'll always have the right type of equipment on hand. Whether you're preparing for regular meals, dinner parties, or grab-and-go snacks, your time in the kitchen will be made a whole lot easier with the following:

countertop blender

A countertop blender with a strong motor is the most effective kitchen tool for making creamy protein shakes and vegetable drinks and mixing salad dressings and soup broths. Choose a heavy-glass, tapered-jar blender that will last over time in the dishwasher. It's also important to buy a large-enough blender to suit your needs, with the right voltage. The more you plan on using your blender, the higher the wattage should be to handle the job. If you're storing your blender on the counter, you may want to choose a colour that matches your kitchen and isn't a continual eyesore. Lastly, after use, take apart your blender, clean it thoroughly with hot water, or run it through the dishwasher. Old food particles settled in the bottom of the blender can be a health hazard.

hand blender

Hand blenders are ideal for smaller blending or puréeing jobs where cleaning an entire blender is not necessary. A high-quality hand blender is powerful enough to chop vegetables and meats and purée sauces, dips, or dressings. To avoid a mess, however, be sure to place all ingredients deep enough in the mixing bowl to reduce splatter.

set of good kitchen knives

Every kitchen should have the following top three knives:
- a paring knife with a firm 3- to 4-inch (8 to 10 cm) blade for peeling vegetables and fruits
- a French knife (also called a chef's knife), which has a broad tapered shape and a fine edge; ideal for chopping vegetables
- an 8-inch (20 cm), or longer, serrated knife for slicing soft vegetables, such as tomatoes, and breads

durable cutting board

There has been great discussion about which type of cutting board is the safest and least likely to provide a breeding ground for bacteria. In truth, if not cleaned and used properly, any type of board can become a vehicle for contamination. Options include wooden, Corian, plastic, or glass boards. Cutting boards should be cleaned with hot soapy water after each use. If your board becomes cracked and overly porous, it's time for a new one.

steamer or steaming basket

Investing in a kitchen steamer or a steaming basket that fits over a stovetop pot is one sure way to preserve the colour, texture, and taste of your vegetables. More importantly, steaming retains more nutrients than any other cooking method and is by far the healthiest method. When steaming, try to cut vegetables into the same size so they steam evenly.

VEGETABLE	STEAMING TIME (MIN)
Artichoke, medium	40
Asparagus, thin spears	3–4
thick spears	5–6
Broccoli, florets	4–5
spears	5–6
Brussels sprouts	7–11
Carrots, cut 1/4-inch (5 mm) thick	6–8
Cauliflower, head	12–15
florets	4–6
Corn on the cob	5
Green beans	4–5
Kale	4–5
Potatoes, new	12
2-inch (5 cm) pieces	15
Spinach	4–5
Sweet potatoes, whole	40–50
1-inch (2.5 cm) pieces	12–15

food journal/notebook

Current research has demonstrated that keeping a daily food journal actually helps with weight loss and health. According to a study soon to be published in the *American Journal of Preventative Medicine*, people who didn't keep a daily diary lost an average of 9 pounds (4 kg), while those who kept a diary six or more days per week lost an average of 18 pounds (8 kg) over a 20-week period. A food journal and/or notebook will help you to record what you've eaten on a specific day, the groceries you need to buy, and the recipes you may want to make. (Please see the sample *Healthy Sin Foods* grocery list on page 82.) Keep this journal handy so it's easy to grab while you're working in the kitchen.

seasoning cupboard or pantry

One of the absolute keys to creating enjoyable meals and snacks is a well-stocked seasoning pantry. A list of starter spices includes:

- basil
- black pepper
- cayenne pepper
- chili powder
- cinnamon
- curry powder
- garlic powder
- minced garlic (jarred in refrigerator)
- minced ginger (jarred in refrigerator)
- onion powder
- oregano
- poultry seasoning
- salt
- white pepper

measuring utensils and kitchen scale

For the novice chef, using proper measurements is critical to ensure that a recipe turns out as intended. There are a variety of kitchen scales, ranging in price from $10 and up, but there's no need to spend a great deal of money. Suggested capacity is a minimum 1 pound (500 g), with both metric and imperial measurements. A removable and washable top tray is recommended. Other must-have measuring utensils include:

- measuring cups, from 1/4 cup (50 mL) to 4 cups (1 L)
- measuring spoons (usually come as a set and include the full range of measurements)

---

1 g of fat = 9 calories

1 g of protein = 4 calories

1 g of carbohydrate = 4 calories

1 g of alcohol = 7 calories

4 g of sugar = 1 tsp of sugar

---

cooking times for grains

DRY MEASURE 1 CUP (250 ML)	WATER OR STOCK	COOKING TIME (h/min)	YIELD
Barley (hulled)	3 cups (750 mL)	1.5 h	3 1/2 cups (875 mL)
Barley (pearl)	3 cups (750 mL)	50 min	3 1/2 cups (875 mL)
Brown rice	2 cups (500 mL)	45 min	3 cups (750 mL)
Buckwheat	2 cups (500 mL)	15 min	2 1/2 cups (625 mL)
Millet	3 cups (750 mL)	45 min	3 1/2 cups (875 mL)
Quinoa	2 cups (500 mL)	15 min	2 1/2 cups (625 mL)
Wild rice	3 cups (750 mL)	1 h	4 cups (1 L)

sample of a healthy sin foods grocery list

GRAINS

- ○ brown rice, millet, and/or quinoa
- ○ slow-cooking oatmeal (steel-cut oats)
- ○ whole grain bread, wraps, or bagels
  (see Product Resource Guide)
- ○ whole grain cereal

FRUITS AND VEGETABLES

- ○ apples, apricots, bananas, berries, clementine oranges, melon, pears, peaches, pineapple, and plums
- ○ broccoli, carrots, cauliflower, celery, cucumbers, eggplant, garlic, kale, mushrooms, onions, spinach, squash, sweet potatoes, tomatoes, endive, and zucchini

PROTEINS

- ○ black cod, haddock, halibut, herring, shrimp, sole, tilapia, wild salmon
- ○ canned fish packed in water
- ○ chicken and turkey breast or lean ground meat
- ○ firm tofu, edamame, vegetarian meats and burgers, tempeh
- ○ omega-3 eggs and egg whites
- ○ protein powder and protein bars (see Product Resource Guide)
- ○ lean ground beef, turkey, or chicken
- ○ salmon, turkey, or chicken burgers
- ○ nitrate free turkey or chicken slices

DAIRY PRODUCTS

- ○ 1% cottage cheese
- ○ light goat cheese
- ○ plain yogurt (flavoured yogurt as well, to mix in if desired)
- ○ skim milk

FATS

- ○ avocados
- ○ black or green olives / extra virgin olive oil
- ○ nuts (almonds, pistachios, walnuts)
- ○ seeds (sesame seeds, sunflower seeds, pumpkin seeds)

TREATS

- ○ dark chocolate chips for baking
- ○ popcorn kernels (for air-popped popcorn)
- ○ spelt or whole wheat flour for baking

healthy sin foods substitutions

When stocking your kitchen, remember the motto "Any recipe can always be made healthier." Here are some healthier options for all your favourites.

INSTEAD OF ...	TRY ...
Cream cheese	Light cream cheese or low-fat ricotta cheese
Flavoured yogurt	Plain yogurt mixed with berries (or 1/2 plain, 1/2 flavoured yogurt)
Whole milk	1% milk or skim milk
Eggs	2 egg whites
Ground beef	Ground turkey or chicken
Hamburger	Veggie, salmon, chicken, or turkey burger
White or whole wheat bread	100% whole grain bread
Juice	Eat the fruit—drink the water!
Sugar for baking	Applesauce or mashed bananas
Pepperoni pizza	Veggie pepperoni pizza
Chips	Baked nachos
Pretzels	Air-popped popcorn

grocery shopping 101

When you shop at the grocery store and eyeball a food label, it can seem like a confusing game of science! What is a serving size? What does "fat free" really mean? Should I buy low calorie or calorie free? To take the guessing game out of interpreting food labels, refer to Nutrient Content Claims for the definitions of a variety of nutrient claims. Once you get the Nutrition Facts panel know-how, you'll be able to interpret all food labels and decide if it's a healthy choice for you and your family.

nutrient content claims

Calorie Free	Less than 5 calories per serving
Low Calorie	40 calories or less per serving
Fat Free	Less than 0.5 g saturated fat per serving
Saturated Fat Free	Less than 0.5 g saturated fat and less than 0.5 g trans fatty acids per serving
Low Fat	3 g or less fat per serving
Low Saturated Fat	1 g or less saturated fat per serving
Sodium Free (or Salt Free)	Less than 5 mg sodium per serving
Very Low Sodium	35 mg of sodium or less per serving
Low Sodium	140 mg of sodium or less per serving
Reduced Sodium	At least 25% less sodium per serving than the regular version
Cholesterol Free	Less than 2 mg cholesterol per serving
Low Cholesterol	20 mg or less cholesterol per serving
Reduced Cholesterol	At least 25% less cholesterol per serving than the regular version
Sugar Free	Less than 500 mg sugar per serving
Reduced Sugar	At least 25% less sugar per serving than the regular version
High Fibre	5 g or more fibre per serving
Good Source of Fibre	2.5–4.9 g fibre per serving

Checking the Nutrition Facts panel is only part of your research, however. For example, a product that is labelled "fat free" may have less than 0.5 g of fat per serving, but it might also be loaded with high fructose corn syrup to enhance taste. To get the full story, you should always check the ingredients list *and* the Nutrition Facts panel to find out the amounts of calories, total fat, saturated and trans fats, cholesterol, sodium, carbohydrate, fibre, sugars, protein, and so on for a specified serving. Here's what to look for:

Nutrition Facts

Serving Size 1 cup (228g)
Servings Per Container 2

Amount Per Serving

Calories 250	Calories from Fat 110

	% Daily Value*
Total Fat 12g	18%
Saturated Fat 3g	15%
Trans Fat 1.5g	
Cholesterol 30mg	10%
Sodium 470mg	20%
Total Carbohydrate 31g	10%
Dietary Fiber 0g	0%
Sugars 5g	
Protein 5g	

Vitamin A	4%
Vitamin C	2%
Calcium	20%
Iron	4%

* Percent Daily Values are based on a 2,000 calorie diet. Your Daily Values may be higher or lower depending on your calorie needs:

	Calories:	2,000	2,500
Total Fat	Less than	65g	80g
Sat Fat	Less than	20g	25g
Cholesterol	Less than	300mg	300mg
Sodium	Less than	2,400mg	2,400mg
Total Carbohydrate		300g	375g
Dietary Fiber		25g	30g

serving size

Serving sizes are located at the top of the panel. These amounts are standardized to make comparison easier with other food items and are provided in familiar units such as cups or grams. It is crucial to pay attention to serving size. While a food item may appear lower in fat or calories, its serving size might be quite small. You have to be careful how many servings you eat. Depending on the amount, you may consume up to two or even three times the serving size, which can mean two or three times the fat, sugar, and sodium!

calories (kcal)

A calorie is a unit of energy and differs from food to food. Calories on the Nutrition Facts panel provide a measurement of how much energy you obtain after eating a serving size (or more) of a specific food.

nutrients listed

The Nutrition Facts panel lists total fat, saturated fat, cholesterol, carbohydrates (including fibre and added sugars), protein, vitamins A and C, calcium, and iron. Other nutrients may be included if the manufacturer decides to do so. Effective January 2006, all labels have to indicate the presence of trans fatty acids.

percent daily values

Percent daily values provide an estimate of the percentage of a nutrient from one serving in a typical 2000-calorie diet.

- 5 percent or less of a nutrient is considered a poor source of that nutrient.
- 10 to 20 percent of a nutrient is considered a good source of that nutrient.
- More than 20 percent of a nutrient is considered a high source of that nutrient.

ingredients list

The ingredients list is always ordered from most to least. If the first word on the ingredients list is *sugar*, the food contains more sugar than any other ingredient. As a rule, it's wise to avoid foods that list the first one or two ingredients as sugar (high fructose corn syrup, sucrose), fats and oils (vegetable oils, soybean oil), or salt. If the packaged or processed food has several ingredients you've never heard of or can't pronounce, put it back on the shelf. Chances are it isn't a healthy food item and is filled with preservatives, flavour enhancers, and/or food colouring.

estimate your portions

Oftentimes, the portions we eat are bigger than we realize. In order to eyeball your food and not suffer from "portion distortion," use the following techniques:

- 3 oz (75 g) meat, fish, chicken = 1 deck of cards
- 4 oz (113 g) tofu = 1/2 baseball
- 2 tbsp (25 mL) peanut butter = 1 golf ball
- 1.5 oz (38 g) cheese = 3 dominos
- 1/2 cup (125 mL) pasta or rice = 1/2 baseball or a small fist
- 1 pancake or waffle = a 4-inch (10 cm) CD
- 1 small muffin = a large egg
- 1/2 cup (125 mL) cooked vegetables = 1/2 baseball or a small fist
- 1 cup (250 mL) salad greens = 1 baseball
- 1 small baked potato = size of a computer mouse
- 1 medium-sized fruit = 1 baseball

top 10 *healthy sin foods* rules

As we come to the end this first section, I want to leave you with the Top 10 *Healthy Sin Foods* Rules to jumpstart your health. Whether you choose to implement some or all of the rules at once is up to you. The key is that now *you* possess a set of health strategies so valuable that you can change your life. Simply refer to these rules from time to time if you find your nutritional choices are "slipping" or if you need a good "health kick" to get you back on track.

1. When food shopping, make 70 to 80 percent of your visit from the periphery of the store, where fresh, whole live foods are stocked. Remember, you must "eat live to feel live." This includes loading up on fruits, vegetables, high-quality dairy products, nuts, seeds, lean meats and fish, and whole grains. Be cautious of foods from the interior of the store, where most of the processed and packaged goodies lie. Check the Nutrition Facts panel to ensure that you are indeed making a healthy choice.

2. Make a commitment to eat two to three raw food choices a day. Your body will thank you for the minerals, vitamins, and enzymes it receives. Keep cut-up broccoli, celery, cucumbers, and carrots in the fridge. Sliced pineapples, berries in a bowl, and small clementine oranges are also instant energy and health boosters. Once home from the grocery store, don't put any vegetables into the fridge without cutting them up. This will take an extra five minutes to do, but it drastically reduces the amount of produce you throw away.

3. Make sure you have grab-and-go protein options on hand to keep weight and insulin levels at bay. Prepare these protein selections when you have an hour on your hands to shop and stock. For example, on a Sunday night, prepare hard-cooked eggs, chicken and turkey slices, grilled chicken breasts, and tuna or salmon salad.

4. Healthy foods are more available than ever before. Buy your nuts and seeds from the bulk section, opt for pre-washed salad for those busy days, visit your local salad bar for a calorie-wise, nutrient-dense lunch, and shop at your local farmers' market. Organic delivery boxes are also now widely available.

5. Whenever you can, avoid foods with added sugars. Sugar is one of the major "health robbers" of our time. Added sugars are linked to being overweight and obesity, type 2 diabetes, heart disease, energy and mood fluctuations, and compromised immune system function.

6. If you were a fly on my office wall, you'd often hear me say, "You're not sick— you're thirsty!" Simply invest in a glass or stainless-steel water bottle and drink, drink, drink! One of the quickest methods to boost energy and stay alert throughout the day is to continually drink water. If you feel that drinking water is a chore, add a small amount of juice or fresh-squeezed lemon into your water to enhance the taste. In addition, put a dot of ink on your hand. Every time you look at the dot, it should remind you to take a sip of water. For the environment and your health, try to avoid drinking from plastic bottles. Also, one cup (250 mL) of coffee a day is just fine (and even contains some antioxidants), but don't overdo it.

7. Go to sleep and wake up at the same time each day. The body has a natural circadian rhythm that it thrives on. The healthiest people in the world fall asleep naturally within five to seven minutes and can wake each day at the same time without an alarm clock. Avoid watching TV, reading the paper, or working out immediately before bed. Also, ensure that you sleep in a completely dark room at

night to promote the secretion of the anti-cancer hormone melatonin (secreted from 2 to 4 a.m.).

8. There is no way around it—you must move! Find a form of exercise you enjoy and engage in physical activity for a minimum of three to five times a week for a minimum of 20 to 30 minutes. Of course, in the summer it's far easier to go for a walk or run. In the winter, if you own a piece of cardiovascular equipment such as a treadmill or elliptical or stationary bike, you're ahead of the game! If a piece of equipment is not an option in your home, during the winter visit your local community centre for an indoor walking/running track, go to the mall for a briskly paced stroll, or join the closest gym. I would also recommend picking up inexpensive free weights and an exercise ball and mat for upper body and abdominal work. Pilates and yoga tapes are also wonderful options for at-home workouts. The more you move, the better you'll feel. The better you feel, the more you'll want to continue!

9. Take a minimum of 20 minutes a day for yourself. Whether you're a busy mother of three or the CEO of a Fortune 500 company, you must engage in daily "you time." "You time" can include listening to music, taking a bath, journalling, meditating, or waking up 20 minutes earlier to enjoy a quiet morning and a cup of tea. You'll find by engaging in a daily "you time" ritual, your day will become far more organized, calm, and balanced.

10. Supplement wisely. Supplements should be your nutritional safety net used in conjunction with a healthy diet. As a starting point, a high-quality multivitamin (taken with food), fish oils, and green powders can help to keep your immune system strong while improving the overall look of your skin and hair.

Please refer to the Product Resource Guide on page 375 for more information.

Now that we've finished Need-to-Know Nutrition, let's move on to Top 50 Superfoods, followed by 101 *Healthy Sin Foods* Recipes!

top 50 superfoods

The term *superfoods* refers to a group of foods that pack a powerful nutritional punch. Superfoods are whole foods close to their original source that haven't been refined, processed, or preserved, such as fruits, vegetables, nuts, seeds, oils, protein, and whole grains. From helping to develop brain function and strengthening the immune system to lowering cholesterol and assisting with weight loss and anti-aging effects, these top 50 superfoods have the unique ability to optimize health and wellness and prevent, and even reverse, a variety of disease processes. To make the most of your meals, you should include these 50 "nutritional superstars" in your diet on a regular basis.

I considered the following criteria when selecting *Healthy Sin Foods'* top 50 super-foods:

- phytonutrient (plant-based chemical) content
- glycemic index and glycemic load rating
- calories and suitability for weight loss
- fibre, mineral, vitamin, and protein content

The following section introduces each of the 50 superfoods and provides quick tips, selection and storage instructions, and preparation methods. These superfoods are also included in the final section, 101 *Healthy Sin Foods* Recipes, to ensure that you'll be enjoying easy-to-prepare, mouth-watering recipes that offer more bang for your nutritional buck.

Note: Certain foods in the following section will not have a glycemic index or glycemic load rating, as it is not applicable (n/a). For example, free-range chicken (mostly protein and some fat) or avocados (fat) do not alter blood sugar levels and thus, scientists do not run glycemic index or load ratings on these types of foods.

almonds

As one of the most popular, versatile, and extensively researched nuts, almonds are a wonderfully healthy addition to any meal or snack. Although nuts tend to be higher in calories and fat, the primary fat in almonds is heart-healthy monounsaturated fat. Almonds are also loaded with an abundant amount of minerals, fibre, and protein, which means that you only need to eat a few to feel satiated. In fact, a good weight-loss tip is to eat five to six almonds prior to a meal to fill you up.

Five large-scale studies (including the Nurses' Health Study) have concluded that eating almonds on a regular basis helps to reduce cholesterol levels. In addition, almonds provide a rich source of vitamin E, which is a fat-soluble antioxidant that promotes cardiovascular health by reducing low-density lipoprotein (LDL, the bad cholesterol). Almonds also help with weight loss. A recent *British Journal of Nutrition* study demonstrated that substituting saturated fats (e.g., full-fat cheeses, red meats) for monounsaturated fats (olive oil, in this study) caused obese patients to lose a significant amount of weight. Even though the calories were exactly the same, monounsaturated fats appeared to have a fat-burning effect. A 2003 study in the *International Journal of Obesity* found that a daily ration of almonds in a low-calorie diet enhanced weight loss and significantly improved risk factors associated with heart disease when compared to a low-fat, low-calorie diet. Researchers cited almonds' heart-healthy monounsaturated fat as being very satiating, which helped prevent overeating.

Eating almonds whole (with the skin) appears to have more heart-healthy and overall health benefits. According to the *Journal of Nutrition*, the flavonoids found in the almond skin tend to "partner up" with vitamin E and more than double the antioxidant value of the nut.

nutritional breakdown

Suitable for weight loss: yes ✓, when consumed in moderation (i.e., 10–15 for the perfect snack size)

Calories per 1 oz (28 g, or about 23 nuts): **162**

Glycemic index rating: **n/a**

Glycemic load rating: **n/a**

Almonds are an excellent source of vitamin E (37% of daily value) and manganese (32% of daily value). They also provide good amounts of magnesium (19% of daily value), riboflavin (17% of daily value), and phosphorus (14% of daily value).

selection and storage

Shelled and unshelled almonds are widely available pre-packaged or in bulk. As with any foods you buy in bulk, to ensure maximum freshness make sure the store has high turnover and the bins are well covered and show no signs of moisture. Unshelled nuts will keep the longest. When selecting unshelled almonds, make sure they're not split, cracked, or stained, which could indicate mould on the nut inside. When selecting shelled almonds, look for ones that are uniform in colour and not limp or shrivelled. Smell is a good indicator of freshness. If their odour is sharp or bitter, chances are they may be rancid.

It's important to store almonds properly because of their high fat content. To preserve freshness, keep shelled almonds in a glass container in the refrigerator or freezer for up to 12 months. Unshelled almonds will stay fresh for up to six months if stored in a cool, dry place or longer if kept in the fridge. Don't shell the almonds until they're ready to be used.

preparation and recipe ideas

Almonds are delicious as is but can also be a tasty addition to many meals.

- Almond butter is a nutritious topping for toast or muffins at breakfast or with slices of apples or stalks of celery for a quick snack. You can make your own almond butter by chopping and puréeing whole shelled almonds in a food processor with a bit of almond oil (or water) until smooth.
- Turn almonds into a healthy breading for chicken or fish or as a topping for casseroles. Add toasted almonds to a food processor and pulse until coarsely ground. Add sea salt, ground pepper, and any combination of spices to suit the dish. Dip chicken or fish in milk or a beaten egg and then dunk in the nut mixture. Cook as usual for a yummy, crunchy topping.

- Almonds are great on salads as croutons. Pre-heat oven to 350°F (180°F). Toss 1 cup (250 mL) slivered almonds with 1 tbsp (15 mL) olive oil in a flat, shallow baking pan. Spread the almonds into a single layer and sprinkle with 1 tbsp (15 mL) grated Parmesan cheese and 1/2 tsp (2 mL) garlic salt. Bake for 5 to 10 minutes or until brown, stirring once and watching closely. Cool. Sprinkle the almond croutons on salads, steamed vegetables, or baked sweet potato.
- Frozen banana-almond pops are sure to please the kid in everyone. In the top of a double boiler, melt a bar of chocolate that has more than 70% cocoa solids. Peel bananas and cut each one in half, crosswise. Insert an ice-pop stick into the cut end of each banana. Line a baking sheet with waxed paper. Dip each banana into the melted chocolate and roll in chopped toasted almonds. Lay bananas on baking sheet and freeze for 4 to 5 hours.

DID YOU KNOW?

Although we think of almonds as a nut, technically they are the seed of a fruit that grows from the almond tree.

apples

Research suggests that, indeed, "an apple a day keeps the doctor away." Phytonutrients found in apples such as phenolics, flavonoids, and carotenoids play a key role in reducing the risk of chronic disease. In fact, the consumption of apples on a regular basis has been linked with the reduction of a variety of cancers, cardiovascular disease, asthma, and diabetes.

Apples contain quercetin, an anti-allergy flavonoid. Quercetin suppresses the release and production of two inflammatory compounds called histamine and leukotrienes, which are responsible for allergic symptoms such as a runny nose, blocked sinuses, itchy eyes, skin blotches, coughing, and wheezing. Quercetin is mainly concentrated in the apple skin, so choose a fresh apple over apple juice or applesauce. Although any variety of apple is a good source of quercetin, red apples tend to have more of the powerful antioxidant than green or yellow apples.

In a recent analysis of a number of studies involving dietary flavonoids, apples were singled out as one of a small number of fruits and vegetables that contributed to a significant reduction in heart disease. One of the antioxidant effects of whole apples, especially their skin, is to protect LDL (bad cholesterol) from oxidation. This protective effect against free radical damage to cholesterol reaches its peak at three hours after apple consumption and drops off after 24 hours, providing yet another good reason to eat a whole fresh apple a day.

nutritional breakdown

Suitable for weight loss: **yes ✓**
Calories per 1 medium raw apple with skin (182 g): **95**
Glycemic index rating: **34 (low)**
Glycemic load rating: **5 (low)**

Apples are a good source of fibre (17% of daily value) and vitamin C (145% of daily value). They also contain beneficial amounts of potassium (6% of daily value) and vitamin K (5% of daily value).

selection and storage

There are more than 25 different kinds of apples, so selection will depend on your taste buds. As a guideline, the Red and Golden Delicious are the sweetest, the Braeburn and Fuji are less sweet, the McIntosh and Empire are tarter, and the Pippin and Granny

Smith are the most tart. Look for firm, crisp apples with rich colour. Avoid apples with bruises or wrinkly skin, and those that feel soft when you apply pressure to the skin.

Apples can stay at room temperature for a few days, but if you want to keep them longer, store them in the crisper drawer of the refrigerator. Don't store apples in a plastic bag, as this encourages moisture and causes them to spoil. You can also store apples for up to three months if done correctly. Select only perfect apples for this because the saying is true: one bad apple spoils the bunch. Wrap each unwashed apple in newspaper and stack in a basket or box. Store in an unheated basement, enclosed porch, pantry, or root cellar—somewhere cool but where the apples won't freeze.

Apples are reported by the Environmental Working Group in the United States as the second most heavily pesticide-contaminated produce product available. Consider purchasing organic apples.

preparation and recipe ideas

The only preparation an apple needs is a gentle rubbing under cool running water. When the apples are sliced, the enzymes in the flesh will oxidize, causing it to turn brown. To avoid this, prepare a bowl of 2 cups (500 mL) water and 2 tbsp (25 mL) fresh lemon juice and place the cut apples in it until you're ready to use them. Here are some apple tips to apply to your diet.

- Toss some apples into your next salad. In a large bowl, whisk together a dressing of 1/3 cup (75 mL) honey, 1/4 cup (50 mL) fresh lemon juice, 1/2 tsp (2 mL) lime zest, and 1 tsp (5 mL) Dijon mustard. Core two Granny Smith apples and cut into thin julienne strips. Shred 4 cups (1 L) of cabbage (use any kind: red, green, Savoy) and chop 2 green onions. Toss everything together and enjoy.
- Enjoy a baked apple on a crisp fall day. Core a McIntosh or Empire apple, place in a glass pan, and fill the apple with a combination of raisins, brown sugar, and walnuts. Cook in a 325°F (160°C) oven for about 30 minutes or until soft. Serve with a dollop of vanilla frozen yogurt or ice cream for an extra treat. Please refer to page 360 for a delicious baked stuffed apple recipe.

DID YOU KNOW?
One hundred grams of apple has the same antioxidant activity as 1500 mg of vitamin C. The average apple is 150 g.

apricots

Thought to have originated in China, this small, velvety golden orange fruit is a low-calorie sweet treat. Apricots are often overlooked as a raw fruit in favour of apples or bananas, but look again because they help protect the heart and eyes and provide the disease-fighting effects of fibre.

Apricots are an abundant source of beta-carotene, the precursor of vitamin A, which helps promote good vision. Vitamin A is an antioxidant that combats the free radical damage that affects the lens of the eye and sets the stage for macular degeneration. Research published in the *Archives of Ophthalmology* suggests that eating three or more servings of fruit a day could lower the risk of age-related macular degeneration by 36 percent.

Apricots are also a rich source of the carotenoid called lycopene, which has had positive effects on heart disease, cataracts, high cholesterol, and a number of cancers, including prostate cancer. A 2007 study found an inverse relationship between men's consumption of lycopene-rich foods such as apricots, tomatoes, watermelon, and papaya and the development of prostate cancer. The men who consumed these foods more frequently were found to have an 82 percent reduced risk of prostate cancer compared to men eating the least amount of lycopene-containing foods. Add green tea to the diet in conjunction with these foods and the protective effect is even stronger.

nutritional breakdown

Suitable for weight loss: **yes** ✓
Calories per 1 raw apricot (35 g): **17**
Glycemic index rating of dried apricots: **31 (low)**
Glycemic load rating of one dried apricot: **1 (low)**

Apricots are a good source of vitamin A (13% of daily value) and contain beneficial amounts of fibre (3% of daily value), vitamin C (6% of daily value), and potassium (3% of daily value).

selection and storage

One of the first fruits of summer, apricots are at their peak in North America from May to July. When selecting fresh apricots, look for an even orange colour without bruising or soft spots. Because apricots are delicate when ripe, they're often picked green, so note that pale yellow or green apricots haven't been tree-ripened and may not be as flavourful. If you need to ripen apricots at home, place a few in a paper bag to trap the ethylene gas that promotes ripening. Check daily. Once the apricots are slightly soft and smell wonderfully sweet, they're ready to eat. Ripe apricots can be stored in the refrigerator for about three days but are best eaten quickly.

When purchasing dried apricots, be aware that most have been preserved with sulphites to prevent discolouration and the growth of bacteria. Sulphites can cause adverse reactions, and asthmatics are at particular risk. Apricots dried without sulphites will be brown instead of bright orange, but their nutritional content is intact.

preparation and recipe ideas

A simple washing under running water is the best way to prepare a fresh apricot. Then slice, remove the pit, and enjoy. When slicing apricots, the enzymes in the flesh will oxidize and cause browning. To avoid this, dip the slices into a mixture of 2 cups (500 mL) water and 2 tbsp (25 mL) fresh lemon juice. In order to boost your apricot intake, consider the following.

- Apricots are a delicious addition to breakfast. Slice them into your oatmeal, muesli, or yogurt, or add them to pancakes, muffins, and quick breads.
- Try apricots on the barbecue. Skewer whole or halved apricots, brush with honey or maple syrup, and grill for 5 to 10 minutes, turning once or twice. For a less sweet approach, mix the honey or maple syrup with steak sauce and brush the apricots often during grilling. Serve as is or with grilled chicken.
- Use apricot in salads, both as the fruit and in the vinaigrette. In a blender, combine 4 or 5 fresh pitted apricots with 1 to 2 tbsp (15 to 25 mL) balsamic vinegar, 1 large minced garlic clove, 1 tsp (5 mL) chopped fresh thyme, and 2 tbsp (25 mL) olive oil. Blend until smooth. Serve with deep greens such as arugula and spinach.

DID YOU KNOW?
Astronauts ate dried apricots on the *Apollo* moon missions.

avocados

Avocados (also called butter pears or alligator pears) are a buttery-rich green fruit that adds flavour and health benefits to salads, appetizers, sandwiches, dips, and wraps. Once considered a luxury food reserved for the tables of royalty, now avocados are enjoyed by people from all walks of life.

Although avocados are high in fat (75 percent), the majority of fat is heart-healthy oleic acid or monounsaturated fat. Avocados are also free of sodium and cholesterol and beneficial for high cholesterol levels. One study of individuals with moderately high cholesterol who ate a diet rich in avocados showed significant decreases in both total cholesterol and low-density lipoprotein (LDL, the bad cholesterol) while also showing an 11 percent increase in high-density lipoprotein (HDL, the good cholesterol). Avocados are very rich in folate and vitamin B6, which work together to help reduce homocysteine, an amino acid that can damage artery walls and promote atherosclerosis (plaque buildup within the arteries, also known as clogging of the arteries).

One of the busiest areas of nutritional research is that of carotenoids, a group of more than 700 compounds that produce the vibrant pigments in fruits and vegetables. Dietary intake of carotenoid-rich foods has been associated with a reduced risk of a variety of diseases, including macular degeneration, cardiovascular disease, and cancer. Avocados have generous amounts of the carotenoids lutein and zeaxanthin, and a *Journal of Nutrition* study found that people absorbed three to five times more carotenoids from an already carotenoid-rich salad when they ate it with avocado than when they ate it without.

nutritional breakdown

Suitable for weight loss: **yes ✓, but watch portion size (avocados are rich in good fat so are higher in calories)**
Calories per 1 avocado (200 g): **322**
Glycemic index: **n/a**
Glycemic load: **n/a**

Avocados are an excellent source of many nutrients, including copper (33% of daily value), potassium (28% of daily value), and vitamins E (21% of daily value) and

K (53% of daily value). Avocados also provide an excellent source of the B vitamins folate (41% of daily value), pantothenic acid or B5 (28% of daily value), and B6 (26% of daily value). With 13.5 g of fibre, one avocado supplies 54% of the daily value for this important nutrient.

Note: While avocados are a heart-healthy fruit, they should be eaten in moderation if on a weight-loss plan (1/4 to 1/2 avocado a day).

selection and storage

Look for avocados that are heavy for their size and free of bruises or dark sunken spots. Avoid ones that rattle when you shake them, as this means they're overripe and the pit has pulled away from the flesh. When an avocado is ripe, its skin will turn from bright green to dark brown-green or almost black and the once-hard skin will yield slightly to pressure.

Avocados will ripen in about five to seven days at room temperature. To speed up the process, place them in a paper bag, which will trap the ethylene gas produced by the avocados, and add a banana or an apple to produce more ethylene gas. Once the avocados are ripe, store them in the refrigerator for two to three days; it's best to eat them within two days. Beyond this, avocados will lose their flavour and begin to turn brown.

Avocados can also be frozen. Remove the skin and the pit and purée the avocado with 1/2 tsp (2 mL) lemon or lime juice. Freeze in an airtight container for up to five months. Avocado slices, however, don't freeze well.

- Classic guacamole is a perennial favourite. Mash 1 medium avocado with 1 tbsp (15 mL) lemon or lime juice, add about 1/4 cup (50 mL) each of minced onion, cilantro, and red peppers or fresh tomatoes. Add sea salt and pepper to taste.
- Instead of butter or mayonnaise on your next sandwich, add thin slices of avocado to add a buttery texture and a hit of nutrients.
- Try mashed avocado on top of chili or a baked sweet potato instead of sour cream.
- Add puréed avocado to oil-and-vinegar salad dressing for a smooth, creamy taste and texture.

DID YOU KNOW?
Similar to bananas, avocados are a climacteric fruit, which means they mature on the tree but only ripen once picked.

black beans

Beans, peas, lentils, and peanuts are collectively known as legumes, which are plants that have pods with tidy rows of seeds inside. Legumes contain many of the nutrients recognized as important in preventing heart disease, cancer, obesity, and other chronic diseases. Black beans (also called turtle beans) are medium-sized oval beans with black skin and white flesh. They have a mild, slightly sweet flavour that has been compared to mushrooms.

Black beans have less fat and more fibre than animal protein and are a popular vegetarian source of protein.

Although beans are mostly carbohydrates, they have a low glycemic index (GI) because of their rich amount of soluble fibre. Thus, beans offer a slow-burning fuel that keeps your metabolism active and keeps blood sugar levels from rising too quickly following a meal.

The low GI rating is good news for weight-loss seekers and diabetics as it's very helpful in the management and prevention of hypoglycemia (low blood sugar), insulin resistance, and diabetes. In fact, in one study, two groups of people with type 2 diabetes followed a diet of either 24 or 50 g of fibre a day. The higher-fibre group reported lower levels of both blood sugar and insulin. As well, they also experienced an almost 7 percent reduction of total cholesterol and a 10 percent reduction in their triglyceride levels.

Beans are also very rich sources of the B vitamin folate. Folate plays a critical role in the reduction of homocysteine levels. When homocysteine accumulates in the body, it is damaging to the blood vessel walls and poses an increased risk for cardiovascular disease. Just 1 cup (250 mL) of cooked black beans contains 64 percent of the daily requirement for folate. Delivered along with the folate in the beans is a healthy dose of magnesium, potassium, and calcium, a mineral-electrolyte combination associated with a reduced risk of high blood pressure and heart disease.

nutritional breakdown
Suitable for weight loss: **yes** ✓
Calories per 1 cup (250 mL) cooked black beans (172 g): **227**
Glycemic index rating: **30 (low)**
Glycemic load rating: **7 (low)**

Black beans are an excellent source of the B vitamins folate (64% of daily value) and thiamin (28% of daily value). They also provide excellent levels of manganese (38% of daily value), magnesium (30% of daily value), phosphorus (24% of daily value), and iron (20% of daily value).

selection and storage

Dried legumes are generally available pre-packaged and in bulk. To ensure maximum freshness, make sure the store has high turnover and the bins are well covered and show no signs of moisture. Look for dried black beans that are uniform in colour and not wrinkled, as this is a sign of age. Store them in an airtight container in a cool, dark, dry place for up to 12 months. When purchasing canned beans, look for brands without added salt. Rinse all canned beans extremely well to reduce sodium (salt) content. Unlike canned vegetables, which have lost much of their nutritional value, there is little difference in the nutritional value of canned black beans and those you cook yourself. Cover cooked beans and store in the refrigerator for about three days.

preparation and recipe ideas

For proper preparation of all legumes, see Chickpeas: Preparation and Recipe Ideas on page 126. Here are a few easy ways to include black beans in your diet.

- Start your day with beans. Scramble an egg, a couple avocado slices, a couple tablespoons (25 to 50 mL) of cooked black beans, and some salsa. Top with chopped cilantro, roll it up in a whole grain wrap, and enjoy.
- Combine cooked black beans with your choice of chopped raw vegetables (peppers, onions, tomato, and cooked corn). Toss with a lime and olive oil dressing, and serve on a bed of quinoa or brown rice.
- Black bean soup is a treat on a cold day. Purée cooked black beans, olive oil, chili powder, and sea salt and pepper to taste. Add stock to desired consistency and top with plain yogurt and chopped cilantro.

DID YOU KNOW?

Black beans are as rich as cranberries in the antioxidant compounds called anthocyanins. The darker the bean's seed coat, the higher its antioxidant capacity.

black cod

Black cod (also called sablefish or butterfish) is found only in the North Pacific. The white flesh of this nutrient-packed large fish has a sweet, rich flavour (because of its high oil content) and a velvety, flaky texture.

Black cod is a lean source of protein and boasts almost as many healthy omega-3 fats as wild salmon. The two omega-3 fats present are docosahexaenoic acid (DHA) and eicosapentaenoic acid (EPA), which perform different functions in the body. DHA is highly concentrated in the brain, where it helps brain cells communicate and protects them from conditions such as Alzheimer's disease. It is also concentrated in the retina, where it's critical for visual function. EPA is important for healthy blood vessels, heart health, and brain function. It has anti-inflammatory and anti-clotting properties that help guard against many chronic diseases.

Black cod contains high amounts of selenium (67% of daily value). An increasing body of evidence suggests a strong inverse relationship between selenium intake and cancer incidence. Certain forms of cancer develop because of free radical oxidation that causes DNA damage in human cells. Because DNA regulates cell multiplication, these damaged cells can begin to multiply abnormally and further damage surrounding healthy tissue. Selenium appears to stop this process because it promotes DNA repair and synthesis in damaged cells. Selenium is also part of glutathione peroxidase, an antioxidant that is particularly important for cancer protection.

nutritional breakdown
Suitable for weight loss: **yes** ✓
Calories per 100 g cooked (dry heat) black cod: **250**
Glycemic index rating: **n/a**
Glycemic load rating: **n/a**

Black cod also contains beneficial amounts of many B vitamins, including excellent levels of niacin or B3 (26% of daily value) and B12 (24% of daily value) and excellent levels of phosphorus (22% of daily value).

selection and storage

When purchasing fresh black cod, ensure that the store has a reliable reputation and high turnover rate, and that the fish is fresh. Find out which day fresh fish is delivered and plan your shopping accordingly. Buy black cod displayed on crushed ice instead of pre-packaged. The flesh should be firm, elastic, and pearly white. The larger the fish, the better the texture and flavour. Smell it to make sure it isn't "fishy": fresh fish should smell more like the ocean than fish. Take the fresh black cod home right after purchasing or bring a cooler with ice if you're going to be at the market for a while. Fresh black cod will keep for a few days in the refrigerator, but it's best to cook it as soon as possible.

preparation and recipe ideas

Rinse the black cod under cold running water and pat dry before cooking. Black cod requires 7 to 10 minutes per inch (2.5 cm) of thickness for cooking. If the fillet, steak, or whole fish is less than 1 inch (2.5 cm) thick, it will take half the time. Black cod is best grilled, broiled, baked, or pan-seared. It can also stand up to long, slow cooking methods such as braising without losing its texture.

- Black cod in miso is one of the most popular ways to enjoy this appetizing fish. In a saucepan, combine 3/4 cup (175 mL) mirin (sweet Japanese cooking wine) and 1/2 cup (125 mL) sake. Boil for 20 seconds over medium heat to evaporate the alcohol. Add 1 cup (250 mL) white miso paste and stir until it dissolves completely. Add 1 cup (250 mL) sugar, turn the heat to high, and stir continuously until the sugar has dissolved. Remove from heat and cool to room temperature. Place the 5-ounce skinless black cod pieces in a glass dish and slather with the miso mixture, setting aside a few spoonfuls for garnish when serving. Cover tightly and refrigerate the fish and sauce for two days. When ready to cook, heat grill, lightly wipe excess miso off the fish, and cook until fish is opaque in the centre. Serve with reheated reserved sauce.

DID YOU KNOW?

Black cod are extremely long-lived fish, estimated to live 90 years. The oldest age reported is 114 years.

blueberries

The small but mighty blueberry should be on everyone's superfoods list. An overwhelming body of research has now firmly established that eating these sweet, scrumptious berries has a positive and profound impact on human health. Blueberries have been shown to limit the development and severity of certain cancers and diseases such as atherosclerosis, stroke, and the neurological decline seen in Alzheimer's disease and other age-related brain conditions.

Blueberries are loaded with powerful antioxidant compounds called flavonoids and proanthocyanidins, which protect brain cells against damaging inflammation and oxidative stress. Both of these processes are thought to be the probable underlying causes of brain aging. In animal experiments, blueberry phytonutrients effectively reversed age-related short-term memory losses. At a 2007 symposium on berry health, research showed that the consumption of blueberries (and similar berry fruits, including cranberries) may help alleviate the cognitive decline occurring in Alzheimer's disease and other conditions of aging.

The richly coloured pigments that give blueberries their red, purple, and blue tones are called anthocyanins. Promising research shows that anthocyanins (also found in strawberries, blackberries, cranberries, red currants, purple cabbage, and eggplant) have a detrimental effect on cancer in all phases: initiation, promotion, and proliferation. Cancer is often initiated when a carcinogen causes cellular DNA damage that goes unrepaired. The antioxidant capacity of blueberries can help prevent this damage. Anthocyanins also help stop the proliferation of cancer because they accelerate the rate of cancer cell death, called apoptosis, essentially making the cancer cells die faster. So be sure to add lots of colour to your plate every day for maximum health benefits. A good rule of thumb is dark blue, purple, or black fruits that easily stain your fingers (or thumb) during picking are great sources of anthocyanins.

nutritional breakdown

Suitable for weight loss: **yes ✓**
Calories per 1 cup (250 mL) raw blueberries (148 g): **84**
Glycemic index rating: **53 (low)**
Glycemic load rating: **6 (low)**

Blueberries contain excellent amounts of vitamins K (36% of daily value) and C (24% of daily value) and manganese (25% of daily value). They are also a good source of fibre (14% of daily value).

selection and storage

When choosing fresh blueberries, look for firm ones with uniform colour and a whitish bloom (which protects the skin from decay). Avoid berries that are soft and watery, as any moisture will cause them to rot. Ripe blueberries will keep covered in the refrigerator for about one week but are best when eaten within a few days. Don't wash the berries until you're going to eat them.

If you're purchasing frozen blueberries, shake the bag to ensure that the berries are loose. If they're clumped together, they may have been previously thawed and refrozen. You can freeze your own ripe blueberries, but be aware that they won't be as firm after they've been thawed (but they'll be good for smoothies and blueberry sauce). Before freezing, wash berries well and pat dry. Spread them out in a single layer on a baking sheet and place flat in the freezer until frozen. Once frozen, transfer to a freezer bag or other container—they will keep in the freezer for about one year.

preparation and recipe ideas

Wash fresh blueberries just before you eat them so you don't remove the whitish bloom that protects the skin. If you're using frozen blueberries in recipes that don't require any cooking, be sure they're thawed first. If the recipe does require cooking, keep the blueberries frozen until you add them to the recipe to ensure the freshest taste. You may have to adjust the cooking time slightly to accommodate the frozen berries. Here are some berrylicious tips.

- Fresh blueberry sauce goes with everything—pound cake, frozen yogurt, ice cream, and whole grain waffles. Simply purée fresh blueberries and use as is, or try a quick-cook sauce. Mix 2 cups (500 mL) of blueberries and 1/3 cup (75 mL) sugar; boil for about 1 minute. Add 1 tbsp (15 mL) fresh lemon juice and 1/2 tsp (2 mL) real vanilla extract. Use hot or cold.
- Add powerful antioxidants to breakfast—in your protein smoothie, on your oatmeal or cereal, in your yogurt, or on your French toast.

- Try blueberries in a salad. Use a mix of dark leafy greens with a bit of peppery arugula and raspberry vinaigrette. Top with lightly toasted walnuts, crumbled feta or goat cheese, and 1 cup (250 mL) fresh blueberries.
- Blueberries are great on grilled salmon. Sauté 1/2 cup (125 mL) chopped onions and 2 to 3 cloves of minced garlic in 1 tbsp (15 mL) olive oil until tender. Add 1 cup (250 mL) blueberries, 1 tsp (5 mL) brown sugar, a dash of balsamic vinegar, and about 1/2 cup (125 mL) chopped fresh basil, and cook for another minute or so. Brush salmon with this before putting it on the grill and also use it to spoon over grilled fish before serving.

DID YOU KNOW?

According to a U.S. Department of Agriculture Agricultural Research Service study, organically grown blueberries have significantly higher levels of total anthocyanins and antioxidant activity than conventionally grown blueberries.

broccoli

Broccoli is a member of the cruciferous family of vegetables, which also includes brussels sprouts, cauliflower, cabbage, kale, bok choy, collard greens, turnip, and horseradish. Although broccoli did not gain popularity in North America until the 1920s, today there are a number of broccoli varieties, such as broccolini (a cross between broccoli and kale), broccoflower (a combination of cauliflower and broccoli), and broccoli raab (a peppery version of broccoli with more leaves and a longer stem).

Like other cruciferous vegetables, broccoli contains phytonutrients that demonstrate significant anti-cancer effects. Compounds called isothiocyanates, specifically indole-3-carbinol, have been shown to deactivate a potent by-product of estrogen metabolism that promotes cancer growth, especially in estrogen-sensitive breast cells. Another phytonutrient in broccoli called sulforaphane boosts the liver's detoxification enzymes and helps to clear potentially carcinogenic substances from the body more quickly.

Broccoli is a rich source of two antioxidants in the carotenoid family, lutein and zeaxanthin. These compounds are concentrated in the lens of the eye. A large study of more than 30,000 people found that those who ate broccoli more than twice a week had a 23 percent lower risk of developing cataracts compared to those who ate broccoli less than once a month. A broccoli-rich diet also provides bone-building vitamin K, calcium, and large amounts of vitamin C, which greatly increases the absorption of calcium.

nutritional breakdown

Suitable for weight loss: **yes ✓**
Calories per 1 cup (250 mL) chopped raw broccoli (91 g): **31**
Glycemic index rating: **n/a** (*Note:* Broccoli doesn't have a GI rating because it's so low.)
Glycemic load rating: **3 (low)**

Broccoli is an excellent source of vitamins C (135% of daily value) and K (116% of daily value) and a good source of folate (14% of daily value) and vitamin A (11% of daily value). Broccoli contains many minerals, including calcium (4% of daily value), potassium (8% of daily value), and manganese (10% of daily value). One cup (250 mL) of chopped broccoli offers 2.4 g of fibre.

selection and storage

A deep colour in broccoli is a good indicator of nutrient value, so look for tightly formed heads that are dark green, purplish, or bluish-green rather than paler yellow. Choose bunches with firm stalks that aren't hollow or woody. Stalks that bend or are rubbery generally indicate broccoli that isn't very fresh. Avoid broccoli with open, flowering, or yellowish bud clusters, which indicates overmaturity. Store broccoli in a plastic bag in the crisper section of the refrigerator. Wash just before using.

preparation and recipe ideas

Broccoli can lose valuable vitamins and phytonutrients when overcooked. To prevent significant nutrient loss and for optimal flavour, steam broccoli for a maximum of 5 to 7 minutes. Steaming is a better way of maintaining nutrients versus boiling as the food is surrounded by water dispersed in air rather than being completely submerged in the water itself. The decreased water contact with the surface of the broccoli results in less nutrient loss. Cut the stems about 1 inch (2.5 cm) below the florets. The broccoli stalk can be peeled, washed, and eaten as well. Stir-frying broccoli lightly in oil is an alternative and equally delicious method of preserving nutrient content.

In order to boost your broccoli intake, add some of these simple tips to your diet.

- Try broccoli slaw. Peel the tough outside layer from the broccoli stems and slice into matchstick size. Toss with shredded carrots and a coleslaw-type dressing for a new twist on an old favourite.
- Add bite-sized broccoli florets to your favourite stir-fry recipe.
- Enjoy broccoli in a hearty soup. Purée cooked broccoli and cauliflower, combine with stock and seasonings of your choice, and sprinkle with freshly ground pepper and a sharp cheese for a simple, savoury soup.
- Try broccoli for breakfast. Add florets and chopped stalks to your morning omelette.

DID YOU KNOW?
One cup (250 mL) of broccoli contains more vitamin C than one orange.

brown rice

As one of the original ancient grains, rice is believed to have been cultivated in China for at least 6000 years. In some parts of Asia, the word for rice is the same as that for food, for agriculture, and even for life itself.

There are thousands of different types of rice around the world. Generally, rice is categorized by its size (long, medium, and short grain) and the method used in processing. Brown rice is minimally processed and has only had the outer hull removed. It still retains the white, starchy interior (endosperm), as well as the nutritious outer layers (the bran) and the embryo (germ). These layers, which give rice its brown colour and nutty flavour, are rich in B vitamins and fibre. The complete milling and polishing that converts brown rice into white rice destroys 67 percent of the vitamin B3, 80 percent of the vitamin B1, 90 percent of the vitamin B6, half of the manganese, half of the phosphorus, 60 percent of the iron, and all of the dietary fibre and essential fatty acids. In fact, fully milled and polished white rice is required to be enriched with vitamins B1, B3, and iron.

There are several health benefits to eating brown rice. For adults, brown rice is optimal for weight loss, can help to lower the risk of type 2 diabetes and cholesterol, promotes regularity, and can reduce the risk of heart disease. For infants, brown rice is often a first introductory grain as it is hypoallergenic and rich in antioxidants.

Brown rice appears to play two important roles in the prevention of colon cancer. First, by being a good source of fibre, it helps reduce the transit time through the bowels, which decreases the amount of time potentially cancer-causing substances spend in contact with colon cells. Second, brown rice contains selenium, an important mineral that functions as a cofactor in the compound glutathione peroxidase, which is one of the body's most powerful antioxidant enzymes and is used in the liver to detoxify a wide range of potentially harmful molecules. When levels of this antioxidant are too low, toxic molecules are not disarmed and can wreak havoc on any cells they come in contact with.

nutritional breakdown
Suitable for weight loss: **yes ✓**
Calories per 1 cup (250 mL) cooked long-grain brown rice (195 g): **216**
Glycemic index rating: **50 (low)**
Glycemic load rating: **16 (medium)**

Brown rice is an excellent source of manganese (88% of daily value), selenium (27% of daily value), and magnesium (21% of daily value). It is also a good source of fibre (14% of daily value).

selection and storage
Brown rice will not keep as long as white rice, so it's important to check the expiration date on pre-packaged rice. When buying in bulk, make sure the store has high turnover and the bins are well covered and show no signs of moisture. Stored in an airtight container, brown rice will keep for up to six months. Refrigeration will extend this by a few months.

preparation and recipe ideas
Before cooking, all grains (except oats) should be rinsed thoroughly under cool running water to remove the dirt and debris. For brown rice, because of its longer cooking time, the ratio of water or broth to rice becomes 2 1/2 cups (625 mL) of liquid to 1 cup (250 mL) of rice. Each rice type is different so follow the instructions on the package, but generally brown rice needs to cook for about 45 minutes.

- Add anything you have on hand to jazz up a rice side dish. Try chopped cilantro, Parmesan cheese, 2 tbsp (25 mL) olive oil, and some lemon zest.
- Brown rice and beans and your choice of vegetables make a hearty, healthy meal.
- Instead of composting leftover rice, add it to soups, broths, and stews. You can also use it to make terrific cold salads by adding chopped vegetables, nuts, herbs, even fruit.
- Try brown rice pasta instead of wheat pasta.
- Homemade sushi rolls are easy to make by wrapping brown rice and sliced cucumber, carrots, and avocado in nori sheets.

DID YOU KNOW?
Brown rice does not contain gluten, making it a good choice for those with food allergies and sensitivities.

cabbage

Cabbage may well be the king of the cruciferous family, named for its cross-shaped (crucifer) flower petals. Hardy and easy to grow, cabbage is a dominant world food crop, available in almost all countries and cultures. While green cabbage is the most popular variety, others include red, Savoy, napa, and bok choy.

One set of characteristics that separates cruciferous vegetables from other vegetables is their particular group of phytonutrients. According to the American Institute for Cancer Research, some of these phytonutrients have the ability to stop and/or slow the growth of cancer cells in the breast, uterine lining (endometrium), lung, colon, liver, and cervix. Sulforaphane, for instance, can stimulate enzymes in the body to detoxify carcinogens before they damage cells. And indole-3-carbinol (I3C) has been shown to increase the rate at which estrogen is broken down through the liver's detoxification pathway by almost 50 percent.

Cruciferous vegetables are also known to reduce free radical damage that may be caused by environmental factors such as pollution, radiation, cigarette smoking, and herbicides and pesticides. In a study funded by the National Cancer Institute in the United States, 20 participants were encouraged to eat 1 to 2 cups (250 to 500 mL) of cruciferous vegetables a day. After three weeks, the amount of oxidative stress in their body dropped 22 percent! Research in this area is ongoing, but it appears that eating cruciferous vegetables is a particularly healthful choice.

nutritional breakdown

Suitable for weight loss: **yes** ✓
Calories per 1 cup (250 mL) shredded cabbage (89 g): **22**
Glycemic index rating: **n/a**
Glycemic load rating: **2 (low)**

Green cabbage is an excellent source of vitamin K (85% of daily value), followed by Savoy (60% of daily value) and red cabbage (42% of daily value). All cabbage types are also excellent sources of vitamin C, starting with red (85% of daily value), green (54% of daily value), and bok choy (52% of daily value).

selection and storage

Look for cabbages that are vibrantly coloured, firm, and heavy, with no cracks or signs of worm damage or decay. Avoid buying pre-cut cabbage, as it starts to lose its vitamins (primarily vitamin C) as soon as it's cut.

To keep cabbage fresh and help maintain its vitamin content, wrap it tightly in a plastic bag and keep it in the crisper drawer of the refrigerator. Green and red cabbage will stay fresh for about two weeks, while Savoy will last about one week.

preparation and recipe ideas

Although the inside of cabbage hasn't been exposed to the environment, wash all the leaves under cool running water. Cutting cabbage into slices of equal thickness will allow it to cook more quickly and evenly, thereby preserving more nutrients.

The healthiest way to cook cabbage is to quickly sauté it or steam it for about 5 minutes. This allows for the cellulose to soften for easier digestion while retaining most of the nutrients. Boiling cabbage causes it to become soggy and lose many of its vitamins, minerals, and phytonutrients, not to mention flavour. Cabbage tips include:

- Grate some raw red and Savoy cabbage into your next green salad for added colour and crunch.
- Top off a burger (or grilled Portobello mushroom) with a crunchy Savoy cabbage leaf instead of lettuce.
- Use large cabbage leaves as the wrap for your burrito. Lightly steam whole cabbage leaves for 2 minutes. Stuff with black beans, rice, chopped cilantro, and some zesty salsa. Roll up and enjoy.
- Try some curried coleslaw. Combine 1 cup (250 mL) each of shredded red and green cabbage with 2 tbsp (25 mL) plain yogurt. Add turmeric, cumin, coriander, and black pepper to taste.

DID YOU KNOW?

Other cruciferous vegetables include arugula, bok choy, broccoli, brussels sprouts, cauliflower, Chinese broccoli, collard greens, kale, kohlrabi, mustard seeds, radishes (red, daikon, horseradish, and wasabi), rapini, rutabaga, turnip root and greens, and watercress.

carrots

With feathery green leaves and orange roots, carrots are a plant of the parsley family. These crunchy nutritional superstars can be consumed raw or cooked. The most commonly found carrots have a long, narrow, cylindrical, cone-shaped root, but other varieties may be thick and short in shape or purple, yellow, or white in colour. The carrot has a sweet flavour and is one of the most popular and versatile root vegetables.

Researchers at the Agricultural Research Service in the U.S. Department of Agriculture are again returning to the deep hues of the original carrots in an effort to capture additional nutritional benefits. The yellow carrots they're developing contain lutein and xanthophylls, which are linked with good eye health. The deep orangey-red carrots contain the carotenoid lycopene, which demonstrates protective properties against heart disease and some cancers. Purple carrots are also being produced that owe their colour to anthocyanins, powerful antioxidants that protect cells from free radical damage.

Carrots are the richest vegetable source of the pro-vitamin A carotenes; prime among them is beta-carotene. In fact, the word *carotenoid* is derived from *carrot* because carrots were the first food linked with these yellow-orange antioxidants. Beta-carotene is converted to vitamin A in the liver. The vitamin A is then deposited in the eye's retina, where it's transformed into rhodopsin, a purple pigment essential for night vision. Beta-carotene also helps protect against macular degeneration and cataracts.

The intake of high-carotenoid foods such as carrots may also be beneficial for blood sugar regulation. A 2005 study in the *American Journal of Clinical Nutrition* suggests that physiological levels and dietary intake of carotenoids may be inversely associated with insulin resistance and high blood sugar levels. In other words, the lower the level of carotenoids in the blood, the worse the blood sugar control was.

nutritional breakdown

Suitable for weight loss: **yes ✓**
Calories per one large raw carrot (72 g): **30**
Calories per 1/2 cup (125 mL) cooked carrots (78 g): **27**
Glycemic index rating: **47 (low)**
Glycemic load rating: **raw: 1 (low); boiled: 4 (low)**

One large raw carrot provides a supply of carotenoids equal to about 241% of the daily value for vitamin A. It is also a good source of vitamin K (12% of daily value), vitamin C (7% of daily value), and potassium (7% of daily value). One carrot also supplies 2 g of fibre (8% of daily value).

selection and storage

Carrots should be deeply coloured and fresh looking. Avoid ones that have cracks and bruises or are limp and rubbery. If the greens are still attached, make sure they're bright green and not wilted. If the tops are not attached, look at the stem end; a darkly coloured end suggests age.

Before storing, cut off the greens to prevent water loss from the carrot itself. Wrap carrots in a paper towel to absorb moisture and store in a plastic bag in the crisper drawer of the refrigerator. Do not wash before storing, as the water will encourage spoilage. Carrots stored this way will stay fresh for up to two weeks.

If you've tried "baby" carrots—large Imperator carrots (bred to grow faster and ripen quickly) cut into smaller pieces and peeled to look more appealing—you may have found that they don't have that "carroty" taste you're used to. Unfortunately, after processing, this type of carrot can have up to 70 percent less of the beta-carotene of a normal carrot.

preparation and recipe ideas

Wash carrots under cool running water and scrub with a vegetable brush. If the skin isn't cracked or discoloured, they don't need to be peeled. Carrots are delicious (and good for you) raw, but cooking enhances the bioavailability of the beta-carotene by breaking down the fibre and making it easier for the body to use.

The best way to cook carrots for preservation of nutrients is to steam them quickly for about 5 minutes so they're still a bit crunchy. Boiling is not recommended as they become soggy and lose not only their flavour but also many of their phytonutrients.

- Raw carrots are a great travel companion. Whole or sliced, they're an easy-to-carry on-the-run snack.
- Grate carrots (for better digestibility) and add to salads and sandwiches.

- Enjoy a refreshing salad of shredded carrots, grated beets, chopped apples, and raisins. Top with oil-and-lemon dressing. Research shows that carotenoids in foods are better absorbed by the body when served with oils.
- Juice your carrots with other vegetables, fruits, ginger, and herbs for a zesty breakfast or pick-me-up snack.
- Add carrots to soups, stews, curries, and pasta sauces.
- Use grated or puréed carrots in muffins, breads, or cakes.

DID YOU KNOW?

An urban legend started during the Second World War when the British success at gunning down German bombers was attributed to the pilots' consumption of carrots. Actually, their covert weapon was a new invention called radar, but the carrot rumour helped protect British security secrets.

cayenne pepper

The cayenne pepper is a red-hot member of the *Capsicum* family, commonly known as chili peppers. Not surprisingly, cayenne peppers are native to Central and South America and have been used for centuries as a food and for medicinal purposes.

The folk remedy uses of cayenne pepper are extensive and include treatments for asthma, sore throats, respiratory tract infections, stomach aches, and digestive issues. Current scientific evidence shows that cayenne pepper does indeed exert a number of beneficial effects, including advantages for the cardiovascular system. Specifically, cayenne pepper appears to reduce platelet aggregation (unwanted blood clotting) and increases the body's ability to dissolve fibrin, which forms blood clots in the body. Cayenne pepper also reduces blood cholesterol levels and triglycerides, thereby reducing the likelihood of developing atherosclerosis (clogging of the arteries). There are much lower rates of heart attack, stroke, and pulmonary embolism in cultures that habitually consume cayenne pepper.

Cayenne pepper also contains a high concentration of capsaicin, the pungent phytonutrient that gives the red pepper its heat. This compound is well recognized as a digestive and anti-ulcer aid and an effective pain reliever. As a pain reliever, it has the ability to cause the nerve cells to release a compound referred to as Substance P. The release of this substance causes pain and irritation, but once released, the capsaicin acts to block its reuptake by the nerves. The net result of this is depletion of Substance P from the nerve fibres, which eventually blocks the pain sensations. This property makes capsaicin-containing ointments popular for the temporary relief of pain from arthritis, herpes zoster, and nerve pain or neuralgia.

nutritional breakdown

Suitable for weight loss: **yes** ✓
Calories per 1 tsp (5 mL) cayenne pepper (2 g): **6**
Glycemic index rating: **n/a**
Glycemic load rating: **n/a**

Cayenne pepper is a rich source of vitamin A (15% of daily value) and has significant amounts of vitamins E (3% of daily value) and C (2% of daily value). It also contains beneficial amounts of manganese (2% of daily value), magnesium (1% of daily value), and potassium (1% of daily value).

selection and storage

Cayenne peppers are available whole and fresh, whole and dried, dried and crushed, or dried and ground. Select the type you need based on the dish you're making. As with all spices, cayenne pepper should be kept in an airtight glass container away from direct sunlight and excessive humidity (not above the stove). You may want to choose organic peppers when purchasing them dried as they are less likely to have been irradiated.

preparation and recipe ideas

There is no preparation required for using ready-made cayenne pepper—but just remember how hot the peppers are! If you eat too much and experience an intense burning in your mouth, do not drink water. Instead, drink milk or eat yogurt because dairy products contain a substance that disrupts the burning.

If you want to dry your own cayenne pepper, simply wash and dry the peppers and place them on parchment paper on a flat baking sheet. Dry them in the oven on the lowest temperature setting until they're crisp. The drying time will vary dramatically with different peppers. When using any hot peppers, consider wearing rubber gloves, as the oils in the peppers can irritate the skin. If you're after a little less spice, remove the seeds with a melon baller (the seeds and veins of the pepper give it its heat). When you're finished cutting the peppers, be sure to wash your hands well with soap and water even if you did wear gloves. Be careful not to touch your eyes (or any other mucous membrane!) as the oils will really burn. Here are a few interesting ways to enjoy cayenne pepper.

- Make your hot chocolate even hotter by adding a dash of cayenne pepper as you're heating the milk.
- Cayenne pepper adds zest to dips and spreads such as hummus and guacamole.
- Whip a little cayenne pepper into some butter or olive oil and drizzle over your favourite cooked vegetables and potatoes or serve as dipping oil for baguettes.
- Cayenne pepper and lemon juice are great complements to cooked bitter greens such as kale, Swiss chard, and mustard greens. Add cayenne to taste to 2 tbsp (25 mL) lemon juice, mix into 3 cups (750 mL) cooked greens, and enjoy.

DID YOU KNOW?
Paprika is another much milder variety of the *Capsicum* family.

celery

Originally cultivated for its medicinal properties, celery is part of the same parsley family of plants as carrots, dill, fennel, and, of course, parsley. While most people associate this crunchy household staple with its stalks, the leaves, root (celeriac), and seeds are also used as food and seasonings. Its low caloric content has made it a favourite for those who are watching their weight, but it also has significant amounts of immune-boosting vitamin C and bone-building vitamin K.

Celery offers several health benefits and has been used for medicinal purposes for centuries. For starters, celery acts as a natural diuretic by helping the body eliminate excess water. Celery also promotes proper elimination by acting as a natural laxative.

Celery also contains compounds known as coumarins, which have been shown to help prevent free radicals from damaging cells. Coumarins are effective in cancer prevention and capable of enhancing the activity of certain white blood cells. Coumarin compounds also lower blood pressure, tone the vascular system, and are possibly effective in the prevention and after the onset of a migraine.

nutritional breakdown

Suitable for weight loss: **yes** ✓
Calories per 1 cup (250 mL) raw celery (101 g): **16**
Glycemic index rating: **n/a**
Glycemic load rating: **1 (low)**

Celery offers excellent amounts of vitamin K (37% of daily value) and significant amounts of vitamins A (9% of daily value) and C (5% of daily value) and folate (9% of daily value). It also contains sodium (3% of daily value), potassium (8% of daily value), and fibre (8% of daily value).

selection and storage

Celery is available year-round but is best at the peak of the season in July and August. Look for firm, bright green, evenly coloured stalks that are tightly clustered around the core. The stalks should make a snapping sound when pulled apart. Celery leaves should be light green and fresh looking. Avoid celery with any sort of discolouration of the stalks or leaves. Limp, rubbery stalks should also be avoided. The

Environmental Working Group in the United States reports that celery is one of the 12 most heavily pesticide-contaminated produce products available. Consider purchasing organic celery.

Celery that is stored properly should keep for up to two weeks. Put unwashed celery in a plastic bag, squeeze the air out, and wrap it tightly. Place in the crisper drawer of the refrigerator. Be sure to keep celery away from the coldest sections of your refrigerator (the back and side walls) since it freezes easily.

preparation and recipe ideas

To clean celery, cut off the base, the leaves, and the tips of the stalks. Separate the ribs and wash thoroughly. Some people like to remove the strings of the celery before eating; use a knife or vegetable peeler to remove the strings lengthwise. Young celery is not as stringy as older stalks. To serve raw or cooked, simply cut to desired length.

- Crisp, raw celery is a popular snack or appetizer as part of a crudités platter served with other raw vegetables such as carrots and broccoli and a favourite dip.
- Use celery in stir-fries to add a crunchy texture.
- Celery leaves are valuable additions to soups, stocks, and stews and can be used like parsley.
- Fill raw celery with a favourite nut butter and top with raisins or sesame seeds for a healthy, quick snack.

DID YOU KNOW?

Celery is rich in both sodium and potassium. Celery-based juices make a great electrolyte replacement drink after a tough workout.

chicken
(free range or
certified organic)

Chicken is a very popular and versatile meat that appeals to people from all cultures. It can be served roasted, broiled, grilled, poached, or with a variety of spices and seasonings. From weight-loss seekers to people wishing to build muscle, the benefits of chicken cannot be beat.

Chicken offers a complete source of lower-fat protein containing all nine essential amino acids. It's also a low-fat and low-cholesterol meat option, containing about half the amount of fat than beef. Chicken is also rich in niacin, vitamin B6, vitamin E, and magnesium. Avoid eating fried chicken or deep-fried chicken wings, which contain inflammatory and high-calorie fat.

Ideally, purchase chicken that is 100 percent certified organic (fed food free of herbicides, pesticides, and fungicides) and/or free range. Free range is a method of farming where animals are allowed to roam freely instead of being constrained in any manner. It is a far more humane way of farming and in general raises healthier animals.

nutritional breakdown
Suitable for weight loss: **yes** ✓
Calories for breast meat only, cooked, roasted (100 g): **165**
Calories for dark meat only, cooked, roasted (100 g): **205**
Glycemic index rating: **n/a**
Glycemic load rating: **n/a**

Chicken breast and dark meat are an excellent source of niacin or B3 (69% and 33% of daily value respectively) and vitamin B6 (30% and 18% of daily value respectively). Both the light and dark meat are also excellent sources of selenium (39% and 26% of daily value respectively), but light meat contains more phosphorus (23% of daily value) and dark meat has much more zinc (19% of daily value).

selection and storage

When buying a whole chicken, look for one that is solid with a round, plump breast and meat that gives a bit when gently pressed. The colour of the skin, yellow or white, is not important from a nutritional perspective; however, ensure the skin is clear and not mottled. A fresh chicken should not have a strong odour—always check the sell-by date. If purchasing frozen chicken, make sure it's frozen solid without any soft spots and doesn't have any freezer burn. Also check for frozen liquid in the packaging, which indicates that the meat has been thawed and refrozen.

Uncooked chicken should be stored in the coldest part of the refrigerator and used within two to three days. Leave the chicken in its original packaging until use, but make sure it's not leaking, because you don't want the chicken to contaminate anything else in the fridge. If you're not going to use the chicken within a few days, freeze it solid and it will keep for up to one year. Leftover cooked chicken is good in the fridge only for about three days.

preparation and recipe ideas

When handling raw chicken, be careful that it doesn't come into contact with other food because it can contain *Salmonella*. Ideally, use separate cutting boards for meat and produce, but if this isn't possible, be sure to wash your hands, utensils, and cutting board with very hot, soapy water after cutting the chicken. Always defrost frozen chicken in the refrigerator. If you're marinating chicken, keep it in the refrigerator for the duration of the marinating time to avoid spoilage. For a whole chicken, cook it until the internal temperature of the breast reaches 175°F to 180°F (80°C to 82°C).

- Chicken is so incredibly versatile; you can choose any spices you want to season it. Poultry seasonings are a standard, but why not try honey mustard or Dijon mustard, basil or cilantro pesto, or lemon and rosemary, or add a little spice with some Cajun seasoning?
- Chicken absorbs flavours around it, so using different marinades can change the taste completely. An Asian-inspired marinade could include mirin (sweet Japanese cooking wine), tamari sauce, curry powder, chopped green onions, some black pepper, and a touch of sugar. Or how about a barbecue marinade, combining orange juice, lemon juice, lime juice, minced garlic, minced onion, some minced parsley, and maybe a splash of beer? Chicken is best marinated at least for a few hours, if not overnight.

- Hot or cold, chicken is a great addition to any type of salad. Try grilled chicken on a crisp romaine Caesar salad with curls of fresh Parmesan or cubed chicken mixed with chopped red pepper, chopped cucumber, chopped onions, and a Greek-inspired dressing of olive oil, lemon juice, and freshly chopped oregano and basil—top with a few black olives and serve on salad greens.
- Instead of a burger, have grilled chicken on a bun at your next barbecue, served with sliced onions, tomatoes, and crisp lettuce leaves.

DID YOU KNOW?
It takes about 4 1/2 lb (2.25 kg) of feed for a chicken to produce a dozen eggs.

chickpeas

These ever-popular legumes are also called garbanzo beans, bengal gram, and Indian peas. *Garbanzo* is the name used in Spanish-speaking countries, whereas the English name *chickpea* comes from the French *chiche*. A very versatile legume, chickpeas have a nutlike taste and a starchy yet buttery texture. Although most people think of chickpeas as being beige in colour, varieties can include black, green, red, and brown.

All legumes, including chickpeas, are rich in both soluble and insoluble dietary fibre. Insoluble fibre adds bulk to the stool and helps prevent constipation, diverticulosis, and other digestive disorders such as irritable bowel syndrome. Soluble fibre, on the other hand, forms a gel-like substance in the intestine that grabs onto bile, which contains cholesterol, and moves it out of the body to reduce cholesterol levels. Research published in the *Annals of Nutrition and Metabolism* showed that adding chickpeas to the diet significantly lowered both the total cholesterol and the LDL (bad cholesterol) in adult subjects.

Chickpeas also offer a rich supply of magnesium, which is involved in glucose and insulin metabolism. A 2008 study in the *European Journal of Nutrition* demonstrated that the lower the intake of magnesium, the greater the risk of metabolic syndrome in both men and women. Metabolic syndrome is a group of symptoms that include abdominal obesity, high blood pressure, elevated triglycerides, low HDL (good cholesterol), and problems with blood sugar control. The American Heart Association estimates that one in five people have metabolic syndrome, which puts them at a greatly increased risk for diabetes and cardiovascular disease.

nutritional breakdown
Suitable for weight loss: **yes** ✓
Calories per 1 cup (250 mL) cooked chickpeas (164 g): **269**
Glycemic index rating: **32 (low)**
Glycemic load rating: **8 (low)**

Chickpeas are an excellent source of folate (71% of daily value) and a good source of the B vitamins thiamin (13% of daily value) and B6 (11% of daily value). They also provide excellent levels of molybdenum (164% of daily value), manganese (84% of daily value), and magnesium (20% of daily value).

selection and storage

Dried legumes are generally available pre-packaged and in bulk. Make sure the store has high turnover and the bins are well covered and show no signs of moisture. Dried beans stored in an airtight container in a cool, dark, dry place will keep for one year. Look for beans that are uniform in colour and not wrinkled (as this is a sign of age). When purchasing canned beans, look for the brands without added salt.

preparation and recipe ideas

Before soaking and cooking, sort through the beans and pick out small stones, debris, and shrivelled beans. Wash under cool running water to remove remaining dirt and dust. Unlike lentils, dried beans require rehydration before cooking. For the quick soak method, cover the beans in a pot with 2 to 3 inches (5 to 8 cm) of water and bring to a boil for about 2 minutes. Once boiled, turn off the heat, cover the pot, and let soak for about 1 hour before cooking. For longer soaking, cover the beans with 2 to 3 inches (5 to 8 cm) of water in a pot. Leave them to soak for 6 to 8 hours or overnight. Be sure to change the soaking water three or more times to help remove the gas-inducing sugars. After either soaking method, you still need to cook the beans. To cook, cover beans with 2 to 3 inches (5 to 8 cm) of fresh water. Bring to a boil, reduce to simmer, and partially cover the pot. Simmer until tender—about 60 to 90 minutes. Skim off any foam that develops while simmering. Do not add salt or acidic ingredients such as tomatoes, lemon, wine, or vinegar to the cooking water as this makes the beans tough—add them once the beans are completely cooked.

- Enjoy chickpea hummus in a wrap for a healthy, quick lunch. Spread the hummus on a whole wheat wrap and garnish with raw vegetables such as cucumber, red pepper, and onion. Roll up and away you go. For a delicious hummus recipe, please see page 252.
- Add chickpeas to salads for additional fibre and protein. Try a Greek garbanzo bean salad by combining beans with chopped tomatoes, celery, and cucumber. Toss with a vinaigrette and top with olives, feta, and fresh parsley.

DID YOU KNOW?

Chickpeas are the most widely consumed legume in the world.

cinnamon

Cinnamon, one of the oldest spices known, was once so highly prized among ancient nations that it was regarded as a gift fit for kings and more valuable than gold. There are more than 200 varieties of cinnamon worldwide, but the two most commonly used are Ceylon cinnamon (or true cinnamon) and Chinese cinnamon (also called cassia). In North America, the term *cinnamon* is used despite the fact that more often than not, the spice is really cassia.

As with most herbs and spices, cinnamon has a long history of both culinary and medicinal uses. In the Ayurvedic tradition, cinnamon was used to treat diabetes. Recent research has supported this finding and demonstrated that extracts of cinnamon increase insulin activity severalfold, which leads to better blood sugar regulation. Sixty people with type 2 diabetes were given from 1/4 tsp to 1 tbsp (1 to 6 g) of cinnamon powder every day for 40 days. At the end of the study, subjects' fasting glucose levels were reduced by 18 to 29 percent, triglycerides by 23 to 30 percent, LDL (bad cholesterol) by 7 to 27 percent, and total cholesterol by 12 to 26 percent.

Additional research has shown cinnamon to be effective for indigestion, nausea, intestinal cramping, diarrhea, and vomiting. Cinnamon oil has been shown to have anti-fungal and anti-bacterial effects. However, cinnamon oil cannot be taken internally and can also be a skin irritant. If using this oil, it must be mixed with a carrier oil to avoid irritation. Cinnamon oil can be inhaled to help with nausea, or a drop can be put on a warm compress to help with stomach upset. Do not use cinnamon oil if pregnant or breastfeeding. Using the cinnamon spice instead of the oil is more convenient and is without precaution.

nutritional breakdown

Suitable for weight loss: **yes ✓**
Calories per 1 tsp (2 g) ground cinnamon: **6**
Glycemic index rating: **n/a**
Glycemic load rating: **n/a**

Cinnamon offers an abundant source of fibre (5% of daily value) and vitamin K (1% of daily value). It is also an excellent source of manganese (22% of daily value) and contains beneficial amounts of calcium (3% of daily value).

selection and storage

Cinnamon is available in stick (quill) or powder form. Both forms should be stored in airtight glass containers in a cool, dark place away from humidity (not above the stove). Ground cinnamon will keep fresh this way for about six months, while the sticks will last up to one year. As with other dried spices, organically grown cinnamon is much less likely to have been irradiated than conventionally grown cinnamon.

preparation and recipe ideas

Cinnamon requires no preparation—just shake out the powder or stir your tea or cider with the cinnamon stick. Here are a few simple and savoury cinnamon ideas.

- Try using cinnamon for breakfast. Mix some into your oatmeal, spread your toast with agave syrup or honey and sprinkle with cinnamon, mix some into your almond butter for another delicious toast spread, or stir some into your batter while making French toast.
- Make cinnamon tea. Boil cinnamon sticks in water for a few minutes and let steep; strain out the sticks. Add a bit of honey if desired and enjoy. This tea is also very refreshing served over ice on a hot day.
- Go beyond the traditional use of cinnamon with the fall foods of apples, squash, and pumpkin and try a dash with your lentils and beans.

DID YOU KNOW?

Cinnamon gets its scent and flavour from a chemical compound called cinnamaldehyde.

cottage cheese

It is with good reason that many health-conscious eaters and weight-loss seekers keep cottage cheese stocked in their fridge. Cottage cheese is high in protein, low in calories, and can be used for a variety of dishes to cut fat and fill you up.

Cottage cheese is made by adding an enzyme (such as rennet, vinegar, or lemon juice) to milk. The action of the enzyme causes the milk to clump (curdle) and the excess liquid is drained off. Different styles of cottage cheese are made from milks with different fat levels and in small-curd or large-curd preparations. Low-fat cottage cheese provides the nutritional benefits of whole-fat cheese, including high protein and mineral content, with less concern about saturated fat. Selenium, a potent antioxidant, is also found in cottage cheese and has been linked with the prevention of numerous chronic diseases including cancer, asthma, and heart disease. Selenium also works synergistically with iodine (found in cottage cheese as well) to ensure proper functioning of the thyroid gland. For interest's sake, 1/2 cup (125 mL) of low-fat cottage cheese (113 g) contains:

- 80 calories
- 1 g of fat
- 0.5 g of saturated fat
- 10 mg of cholesterol
- 380 mg of sodium
- 130 mg of potassium
- 7 g of carbohydrates
- 3 g of sugar
- 12 g of protein

In addition to the health benefits above, cottage cheese and other dairy products contain a fatty acid called conjugated linoleic acid (CLA). Studies have shown CLA to boost immune function, reduce atherosclerosis (clogging of the arteries), and reduce body fat. In fact, a study involving 2375 Welsh men found that including dairy products in a healthful diet lowered the risk of metabolic syndrome by up to 62 percent. Researchers proposed that the CLA may have improved the action of insulin and reduced blood sugar levels.

nutritional breakdown
Suitable for weight loss: **yes** ✓
Calories per 1 cup (250 mL) low-fat 1% milk fat cottage cheese (226 g): **163**
Glycemic index rating: **n/a**
Glycemic load rating: **6 (low)**

Cottage cheese is an excellent source of B12 (24% of daily value) and riboflavin (22% of daily value) as well as phosphorus (30% of daily value), selenium (29% of daily value), and calcium (14% of daily value).

selection and storage
Cottage cheese is readily found in the dairy section of all grocery and health food stores. Since it is a fresh cheese, it is highly perishable and should ideally be eaten within 10 days, so check the expiry date on the container. There are a number of varieties, from low fat to creamy, small curd to large, dry to moist, and fruit flavoured. Keep cottage cheese in its original container and store in the refrigerator.

preparation and recipe ideas
- Purée cottage cheese in a blender or food processor and use it in lasagna, cheese blintzes, and cannelloni, or spread on homemade pizza.
- Make your baked sweet potato into a meal by topping it with cottage cheese and lightly sautéed vegetables.
- Add cottage cheese to a green salad for a quick, healthy lunch. Combine romaine lettuce, chopped green and red pepper, chopped onions, halved cherry tomatoes, and some pitted Kalamata olives. Mix together cottage cheese and your favourite vinaigrette, and add to the salad.
- Cottage cheese mixes well with salsa for a delicious and healthy dip for raw veggies or toasted whole wheat chips.

DID YOU KNOW?
It takes 100 lb (45 kg) of milk to make 15 lb (7 kg) of cottage cheese.

dark chocolate/
cocoa powder

Ah, chocolate … one of life's greatest pleasures! Not surprisingly, the scientific name for the cocoa tree (*Theobroma cacao*) from which cocoa is derived translates directly to "food of the gods." Chocolate or, more correctly, the seeds of the cocoa tree have figured prominently in many civilizations, including the Mayan and Aztec cultures, where they had religious, medical, and economic importance. Today, chocolate still offers medicinal benefits all the while being one of greatest indulgences of our time.

There are several different types of chocolate, including white chocolate, milk chocolate, and dark chocolate. Yet not all chocolate is created equal. All chocolate begins with the cocoa bean. The cocoa bean is extremely rich in flavonols, which are powerful antioxidant compounds that prevent damage to cells. However, depending on how the beans are processed, many of the beneficial compounds can be destroyed. Dark chocolate has the highest antioxidant capacity, followed by milk chocolate and then white, which has very little.

When recent research demonstrated that dark chocolate was indeed good for overall health, chocolate lovers worldwide celebrated. A 2007 study in the *Journal of the American Medical Association* found that the health benefits of dark chocolate may include lowering high blood pressure. Participants were given either a small amount (30 calories' worth) of dark chocolate or the same amount of white chocolate every day for 18 weeks. At the end of the study, there was a small but statistically significant drop in the blood pressure of the participants in the dark chocolate group.

Other studies have found further heart-healthy effects, including preventing damage to LDL (bad cholesterol) (when LDL is damaged, it is more likely to form plaque in the artery walls), reducing platelet aggregation (which reduces the risk of heart attack), and increasing the production of nitric oxide, a compound that is an indicator of healthy blood vessel function. In the October 2008 *Journal of Nutrition*, researchers reported that regular consumption of small doses of dark chocolate helped reduce inflammation as measured by C-reactive protein (CRP). CRP is a general marker for inflammation in the body, and research suggests that people with elevated CRP are at an increased risk of diabetes, high blood pressure, and cardiovascular disease.

nutritional breakdown: dark chocolate

Suitable for weight loss: **yes ✓, in limited amounts**
Calories per 1 oz (28 g) dark chocolate (70% to 85% cocoa solids): **168**
Glycemic index rating: **22 (low)**
Glycemic load rating: **4 (low)**

Dark chocolate is an excellent source of manganese (27% of daily value) and copper (25% of daily value) and a good source of iron (19% of daily value) and magnesium (16% of daily value).

nutritional breakdown: cocoa powder

Suitable for weight loss: **yes ✓, in limited amounts**
Calories per 1 oz (28 g) of dry, unsweetened cocoa powder: **64**
Glycemic index rating: **20 (low)**
Glycemic load rating: **1 (low)**

Unsweetened cocoa powder is an excellent source of many minerals, including manganese (54% of daily value), copper (53% of daily value), magnesium (35% of daily value), and iron (22% of daily value).

selection and storage

For the most flavonoids and the least amount of fat and calories, seek out dark chocolate that contains at least 70 percent cocoa solids. Check the ingredients list to know exactly what you're getting along with your flavonoids. Cocoa butter is the naturally occurring fat in the cocoa bean and is preferable to other oils (such as vegetable) that may be added. As a general rule, the higher the cocoa solids content, the lower the added sugar. There are two types of unsweetened cocoa powder: natural or Dutch-process cocoa. While the Dutch-process cocoa has a milder, less acidic taste, it has also been processed in a way that removes many of the flavonoids, thereby greatly reducing its health benefits.

Dark chocolate should be stored in an airtight container in a cool, dark place. When the chocolate is exposed to warm temperatures, a white "bloom" can form on the surface, which is the result of the cocoa butter rising to the surface. Dampness can also cause tiny crystals to form on the surface. Neither means the chocolate has spoiled, but the flavour and texture may be affected.

preparation and recipe ideas

There is no preparation for eating dark chocolate except undoing the wrapper. To melt it, put the chocolate in the top of a double boiler over simmering water as this will help prevent it from scorching. There are many chocolate-friendly ideas to choose from.

- Why not eat chocolate for breakfast on occasion? Simply add a spoonful of unsweetened cocoa powder to your morning smoothie mixed with puréed bananas or strawberries.
- Dark chocolate fondue is a great way to give you and your guests a flavonoid burst! Serve melted dark chocolate with freshly washed strawberries, raspberries, chunks of sweet pineapple, banana, and apple slices.
- Dark chocolate or cocoa powder makes an interesting addition to regular or vegetarian chili. Add 1 or 2 tbsp (15 to 25 mL) cocoa powder to your favourite recipe when you mix in the rest of the spices. The chocolate adds a wonderfully rich flavour.
- Spice up your hot chocolate with a bit of cayenne pepper. Mix 1 tsp (5 mL) unsweetened cocoa powder with 2 tsp (10 mL) sugar and a pinch of cayenne pepper. Add 1 tbsp (15 mL) of cold milk and mix into a paste. Heat 1 cup (250 mL) milk, add to the paste, stir well, and enjoy the sweet heat.

DID YOU KNOW?

White chocolate isn't really chocolate. It is made of cocoa butter, milk, and sugar but does not contain any cocoa solids.

edamame

Edamame (pronounced eh-da-*mah*-may) is perhaps one of the world's oldest, and healthiest, snack foods. Meaning "twig bean" or "branched bean" in Japanese, it is known as *mao dou* ("hairy bean") in China, where it originated. Edamame is the immature green form of edible soybeans and differs from field soybeans (used for tofu and soybean oil) by having larger seeds and being milder tasting, more tender, and more digestible. Also known as fresh green soybean, sweet bean, and vegetable soybean, edamame has become increasingly popular with health-conscious North Americans.

Despite its fun-loving reputation as a snack food often served with beer, edamame is a seriously healthy food. Not only is it high in fibre, which helps to reduce cholesterol levels, edamame is a complete protein source, meaning that it contains the nine essential amino acids that are the building blocks for all the proteins in the body.

Numerous studies suggest that soy may reduce the risk of several types of cancer, including breast, endometrial, and prostate, and much research has focused on the role of isoflavones, a phytonutrient compound in soybeans. Soy isoflavones have antioxidant properties that reduce free radical damage to fats and DNA. They have also been shown to decrease the oxidation of LDL (bad cholesterol), improve blood vessel flexibility, which helps decrease blood pressure, and induce specific liver enzymes that help the body eliminate potentially carcinogenic toxins. Additionally, soybeans may help strengthen bones in postmenopausal women, and studies have shown that women who consume soy foods report a significant reduction in the amount of hot flashes during menopause.

nutritional breakdown

Suitable for weight loss: **yes** ✓
Calories per 1 cup (250 mL) plain edamame: **130**
Glycemic index rating: **n/a**
Glycemic load rating: **4 (low)**

Edamame offers an excellent source of folate (89% of daily value), manganese (60% of daily value), and vitamin K (46% of daily value). It is also high in many minerals, including phosphorus (19% of daily value) and magnesium (18% of daily value), yet very low in sodium (less than 1% of daily value).

selection and storage
Thanks to the new-found popularity of the beans, fresh edamame can be found in Asian and specialty stores but mostly it's available frozen, both in and out of the pods, in many grocery and health food stores. When shopping for fresh edamame, look for pods that are firm, not bruised, and dark green. Fresh edamame can be stored in the refrigerator for two days, while frozen edamame can be kept frozen for four to six months.

preparation and recipe ideas
Edamame is so versatile it can be served hot as a side dish, cold in a salad, or on its own as a great quick snack. To prepare, boil the pods in salted water for about 10 to 12 minutes. Once drained, squeeze the beans from the pod directly into your mouth. To ensure that frozen edamame is not overcooked, follow the instructions on the package.

- Add a nutty flavour and a crispy texture to a cold salad with shelled edamame. Try them with diced red pepper, fresh cooked corn, sliced green onions, and a Japanese-inspired dressing.
- Edamame can substitute for green peas or lima beans in any recipe.
- Toss shelled beans in with other vegetables, sesame oil, grated ginger, and tamari for a flavourful stir-fry.
- The buttery mild flavour of edamame means they can be used mashed as well. Purée them with garlic and serve with pita chips for an edamame hummus, or mash them and add to your favourite mashed sweet potato recipe.
- Watching a movie? Why not snack on some protein-rich lightly salted edamame instead of popcorn?

DID YOU KNOW?
Soybeans are the most widely grown and utilized legume in the world. The United States is responsible for more than 50 percent of the world's soy production.

eggs

Eggs are not just for breakfast anymore! In fact, eggs offer a multitude of nutritional benefits, such as being an excellent source of protein (5.5 g per egg) and containing only 70 to 80 calories per egg. The egg yolk also contains lecithin and choline, a substance that assists in transporting and metabolizing fats in the body. In addition, eggs provide lutein and zeaxanthin, antioxidants that help prevent macular degeneration and cataracts.

Unfortunately, about 20 years ago, eggs were given a bad nutritional rap. It was once thought that the cholesterol in eggs was translating into artery-clogging cholesterol in the blood. Research done since that time has confirmed that eggs are not the underlying cause of high cholesterol and can be consumed on a regular basis (i.e., one a day). In fact, researchers at the Harvard School of Public Health examined a population of 117,000 nurses who had been studied for 8 to 14 years and found no difference in the heart disease risk between those who ate one egg a week and those who ate more than one egg a day.

In another study, participants ate a breakfast of either two eggs or a bagel that supplied the same amount of calories. After eight weeks, the egg eaters had lost twice as much weight as the bagel eaters (6 lb versus 3.5 lb/2.75 kg versus 1.5 kg). In addition, there were no significant differences between blood levels of total cholesterol, triglycerides, or LDL (bad cholesterol) in either group. Thus it was concluded that healthy people can safely enjoy the numerous benefits of eggs without increasing their risk of heart attack. For those who have a diagnosed cardiovascular condition, type 2 diabetes, or high cholesterol, the American Heart Association recommends choosing a small egg over a large one and to consider using egg whites, which are cholesterol free.

nutritional breakdown

Suitable for weight loss: **yes** ✓
Calories per 1 large, whole egg, cooked (50 g): **71**
Glycemic index rating: **n/a**
Glycemic load rating: **n/a**

Eggs are an excellent source of selenium (23% of daily value). They're also a good source of many of the B vitamins, including riboflavin (12% of daily value) and B12 (11% of daily value).

selection and storage

Before buying eggs, check them for cracks or breaks. Eggs can be stored in the refrigerator for up to one month, especially if stored in the coldest part of the fridge. Storing eggs in the door exposes them to changes in temperature every time the door is opened, which reduces shelf life. Eggshells are porous, so keeping eggs in their original containers helps keep them fresh by reducing the air exchange. Store the eggs with their points down to help prevent the yolk and air chamber inside the shell from becoming displaced.

When shopping for eggs, opt for omega-3 eggs, which are now widely available. Omega-3 eggs are similar to normal eggs in look, taste, storage instructions, and cooking versatility. The difference lies in the fact that omega-3 eggs are produced by chickens that have been fed with alfalfa, corn, soybean, and flaxseed. Flaxseed is an excellent source of omega-3 essential fat, which has been shown to be beneficial to human health. In fact, an average-sized omega-3 egg contains about 320 mg of omega 3, while a regular egg contains about 63 mg.

preparation and recipe ideas

Eggs can be pickled, hard-cooked, soft-boiled, poached, scrambled, or fried. It is not recommended to eat raw eggs because of the potential *Salmonella* contamination (about 1 in 200,000). When using more than one egg, in order to prevent any possible contamination by a spoiled egg, break each egg separately into a small bowl before combining with the others. To "get cracking" with more eggs, follow these simple tips.

- There are so many ways to enjoy eggs for breakfast—poached on whole grain bread with a slice of fresh tomato, in omelettes with spinach and mushrooms, and in whole grain French toast.
- Hard-cooked eggs are a terrific solution for on-the-go eating. They also make a great protein addition to almost any salad. Combine 1 can of drained and rinsed cannellini beans, 1/2 cup (125 mL) chopped fresh tomato, 1/2 cup (125 mL) chopped cucumber, 2 tbsp (25 mL) chopped fresh parsley, and 2 cups (500 mL) baby spinach greens. Dress with your favourite vinaigrette and some fresh chives and a sliced hard-cooked egg on top.

DID YOU KNOW?

There is no nutritional difference between brown-shelled eggs and white-shelled eggs. The breed of hen determines the colour of the egg.

flaxseed

Flaxseed is truly one of the healthiest foods on the planet. In most grocery and health food stores, brown and golden flaxseed should be available. Both types provide the same nutritional benefits, boasting more than 50 percent alpha-linolenic acid, the essential omega-3 fat that offers several health benefits. Research has shown omega-3 fats to have a natural anti-inflammatory effect and to be beneficial for digestion, weight loss, and mood control. Flaxseed also offers plenty of dietary fibre and a whole host of health-promoting vitamins and minerals. Other health benefits include relief from chronic constipation, balancing of blood sugar, and reducing cholesterol levels.

Whole flaxseed is difficult to eat because it's hard to crack, even with lots of chewing, and may pass through the body completely intact. Thus, when using flaxseed on your morning meals, in salads, or other dishes, it's important to grind it first in a coffee grinder or purchase pre-ground flaxseed. Ground flaxseed contains lignans, a type of dietary plant fibre that protects against a variety of cancers, such as breast and prostate, by aiding the body's elimination of excess hormones.

When adding ground flaxseed to your diet, start slowly with about 1 tsp (5 mL) a day. If too much flax is consumed initially, bloating can be experienced. When introducing excess fibre into the diet, be sure to increase your water intake as well.

nutritional breakdown

Suitable for weight loss: **yes** ✓
Calories per 2 tbsp (25 mL) ground flaxseed (14 g): **75**
Glycemic index rating: **n/a**
Glycemic load rating: **n/a**

Flaxseed is one of the richest sources of omega-3 essential fatty acids and a very good source of dietary fibre (15% of daily value). It's a great source of manganese (15% of daily value) and magnesium (14% of daily value) and provides good levels of folate (13.5%) and vitamin B6 (9%).

selection and storage

Flaxseed is available pre-packaged and in bulk in most grocery and health food stores. Due to the protection provided by the hard skin of the flaxseed, whole seeds can be purchased in bulk, but be sure the store has high turnover and the bins are well covered and show no signs of moisture. Whole seeds can be stored in an airtight glass container in a dry, dark, cool place for several months.

Ground flaxseed, however, should always be purchased in a vacuum-packed refrigerated container because once the seeds are ground, the unsaturated oils are very susceptible to oxidization and rancidity. You can grind your own flaxseed in a coffee grinder, blender, or food processor, but be sure to store it in a glass jar in the refrigerator or freezer and use it quickly.

Flaxseed oil is very perishable and should always be bought in opaque refrigerated bottles. It must be stored in the refrigerator, should never be used for cooking, and should be consumed cold: 1 tsp (5 mL) in your morning smoothie or as a healthy topper to air-popped popcorn. When it is fresh, flaxseed oil has a light nutty flavour.

preparation and recipe ideas

- Use ground flaxseed as a substitute for eggs in baking. For every egg being replaced, mix 3 tbsp (50 mL) water with 1 tbsp (15 mL) ground flaxseed and let sit for 1 or 2 minutes until the mixture becomes gelatinous. (*Note:* This mixture does not have a leavening effect.)
- For heart-healthy eating, drizzle flaxseed oil and sprinkle ground flaxseeds on grilled vegetables after they've been cooked.
- At breakfast, add ground flaxseed to hot or cold cereals, yogurt, or smoothies for added fibre.
- Use flaxseed oil for a healthy homemade salad dressing.
- On movie night, top air-popped popcorn with flaxseed oil and sea salt to taste.

DID YOU KNOW?
Flax is the best plant source of the health-promoting omega-3 fat alpha-linolenic acid (ALA).

garlic

In addition to making food taste delicious, garlic is loaded with nutritional health benefits that can't be beat. Belonging to the same family as onions, chives, leeks, and shallots, garlic has a long history of both culinary and medicinal use. Raw garlic has a spicy, pungent flavour, but cooked garlic becomes much more mellow, sweet, and creamy and can even be used as a spread on whole grain bread.

Garlic has been used around the world for thousands of years to treat many conditions, including snakebites, infections, cancer, and cardiovascular disease. One of the most potent active substances in garlic is called allicin, which has antimicrobial, antiyeast (*Candida albicans*), and natural antibiotic properties. The finer the chopping and the more crushed the garlic, the more allicin it releases and the greater the health benefits.

Some evidence suggests that people whose diets are rich in onions and garlic have a lower risk of several types of cancer than those who avoid them altogether. A 2006 Italian study in the *American Journal of Clinical Nutrition* indicated that moderate use of dietary garlic appeared to reduce the risk of colorectal and renal (kidney) cancers, while the moderate consumption of onions was associated with a lower risk of breast, ovary, and prostate cancers.

nutritional breakdown

Suitable for weight loss: **yes** ✓
Calories per 3 raw garlic cloves: **13**
Glycemic index rating: **n/a**
Glycemic load rating: **1 (low)**

Garlic contains beneficial amounts of manganese (8% of daily value), calcium (2% of daily value), and selenium (2% of daily value). It's also abundant in vitamins B6 (6% of daily value) and C (5% of daily value).

selection and storage

Garlic is widely available in many forms, including powder, paste, flaked, and frozen. While these forms may be convenient, they are not as flavourful in comparison to fresh garlic. When purchasing fresh garlic, select bulbs that are plump with tightly packed cloves. Avoid garlic that is soft, shrivelled, or sprouting. A whole garlic bulb can be stored for up to one month if placed either uncovered or loosely covered in a cool, dark place away from heat and sunlight. Don't store garlic in the refrigerator as the moisture will cause it to soften and sprout.

preparation and recipe ideas

Unless you're roasting the entire bulb, you'll need to separate the individual cloves you need from the bulb. You can use your fingers or a paring knife, or place the whole bulb on a cutting board and firmly push on it on an angle. This will loosen the skin between the cloves and make them easier to separate.

To loosen the skin of the individual cloves, place the side of a large chef's knife on the clove and whack it with the side of your fist. You can also twist the clove between the fingers of both hands or peel it with a paring knife. Now you're ready either to chop the garlic or put it through a garlic press. Let it sit for 5 to 10 minutes after chopping or pressing to activate the health-promoting compounds. Add the garlic at the end of your cooking so it's exposed to heat for no more than 3 minutes. The longer or hotter it cooks, the more it loses its flavour and health benefits.

For roasted whole garlic, remove any loose skin on the outside of the bulb but leave the rest of the skin intact. Lightly coat the bulb in olive oil, wrap in foil, and place in a 350°F (180°C) oven or barbecue for about 45 minutes. To serve, remove foil and squeeze cooked garlic out of each clove.

- Add some flavour to your mashed sweet potatoes. Use 3 pressed cloves for 4 cups (1 L) of mashed potatoes, season with sea salt and freshly ground pepper, top with a sprinkle of paprika.
- Try minced or pressed garlic in your guacamole or hummus. For bruschetta, add garlic to a mixture of chopped tomato, basil, onions, and olive oil.

DID YOU KNOW?

Raw garlic juice was used as an antimicrobial field dressing in the trenches during the First World War.

goat cheese

Since goats are one of the oldest domesticated animals, goat cheese is probably one of the earliest man-made dairy products. In its simplest form, goat cheese is made by warming goat milk, mixing it with rennet to curdle it, and then draining and pressing the curds. Also called chèvre, most goat cheese is soft, easily spreadable, and delicious.

Most people who are allergic to cow's milk or who are lactose intolerant can safely use goat dairy products because there's a different type of milk protein, or casein, in goat milk that's easier to digest. The fat molecules in goat cheese are also smaller, with more short-chain fatty acids that produce a softer curd, which makes them easier to break down than the larger, long-chain fatty acids of cow cheese. When compared to cow milk products, goat cheese is lower in fat, calories, and cholesterol and provides more calcium and fewer carbohydrates—the perfect complement to a heart-healthy diet. Despite the lower fat, goat cheese maintains a full, rich, and creamy flavour.

If you're looking to boost your calcium intake, the harder versions of goat milk, such as goat milk feta, have a higher percentage of calcium than the softest ones. All varieties provide a good source of high-quality protein necessary to repair and build muscles, tissues, enzymes, and antibodies. Protein also helps keep our blood sugar stable and helps us feel full longer.

nutritional breakdown
Suitable for weight loss: **yes** ✓
Calories per 1 oz (28 g): **75 (soft goat cheese) to 127 (hard goat cheese)**
Glycemic index rating: **n/a**
Glycemic load rating: **n/a**

Goat cheese is a good source of copper (10% of daily value) and provides beneficial amounts of phosphorus (7% of daily value), riboflavin (6% of daily value), and vitamin A (6% of daily value). Hard goat cheese contains higher percentages of these nutrients because there's less water in the cheese. One ounce of hard goat cheese can contain 25% of the daily intake for calcium.

selection and storage

If you can, purchase cheese from a specialty cheese shop, as it is likely fresher. When storing cheese, the goal is to avoid moisture loss, which can happen quickly in a refrigerator. Wrap the cheese in waxed or butcher's paper and put it in an enclosed box (a plastic container will do) to protect it from the dry air. The softer the cheese, the shorter the shelf life, so simply select the amount you're going to use within 10 days to two weeks.

preparation and recipe ideas

Take goat cheese out of the refrigerator at least 1 hour before serving it. The cheese should be served at room temperature to maximize the wonderful, creamy texture. Go beyond the standard crackers and cheese with the following tips to fully enjoy the goodness of goat cheese.

- Goat cheese is wonderful in a salad. Slice cooked, cooled beets into julienne strips. Place washed and dried arugula in the centre of a plate and top with julienned beets, chopped walnuts, and thinly sliced goat cheese. Drizzle with a balsamic vinaigrette and enjoy.
- What about baked cheese? Coat a small ramekin with olive oil and fill with fresh goat cheese. Poke several cloves of roasted garlic into the cheese (roast the garlic for 20 minutes in a 350°F/180°C oven). Drizzle some olive oil over the cheese and garlic and add some freshly chopped rosemary. Bake for 10 minutes at 400°F (200°C) until bubbly. Serve with a fresh multigrain baguette or endive leaves and raw baby asparagus spears for dipping.
- Add slices of goat cheese to your next homemade pizza for a creamy variation of the traditional mozzarella. The fat in the goat cheese will help your body absorb more of the carotenoids in the tomato sauce.

DID YOU KNOW?
Worldwide, more people drink goat milk than cow milk.

kidney beans

Just as the name suggests, the kidney bean is shaped like a kidney and comes in two colours: a deep, glossy red and a light pink. This extremely versatile legume is chock full of complex carbohydrates and other nutrients and helps prevent heart disease, diabetes, cancer, and obesity.

The kidney bean's contribution to health is due, in no small part, to its significant amount of antioxidants. Oxidative stress caused by free radicals in the body has been associated with the development of many chronic diseases, including cancer and heart disease. These free radicals are produced during normal metabolism and are also a result of external sources such as pollutants, chemicals, and environmental toxins. In order to decrease the damage by free radicals, dietary antioxidants are needed. A 2004 study in the *Journal of Agricultural and Food Chemistry* indicated that red kidney beans ranked third highest in antioxidant capacity as measured by the ORAC (oxygen radical absorbance capacity) analysis.

The high antioxidant capacity of beans may partially explain why they are protective against cancer. In an analysis of data collected from the Nurses' Health Study II, researchers found a significant reduction in the frequency of breast cancer among women who had a higher intake of beans and lentils. Even when the intake of other antioxidant-rich foods such as green tea, blueberries, and apples was removed from the analysis, eating beans or lentils two or more times a week was associated with a 24 percent reduced risk of breast cancer.

Many people avoid beans because of the embarrassment or discomfort of the intestinal gas or flatulence that can be produced. Humans are lacking the enzyme required to break down the raffinose sugars found in beans. The bacteria in our gut feed on these sugars, giving off hydrogen and carbon dioxide and causing the dreaded gas. But there are ways to help reduce these emissions and help you enjoy the huge health benefits beans have to offer.

1. Add a pinch of baking soda to the soaking water. This can help break down the indigestible sugars.
2. Change the water several times during soaking.
3. Never cook the beans in the water they have been soaking in—always use fresh water.
4. Gradually increase the amount of beans you eat over several weeks to allow the gut to adapt to the increase in fibre.

nutritional breakdown

Suitable for weight loss: **yes ✓, in moderation**
Calories per 1 cup (250 mL) cooked kidney beans (177 g): **225**
Glycemic index rating: **28 (low)**
Glycemic load rating: **7 (low)**

Kidney beans are an excellent source of manganese (42% of daily value), iron (29% of daily value), phosphorus (25% of daily value), and copper (21% of daily value). They are also very high in folate (58% of daily value), thiamin (19% of daily value), and vitamin K (19% of daily value).

selection and storage

For selection, storage, and preparation of all beans, see Chickpeas: Selection and Storage.

preparation and recipe ideas

- Cozy up with a bowl of steaming chili in the fall and winter. Choose the classic meat chili by combining lean ground beef or turkey with kidney beans and vegetables, or try a vegetarian version with kidney beans, chickpeas, and black beans with lots of carrots, peppers, and onions. Top with green onions and plain yogurt.
- Serve kidney bean dip at your next get-together. With a handheld blender, combine cooked kidney beans with chopped garlic, a touch of cumin, and a dash of red pepper flakes; serve with crudités, small toasts, or breadsticks.
- Try a kidney bean tortilla. Combine cooked kidney beans with diced avocado, diced tomatoes, chopped onion, olive oil, and lime juice. Top with grated cheese, roll in a tortilla, serve with salsa, and enjoy.

DID YOU KNOW?

Beans, squash, and maize are the "Three Sisters" that provided the foundation of Native American agriculture.

lentils

There are hundreds of lentil varieties, with as many as 50 or more cultivated for food. Lentils are available in a spectrum of colours from yellow to orange to black, but red, brown, and green are the most popular. Lentils also vary in consistency, with some becoming soft and mushy after cooking while others retain their shape and texture. All types of this superfood provide enormous benefits such as a lean protein option and cholesterol-lowering soluble fibre. Lentils are also rich in the B vitamins, especially folate, which is particularly important for heart health and women of childbearing age. Folate has been shown to reduce the risk of certain kinds of birth defects.

Lentils are one of the best vegetable sources of iron, which makes them an important part of a vegetarian diet. Lentils contain non-heme iron, which is better absorbed when eaten with a good source of vitamin C such as red peppers and leafy green vegetables. Vegetarians who exclude all animal products from their diet may need almost twice as much dietary iron each day as non-vegetarians because of the lower intestinal absorption of non-heme iron in plant foods. Iron is particularly important for adolescents and pregnant women. A pregnant woman's iron requirements about double because of the increased blood volume during pregnancy and the nutrient needs of the fetus.

With about 26 percent protein, lentils have the third highest level of protein from any plant-based food after soybeans and hemp. However, lentils are not complete proteins. (A complete protein provides your body with essential amino acids in the right ratio to one another.) Lentils are low in the essential amino acids methionine and cysteine, so combining them with foods that provide these amino acids, such as brown rice, quinoa, and vegetables, will provide the body with the right amino acid combination. Other foods that boast similar high protein content to lentils generally have a higher total fat and saturated fat content. Lentils are low in fat, with 1 cup (250 mL) cooked lentils offering 18 g of protein, less than 1 g of fat, and only 0.1 g of saturated fat. This makes lentils an excellent choice for combating heart disease, obesity, diabetes, and cancer.

nutritional breakdown

Suitable for weight loss: **yes** ✓
Calories per 1 cup (250 mL) cooked lentils (198 g): **230**
Glycemic index rating: **29 (low)**
Glycemic load rating: **5 (low)**

Lentils are an excellent source of fibre (63% of daily value) and the B vitamins folate (90% of daily value) and thiamin (22% of daily value). They also offer excellent levels of manganese (49% of daily value), iron (37% of daily value), phosphorus (36% of daily value), and copper (25% of daily value).

selection and storage

Lentils are available dried or canned—they are not used fresh. Dried lentils are found pre-packaged and in bulk. When buying in bulk, make sure the store has high turnover and the bins are well covered and show no signs of moisture. Look for lentils that are dry, firm, unshrivelled, and of uniform colour. Faded colours and wrinkles are indications that the lentils are too old. If you buy lentils at different times, keep them separate because lentils of differing ages will need different cooking times. When buying canned lentils, look for ones without added salt. You can store dried lentils in an airtight container in a dry, cool place for up to one year.

If your recipe calls for lentils that will keep their shape and texture after cooking (for use in salads and casseroles), use the green or brown variety. Most red, orange, and yellow lentils have had their hulls removed and are generally split, making them lose their shape and disintegrate more quickly with cooking. These varieties are best used for soups, purées, and stews. According to many, the most flavourful (and most expensive) variety is the French verte du Puy.

preparation and recipe ideas

Dried lentils, unlike beans, do not need to be soaked in water before cooking. Simply pick over the lentils to remove pebbles, debris, and shrivelled ones, then rinse and drain. The water or broth used for cooking should be about 1 to 2 inches (2.5 to 5 cm) above the top of the lentils as they expand in volume when cooked. Boil the liquid first, add the lentils, return to a boil, reduce to a simmer, and cover. Different varieties of lentils will have different cooking times: brown lentils take the longest at about 45 minutes, green at about 30 to 40 minutes, followed by red and orange at about 20 to 30 minutes. If you're using canned lentils, be sure to rinse them well to reduce the sodium levels.

- Lentil soup is a hearty meal. Sauté onions, garlic, and some of your favourite vegetables. Add to cooked lentils, season with curry and/or ginger or other spices, purée, and add enough chicken or vegetable stock until you reach the desired consistency.

- Enjoy lentils in a cool protein-packed salad. Combine cooked green or brown lentils with chopped tomatoes, chopped bell peppers, minced sweet onion, and fresh mint. Add a yogurt or vinaigrette dressing.
- For a complete protein meal, add cooked lentils to brown rice, whole wheat couscous, or quinoa, mix with seasonal vegetables, add your favourite spices, and enjoy.

DID YOU KNOW?
Lentils are most likely the oldest cultivated legume. Archaeologists have discovered lentil seeds in villages that date back to 6000 BC.

mangoes

Mangoes are the quintessential taste of the tropics that can be enjoyed year-round. There are hundreds of varieties of mango available in a range of colours, including shades of green, yellow, and red. In addition to their sumptuous flavour, mangoes deliver a host of nutrients.

Along with their high vitamin C content, mangoes contain beneficial amounts of many of the B vitamins, especially B6. B6 plays a key role in the formation of new cells and is especially important for the healthy function of body tissues that regenerate quickly, such as the skin. A deficiency of vitamin B6 is associated with skin problems such as eczema and seborrheic dermatitis.

Copper is found in significant amounts in mangoes. Copper is involved in several important, and varied, enzymatic reactions in the body. Among other things, copper promotes collagen maintenance, proper iron absorption, and antioxidant activity. Because of its many functions, an imbalance in copper produces an extensive range of symptoms, including joint problems, elevated LDL (bad cholesterol) and reduced HDL (good cholesterol), skin sores, poor thyroid function, weakness, and irregular heartbeat. Copper can be reduced dramatically when foods are cooked, so eating mangoes raw maximizes their beneficial copper content.

nutritional breakdown

Suitable for weight loss: **yes** ✓
Calories per 1 cup (250 mL) sliced raw mango (165 g): **107**
Glycemic index rating: **51 (low)**
Glycemic load rating: **8 (low)**

Mangoes are an excellent source of both vitamin C (76% of daily value) and vitamin A (25% of daily value) and a good source of vitamin B6 (11% of daily value). They also contain significant amounts of copper (9% of daily value) and potassium (7% of daily value).

selection and storage

When selecting fresh mangoes, don't go by colour alone. Look for firm, unblemished skin and a fruity aroma at the stem end. Give the mango a light but firm squeeze—it should give slightly to this pressure when ripe. You can ripen green mangoes the same way you ripen most fruit: by storing it in a paper bag at room temperature for a few days. Once ripe, mangoes should be moved to the refrigerator, which will slow down the ripening process. Whole, ripe mangoes can be stored for up to five days in the refrigerator. Mangoes that have been peeled and cut should be stored in an airtight container in the refrigerator for several days. Cut mangoes can also be frozen for up to six months.

preparation and recipe ideas

Mangoes should be gently scrubbed under running water with a vegetable brush before peeling. Since mango peels may be irritating to the skin, some people wear rubber gloves, especially if they're cutting a number of them. The mango is not the easiest fruit to cut because the pit clings tightly to the flesh. The traditional way to eat mango in the tropics is to roll the fruit back and forth under gentle pressure on a hard surface to soften the pulp under the skin. The tip is then cut off the stem end and the delicious mashed pulp and juice is sucked out.

If you want to have mango cubes, place the whole mango on its side and cut a "cheek" off either side of the pit. Then cut off the remaining two "fingers." Take each "cheek" and cut crosshatch lines all the way through the flesh but not the peel. Then gently turn the "cheek" inside out so it looks somewhat like a mango porcupine. Slice off the exposed cubes.

- Mangoes are perfect for breakfast. Dip chunks of mango into yogurt first and then into hemp seeds for a healthy start. Purée mango, pineapple, and banana with yogurt or soft tofu for a tropical smoothie.
- Beat the heat with mango ice pops on a hot day. Purée fresh-cut mango in a blender, pour into ice cube or ice pop trays, stick in an ice pop stick or a toothpick, and freeze until solid. You can even make mango ice cubes without the sticks and serve with cold sparkling mineral water for a colourful touch.
- Sweeten up your black bean salad with a little mango. Mix chopped onion, red peppers, and cilantro with some olive oil, lime juice, and a few red pepper flakes. Add a can of rinsed and drained black beans.

DID YOU KNOW?

Mangoes are consumed by more people in the world than apples.

millet

Although it's the main ingredient in many bird seeds, millet is anything but "for the birds." Millet is a small seed that is commonly thought of as a whole grain. The tiny, round millet seeds are encased in an indigestible hull that must be removed before human consumption. Once released, the seeds look like pale yellow beads.

Millet is very versatile, and its texture can be like couscous or mashed potatoes, depending on how long it's cooked. Millet doesn't contain any gluten and is not acid forming in the body, which makes it a soothing and easy-to-digest grain alternative for those with allergies or gluten intolerance.

One of the reasons millet is considered a superfood is because of its magnesium content. Magnesium is considered the "anti-stress" mineral. It relaxes skeletal muscles as well as the smooth muscles of the blood vessels and gastrointestinal tract and acts like a natural tranquilizer. Some studies have also shown that magnesium can reduce the severity of asthma and the frequency of migraine headache attacks.

In the Physicians' Health Study, researchers at Harvard followed more than 21,000 people for 19.6 years. After adjusting for variables such as smoking, alcohol consumption, and history of heart disease, they found that the participants who had a morning bowl of whole grain (not refined) cereal had a 29 percent lower risk of heart failure. Millet has all the healthy nutrition of a whole grain, not to mention a good dose of niacin and fibre, both of which may be helpful in reducing cholesterol levels.

nutritional breakdown

Suitable for weight loss: **low in calories but high on the glycemic index so should be eaten in moderation and always matched with a protein and/or fat**
Calories per 1 cup (250 mL) cooked millet (174 g): **174**
Glycemic index rating: **71 (high)**
Glycemic load rating: **25 (high)**

Millet offers an excellent source of manganese (24% of daily value), magnesium (19% of daily value), phosphorus (17% of daily value), and copper (14% of daily value). It's also a good source of the B vitamins thiamin (12% of daily value) and niacin (12% of daily value).

selection and storage

Properly stored in an airtight container (preferably glass) in a cool, dry place or in the refrigerator, millet can last up to two years. Millet flour, however, can become rancid quickly after it's ground, so look for an expiry date on the package and store it in the refrigerator. If grinding fresh millet flour, it's best to grind only the amount needed each time.

preparation and recipe ideas

There are many cooking variations for millet, but a general guideline is to use 3 parts liquid to 1 part millet. Add the millet to the boiling liquid, simmer covered for about 30 minutes or until the liquid is absorbed, remove from heat, and let steam for 10 minutes. The flavour of the "grain" is enhanced by lightly roasting the grains in a dry pan before cooking; stir constantly over medium heat for about 3 minutes until you notice a mild nutty aroma.

- For a healthy alternative to mashed potatoes, boil a head of cauliflower with millet and blend until creamy with an immersion blender.
- Use millet instead of rice or potatoes in casseroles, stews, soups, and stuffing.
- Enjoy cooked millet as a hot breakfast cereal; add berries, dried fruit, and a few walnuts or almonds for a terrific start to the day.
- Millet can be sprouted for use in salads and sandwiches.

DID YOU KNOW?

Millet can be popped like popcorn to be eaten as a snack or breakfast cereal.

mint

The mint family has more than 30 different species and hundreds of varieties, with the two most popular being peppermint and spearmint. Peppermint is often used in cosmetic and medicinal products such as mouthwash, toothpaste, and chewing gum, while milder spearmint is used in the kitchen. Other unusual but delicious varieties include pineapple mint, lemon mint, apple mint, and hard-to-resist chocolate mint.

Mint has long been used medicinally to treat stomach ache and indigestion. It is well recognized as a carminative herb, which means it stimulates peristalsis in the digestive system and relaxes the stomach, thereby supporting digestion and helping to reduce gas in the intestine. Peppermint also plays a role in the treatment of irritable bowel syndrome (IBS), ulcerative colitis, and Crohn's disease. A number of clinical trials have demonstrated a significant decrease in the symptoms of the participants with IBS when enteric-coated peppermint oil capsules were administered between meals. In order for peppermint oil to be effective, it needs to reach the intestine in its original state and, therefore, is taken in capsule form. (Peppermint oil would be digested before it reached the intestine.)

Along with a number of other herbs, mint demonstrates antimicrobial activity. *In vitro* testing (testing done in a laboratory) shows that mint inhibits the growth of a number of bacteria, including *Streptococcus aureus* and *Escherichia coli* and is effective against the fungus *Candida albicans* (yeast) and the herpes simplex virus.

nutritional breakdown

Suitable for weight loss: **yes** ✓
Calories per 2 tbsp (25 mL) mint (3 g): **2**
Glycemic index rating: **n/a**
Glycemic load rating: **n/a**

Mint is rich in vitamin A (3% of daily value) and the antioxidant vitamin C (2% of daily value). It also supplies an array of essential minerals, including manganese (2% of daily value), calcium (1% of daily value), iron (1% of daily value), and magnesium (1% of daily value).

selection and storage

Mint can be used fresh or dried. When purchasing dried mint, look for green leaves (either light or dark) that don't look dusty or show any bits of yellow stalk. Store in an airtight package in a cool, dark place away from humidity (not above the stove). You can also dry your own: hang mint in bundles of four to six stalks to dry or lay leaves in a single layer on paper towels and leave to dry, again in a cool, dark, dry place.

If you have a choice, use fresh mint for a smoother, less assertive flavour. Choose mint that has vibrant green leaves. Avoid bunches that have dark or yellowing colours. Fresh mint stores well in the refrigerator when placed stem down in 1 cup (250 mL) water and lightly covered with a plastic bag. Change the water every two days and the mint will stay fresh for about one week. Be sure to wash it before using.

preparation and recipe ideas

Simply wash and pat the leaves dry. Generally fresh mint is used chopped or minced with a sharp chef's knife or ground with a mortar and pestle. The whole leaves are also used in teas or as a garnish.

- Try mint with your veggies. In a blender, mix together 2 parts olive oil, 1 part lemon juice, and 2 parts fresh mint leaves. Toss with hot or cold vegetables such as green beans and sugar snap peas.
- Mint goes well with tomatoes. Thinly slice mint and basil leaves and sprinkle over sliced tomatoes and slices of bocconcini cheese. Top with freshly ground pepper and sea salt.
- Sprinkle chopped mint on your next fruit salad or mix it with the raisins in baked apples for a fresh taste.
- Use mint in your next power smoothie—especially if it's chocolate. Mix banana, plain or vanilla yogurt, and a handful of mint leaves in a blender; thin with water if needed. Add a good-quality chocolate protein powder, mix, and enjoy a minty chocolate breakfast or snack.

DID YOU KNOW?

The mint family also includes herbs such as basil, rosemary, sage, oregano, thyme, and lavender.

miso

The refined and sometimes complex process of making miso, a Japanese culinary staple, is said to be equivalent to the art of making fine wine or cheese. To make miso, a combination of rice, barley, and/or soybeans is inoculated with the fungus *Aspergillus oryzae*. This combination is then added to a preparation of ground soybeans and salt and left to ferment for days (or years) before it's ground into a paste the consistency of peanut butter. Depending on the various ingredients used and the length of fermentation, different varieties of miso range in colour from white to dark brown and in taste from salty and savoury to sweet and fruity.

Soy in all its forms, including miso, has been the subject of much study in the past decade. In laboratory tests, the isoflavones in soy have been shown to inhibit breast cancer, but the associations between isoflavone-containing foods and breast cancer have been inconsistent in population studies. A 2003 study, however, in the *Journal of the National Cancer Institute* followed 21,000 Japanese women for 10 years. It found that consumption of miso soup was inversely associated with the risk of breast cancer. Even when other things were considered, including consumption of other soy foods such as tofu, reproductive history, and family history, women who consumed three or more bowls of miso soup daily had half the risk of breast cancer than those who ate less than one bowl a day. The greatest benefit was seen in postmenopausal women.

Fermented foods are gaining recognition as nutritional superstars loaded with antibacterial and antiviral properties that aid in digestion. Historically, people discovered that by storing food in brine or inoculating it with live bacteria, they were able to keep the food safely for longer periods of time. This process of lacto-fermentation causes the sugars in the food to be digested by a good bacteria called lactobacillus. Lactobacillus provides protection against harmful bacteria, creates an environment where beneficial bacteria can grow in the gut, and produces vitamin K and some B vitamins. When we eat these fermented foods, not only do we benefit from these nutrients, but the good and bad bacteria in our intestines are kept in balance, resulting in increased immunity and better digestion.

nutritional breakdown

Suitable for weight loss: **yes** ✓
Calories per 1 oz (28 g) miso: **56**

Glycemic index rating: **n/a**
Glycemic load rating: **3 (low)**

Miso is a good source of manganese (12% of daily value) and vitamin K (10% of daily value). It also contains beneficial amounts of zinc (5% of daily value) and iron (4% of daily value). It should be noted, however, that miso is also very high in sodium (43% of daily value).

selection and storage

Miso is widely available in natural food stores, in Asian markets, and increasingly, in local grocery stores. It typically comes as a paste in a sealed container and should be stored in the refrigerator after opening, where it will keep for up to one year. Look for the best-before date to check for freshness.

Certain types of miso are recommended for certain recipes, but as a rule of thumb, the lighter the miso, the less salty and mellower tasting.

preparation and recipe ideas

Miso should be eaten raw, as cooking will change its flavour and nutritional value. When used in soup, do not allow the miso to come to a full boil. It is very versatile and can be used in sauces, patés, dressings, marinades, and soups. Miso can be used in place of salt or soy sauce in many recipes. One-quarter cup (50 mL) of miso in 4 cups (1 L) of water makes a savoury soup stock.

- Traditional miso soup is a wonderful way to warm up on a cool day. Cover 1/2 cup (125 mL) wakame (a type of seaweed) with 1 inch (2.5 cm) of warm water and let stand for 15 minutes. Drain in a sieve. Mix together 1/4 cup (50 mL) white soybean miso and 1/2 cup (125 mL) dashi (a stock generally made from sea vegetables, available in powder or liquid). Heat 5 1/2 cups (1.75 L) dashi in a saucepan over medium-high heat until hot and stir in 1/2 lb (250 g) cubed soft tofu and the wakame. Simmer for 1 minute, remove from heat, stir in the miso mixture, add 1/2 cup (50 mL) thinly cut green onion, and serve.

- Miso adds tremendous flavour to marinades and dressings. Try this versatile dressing on salads or as a basic marinade for a mild fish such as tilapia: Mix 3 tbsp (50 mL) miso in 1/2 cup (125 mL) water, add 1/4 cup (50 mL) olive oil, 1 tsp (5 mL) sesame oil, 2 tbsp (25 mL) rice vinegar, and 1 tsp (5 mL) Dijon mustard. Mix well.
- Use miso as a spread or mix with a pesto recipe and serve with crispy baguette or on fresh pasta. Basil miso pesto is a favourite. In a food processor, chop 2 cloves of garlic. Add 3 cups (750 mL) chopped fresh basil leaves and pulse until coarsely chopped. Add 2 tbsp (25 mL) brown rice or barley miso and 1/2 cup (125 mL) pine nuts or walnuts or a mixture of the two and process until well chopped. With the food processor running, slowly pour in 1/4 cup (50 mL) olive oil and process until blended.

DID YOU KNOW?

Miso, which we usually think of as a traditional Japanese food, actually has its origins in ancient China and was known as hisio. It was introduced to Japan in the sixth or seventh century.

mushrooms

Mushrooms are often classified as a vegetable, but in fact they're from the fungi family. Mushrooms offer myriad nutrients and health benefits, such as being low in calories, fat, and sodium and high in selenium, riboflavin, and niacin. They contain about 80 percent water, making them a great addition to any weight management program. Mushrooms are also superior in protein in comparison to other vegetable proteins on account of their essential amino acid content. Between 70 percent and 90 percent of the vegetable protein present can be easily digested.

The white button mushroom is the most commonly consumed mushroom in North America, but other popular types include shiitake, maitake, reishi, oyster, Portobello, and crimini; each has its own unique taste and texture. Portobello mushrooms are actually crimini mushrooms that have been allowed to grow longer and larger.

Mushrooms contain a variety of B complex vitamins necessary for carbohydrate, protein, and lipid metabolism. These edible fungi are also a rich source of antioxidants, including selenium and L-ergothioneine. Selenium is a cofactor in one of the body's most important internally produced antioxidants, glutathione peroxidase, which works to reduce the levels of damaging free radicals in the body. L-ergothioneine is an antioxidant that protects the body on a cellular level.

Prized for thousands of years for their therapeutic value, mushrooms have played an essential role in Asian medicinal traditions and have been noted in the earliest botanical medicine texts. Among other things, they appear to modulate the immune system, help fight infection, and provide potent antioxidant protection. Shiitake, maitake, and reishi varieties have been studied for more than 20 years for their anti-cancer effects, but recent clinical trials have shown that white button mushrooms contain substances that inhibit the activity of aromatase (an enzyme involved in estrogen production) and 5-alpha-reductase (an enzyme that converts testosterone to DHT). These latest findings show that white button mushrooms may reduce the risk of breast cancer and prostate cancer. The chemoprotective effect was seen with an intake of about 3.5 oz (100 g) of mushrooms a day.

nutritional breakdown

Suitable for weight loss: **yes** ✓
Calories per 1 cup (250 mL) sliced, raw white button mushrooms (70 g): **22**
Glycemic index rating: **n/a**
Glycemic load rating: **2 (low)**

Mushrooms are generally an excellent source of the B vitamins riboflavin (21% of daily value) and niacin (23% of daily value) and a good source of B5 or pantothenic acid (13% of daily value). They are also a good source of selenium, potassium (12% of daily value), and phosphorus (11% of daily value). Although the white button, crimini, and maitake mushrooms are rich sources of these nutrients, the Portobello comes out ahead with even more of each of these important vitamins and minerals.

selection and storage

When selecting mushrooms, look for ones that are firm, plump, and relatively clean. Always avoid ones that are wet and slimy or have wrinkled patches. Mushrooms do not generally store well and can lose up to 30 percent of their nutrients and flavour if not stored properly. The best way to store most mushrooms is to wrap them loosely in a damp cloth and place them in a paper bag in the crisper of the refrigerator. They will last about three days in the refrigerator.

Mushrooms are extremely porous and therefore, if soaked in water, will become soggy quickly. The best way to clean mushrooms is to wipe them gently with a damp paper towel or mushroom brush.

preparation and recipe ideas

The flavour of mushrooms normally intensifies during cooking, and their texture holds up well to stir-frying and sautéing. Don't boil or steam mushrooms, as they'll become watery and lose much of their flavour.

- Have a Portobello burger! Grill up a juicy, meaty Portobello mushroom cap and serve with all the usual burger fixings. Portobello mushrooms can be marinated in olive oil, balsamic vinegar, garlic, rosemary, and freshly ground pepper.
- To give vegetable stock more depth and flavour, add shiitake or reishi mushrooms.

DID YOU KNOW?

White button mushrooms are the only fruit or vegetable that contains vitamin D. About 15 IUs (international units) of vitamin D (7.5% of the recommended daily value) are found in four or five button mushrooms.

olives and
olive oil

Olives and olive oil are truly one of nature's biggest gifts in terms of health benefits and flavour. Derived from the olive tree, the olive fruit has been one of the most researched superfoods to date.

The predominant type of fat found in olive oil is monounsaturated fats at 73 percent of total fat. It is thought that one of the reasons the Mediterranean diet boasts significantly lower levels of heart disease, cholesterol levels, and stroke is the higher consumption of heart-healthy monounsaturated fats found in olive oil. The monounsaturated fat in olive oil, specifically oleic acid, helps prevent LDL (bad cholesterol) from becoming oxidized and sticking to the artery walls. Additionally, olive oil contains an array of health-promoting plant compounds, such as oleurpein and hydroxytyrosol, which have strong antioxidant and anti-inflammatory effects on the body. Extra virgin olive oil has the highest amounts of these disease-fighting compounds and is also the least processed.

Other health benefits associated with olive oil consumption include:

- Protection against certain types of cancers, such as breast cancer and colon cancer. It's unclear if this is due to the antioxidants or fat content of olive oil.
- Monounsaturated fat is high in vitamin E, a very potent antioxidant vitamin.
- Weight loss. Preliminary research shows substituting olive oil for saturated fat in the diet can translate into a small but significant loss of both body weight and fat mass.
- Regular olive oil consumption may help to prevent belly fat accumulation and can assist with blood sugar control (i.e., insulin resistance).

nutritional breakdown

Suitable for weight loss: **yes** ✓
Calories per 1 tbsp (15 mL) olive oil (14 g): **119**
Calories per 1 oz (28 g, about 10 medium) olives: **32–41**
Glycemic index rating: **n/a**
Glycemic load rating: **n/a**

Olive oil is a good source of vitamins A (10% of daily value) and E (10% of daily value). Olives contain beneficial amounts of iron (5% of daily value), copper (4% of daily value), and vitamins A and E (both 2% of daily value).

selection and storage

Both olives and olive oil are readily available in all grocery and specialty stores. The classification of olive oil worldwide (except for the United States) is governed by the International Olive Oil Council and includes the following standards:

Extra virgin olive oil: The superior form of the oil has the least acidity and the most abundant nutrients. It is made using only mechanical pressing methods with no chemical or heat extraction of the oil.

Virgin olive oil: Slightly more acidic than extra virgin oil, with less antioxidant nutrients, it's also made using mechanical pressing only.

Pure olive oil: This refined oil is created by using charcoal and/or chemicals to extract and filter the oil. It's generally a mixture of different olive oils.

Light olive oil: This is the most refined of all olive oils. Light refers to the taste and light colour but not the fat content. It still has the same fat calories without the nutrients.

Olive oil should be stored in dark glass away from heat or light in a cupboard or the refrigerator as opposed to beside the stove. The oil will remain fresh for one year from the time it's bottled (check expiration dates).

Green or black olives are available in cans or jars and increasingly at olive bars in grocery and specialty stores. When buying in bulk, be sure there is a good turnover in the store and that the olives are immersed in brine or oil to maintain freshness and keep them moist. Store olives in an airtight container in the refrigerator, ensuring that there is enough oil or brine to prevent them from drying out. You can add more olive oil to keep them covered if you need to. The olives will keep for a couple of months if covered with oil or brine.

preparation and recipe ideas

Some olives are very salty and can be rinsed under cold water before serving. To remove the pits, use the flat side of a large knife to crush the olive, making the pit easier to get at.

If you refrigerate your olive oil, it may become temporarily cloudy, so allow it to come to room temperature before serving. Here are some *Healthy Sin Foods* tips to include olives and olive oil in your recipes.

- Both olives and olive oil are delicious as is. Serve olive oil in a shallow dish for dipping with crusty baguette instead of butter. For variety, add a splash of balsamic vinegar or freshly ground black pepper to the oil.
- Good olive oil is the foundation of a good salad dressing. This basic recipe can be modified to suit the dish. Press 4 to 5 cloves garlic and let sit for a few minutes to release the health-promoting compounds. Whisk together 1/3 cup (75 mL) fresh lemon juice (or balsamic vinegar), garlic, and sea salt and ground pepper to taste. Slowly pour the olive oil into this mixture, whisking constantly. The faster you whisk and more slowly you pour the oil, the thicker and creamier the dressing will be.
- Olive tapenade can be used as a dip, a spread on sandwiches instead of mayonnaise or butter, or as a topping for grilled fish or chicken. Combine 1 cup (250 mL) Kalamata olives, pitted and minced, with 3 minced garlic cloves, 2 tbsp (25 mL) rinsed and drained capers, 2 tbsp (25 mL) minced Italian parsley, 2 tsp (10 mL) minced organic lemon peel, 3 tbsp (50 mL) extra virgin olive oil, and freshly ground black pepper to taste.

DID YOU KNOW?

Olives are technically a fruit, with the green and black colours generally indicating different degrees of ripeness. Regardless of their ripeness, olives are too bitter to be eaten directly from the tree and must be cured or pickled first.

oranges

Oranges, once rare and extremely expensive, were reserved for special occasions such as weddings and Christmas. To the benefit of our health and taste buds, oranges are now widely available and one of the most popular fruits in the world. Oranges are classified as bitter or sweet varieties, with the bitter variety used for marmalades and liqueurs. The sweet variety, which includes Valencia, navel, Jaffa, and blood oranges, is delicious for eating and juicing.

Oranges are best known for their vitamin C, but the health benefits go beyond this important nutrient. The bioflavonoid hesperidin is also found in oranges, and it enhances vitamin C activity within the body; shows impressive anti-inflammatory, anti-carcinogenic, and cholesterol-lowering actions; and improves the health of capillaries by keeping them strong and reducing their permeability to maintain healthy blood flow. The highest concentration of hesperidin is in the white parts and pulp of the citrus peel, so orange juice with pulp will have more than pulp-free juice.

Recent research demonstrates that the citrus found in oranges can provide significant protection against a variety of cancers, such as esophageal, mouth, and stomach cancer. Reduction of rates can be as dramatic as 50 percent!

nutritional breakdown
Suitable for weight loss: **yes** ✓
Calories per 1 medium raw orange (131 g): **62**
Glycemic index rating: **40 (low)**
Glycemic load rating: **4 (low)**

Oranges are, of course, an excellent source of vitamin C (116% of daily value). They are also a good source of folate (10% of daily value) and offer beneficial amounts of vitamin A (6% of daily value) and potassium (7% of daily value).

selection and storage
Oranges won't ripen after they've been picked, so selecting ones that are heavy for their size helps ensure that you're getting ripe ones with high juice content. Avoid ones that are soft or bruised. Colour is not a good way to choose oranges because some may have their skins injected with an artificial dye (Citrus Rd No. 2) to promote uniform colour. Oranges don't necessarily have to be bright orange; ripe ones may

also be partly green or brown. Oranges can be stored at room temperature for about one week or longer in the refrigerator, where they should be unwrapped so they don't gather moisture and spoil.

preparation and recipe ideas

Oranges need to be washed well first, even if you are peeling them. Scrub oranges gently under running water with a vegetable brush. Thin-skinned oranges can be peeled with your fingers, but thicker-skinned ones may need longitudinal cuts from the top to the bottom with a sharp knife to be able to peel away the sections of skin.

If you're juicing oranges, they'll produce more juice if they're at room temperature. After washing the orange, roll it on the counter with gentle pressure to help burst the cell walls and liberate the juice. Orange zest is called for in many recipes, and since conventionally grown oranges will have pesticide residue in the peel even after washing, consider using organic oranges. To boost your intake of oranges, follow these simple tips.

- Freshly squeezed orange juice is a delicious addition to any breakfast or brunch. For added colour and nutrients, float a couple of fresh raspberries on top of the juice.
- Include oranges in your fruit salad or make a more savoury salad by combining orange segments with chopped fennel, shaved Parmesan cheese, and light vinaigrette. Top with freshly ground black pepper.
- Orange salsa is a sweet addition served over chicken or fish. Combine 1 diced orange, 1/4 cup (50 mL) diced red onion, 1 tbsp (15 mL) fresh lemon or lime juice, 1 tsp (5 mL) Dijon mustard, 2 tbsp (25 mL) olive oil, and 1 tsp (5 mL) chopped mint or cilantro.
- Make your own ice pops. Pour the juice of fresh oranges into ice cube or ice pop trays and enjoy on the next hot day. You can also add other juices for a more exotic taste or some vanilla yogurt for a frozen yogurt treat.

DID YOU KNOW?

Oranges (especially Valencia) that look green have undergone a natural process called regreening. This is due to a ripe orange pulling green chlorophyll pigment from the leaves. These oranges may be very sweet.

oregano

Oregano is an important aromatic herb that greatly contributes to the distinctive flavour and character of both Greek and Italian cuisine. It's hard to imagine pizza or tomato sauce without oregano. Not only do herbs such as oregano make food tastier, they contribute a multitude of health benefits when used instead of salt, sugar, and synthetic flavourings.

According to researchers at the U.S. Department of Agriculture, herbs have higher antioxidant activity than fruits, vegetables, and some spices, including garlic. Using a variety of chemical tests including the ORAC (oxygen radical absorbance capacity) analysis, the researchers studied 27 culinary and 12 medicinal herbs. To the delight of pizza lovers everywhere, the herbs with the highest antioxidant activity belonged to the oregano family, which showed 3 to 20 times higher antioxidant activity than the other herbs in the study. Antioxidants are a class of compounds associated with reducing the tissue damage caused by free radicals in the body—tissue damage that can lead to cancer, heart disease, and stroke.

In another study, Australian researchers reported that the antioxidant content of a salad could be more than doubled with the right dressing. The researchers tested Greek, Italian, and Thai-style dressings and kept the vegetable content of the salad consistent. The Greek dressing came out on top, followed by the Italian and the Thai. The Greek dressing contained olive oil, lemon juice, garlic, rosemary, oregano, and mint. The Italian dressing also included olive oil, garlic, and oregano, while the Thai had only the garlic in common. For all the dressings, fresh herbs were used. For an aromatic mixed-herb red wine vinaigrette dressing, see page 262.

nutritional breakdown

Suitable for weight loss: **yes** ✓
Calories per 1 tsp (5 mL) dried leaves (1 g): **3**
Glycemic index rating: **n/a**
Glycemic load rating: **n/a**

Oregano is a very rich source of vitamin K (8% of daily value) and contains vitamins B6, A, C, and E (all 1% of daily value). It also contains beneficial amounts of calcium (2% of daily value), iron (2% of daily value), and manganese (2% of daily value).

selection and storage

Oregano can be purchased fresh or dried (the dried herb has a stronger flavour). When buying fresh oregano, look for vibrant green leaves without any yellowing or dark spots. Wrap the fresh herb in damp paper towels and store in the refrigerator, where it will keep for about one week. A clever way of preserving oregano is to freeze it. Chop up the fresh herb, put it in an ice cube tray, and cover with water or stock and freeze. Pop out frozen blocks and store in the freezer in airtight containers or freezer bags. This is an easy way to have fresh-tasting oregano available at all times for sauces and stews.

You can also dry your own oregano. Hang bundles of four to six stems in a dry, dark place. When the leaves are crisp, rub off the stems and store in an airtight glass jar in a dark, cool place away from humidity (not by the stove).

preparation and recipe ideas

Simply wash and dry fresh herbs before use. If you're using fresh oregano, strip the leaves from the fibrous stem before chopping or using whole. Add oregano toward the end of the cooking process to maximize the flavour and prevent it from becoming bitter. If you're using dried oregano, crush the leaves in the palm of your hand before cooking to help release the essential oils. Here are some tasty oregano ideas.

- Add oregano to your next omelette or soufflé for an Italian twist.
- Maximize the flavour and health benefits of your next salad by adding whole or chopped oregano leaves to the greens or finely mince the oregano leaves and mix with the dressing.
- Nothing beats the taste of oregano, basil, garlic, and tomatoes together. Combine them in a savoury sauce over whitefish or tilapia, or use them raw, chopped all together, and served on multigrain toast.
- Sauté some garlic and onions, add zucchini, and cook until just tender. Toss in some chopped fresh oregano at the end and serve with freshly ground pepper and sea salt.

DID YOU KNOW?

Oregano has 42 times more antioxidant activity than apples, 30 times more than potatoes, 12 times more than oranges, and four times more than blueberries.

peaches

Originating in China, succulent peaches have become one of our favourite summer fruits. Peaches can be red, pink, yellow, or orange (or a combination of these colours) and are divided into two types: clingstone or freestone, depending on whether the flesh of the fruit sticks to the stone. Both types have juicy white or yellow flesh with distinctive red stains near the pit and are chock full of health-promoting nutrients.

Peaches contain a significant amount of vitamin C, which is a powerful antioxidant and anti-inflammatory agent. Its anti-inflammatory activity may decrease the incidence of asthma symptoms characterized by bronchial spasm and swelling in the lining of the lungs. Antioxidants in general are thought to provide important defence mechanisms for maintaining the health of the lungs; however, vitamin C is especially important as it's present in larger amounts in the lining of the airway surfaces. A study from the *American Journal of Clinical Nutrition* indicates that vitamin C in the general population appears to correlate with the incidence of asthma. In other words, when vitamin C intake is low, the rate of asthma is high. Another large study conducted in Italy has shown that young children with asthma experience significantly less wheezing if they eat a diet high in fruits rich in vitamin C.

Carotenes and flavonoids such as lycopene and lutein are also found in good supply in peaches, giving them their red, orange, and yellow colours. Different phytonutrients have been found to possess a range of activities, which may help inhibit cancer cell proliferation, regulate inflammatory and immune response, and protect against lipid oxidation—a major contributor to cardiovascular disease. A significant role of the phytonutrients is protection against oxidation. We live in an environment that creates a lot of oxidation, and many processes involved in metabolism in the body also result in oxidation. It has been estimated that there are 10,000 oxidative hits to DNA per cell a day in humans. Add that to the top of the list of reasons to eat as close to 10 servings of fruits and vegetables as possible a day.

nutritional breakdown

Suitable for weight loss: **yes** ✓
Calories per 1 raw, medium peach (150 g): **59**
Glycemic index rating: **28 (low)**
Glycemic load rating: **5 (low)**

Peaches are a very good source of vitamin C (17% of daily value) and contain significant amounts of vitamins A (10% of daily value) and E (5% of daily value). They are also rich in potassium (8% of daily value), copper (5% of daily value), and manganese (5% of daily value).

selection and storage

Be sure to select peaches at the peak of the season—from June through August. The amount of red on peaches depends on the variety and is not always a sign of ripeness. When selecting fresh peaches, look for ones that have a rich yellow hue; those with a green undertone will never ripen. Ripe peaches should yield to gentle pressure on the skin and should smell deliciously sweet.

Harder peaches can be softened and ripened at room temperature for a few days. When the fruit is soft, it should be eaten right away, but if you must wait, it will keep in the refrigerator for two or three days.

Peaches have been reported by the Environmental Working Group in the United States to be the type of produce that is the most heavily contaminated by pesticides. Consider purchasing organic peaches.

preparation and recipe ideas

Wash peaches gently but thoroughly under cool running water. Much of the peach fuzz can be eliminated with gentle rubbing. If you're slicing the peaches, they may show some enzymatic browning after being cut. To delay this process, dip the slices into a mixture of 2 cups (500 mL) water and 2 tbsp (25 mL) fresh lemon juice. Fresh peaches don't last very long so they're generally preserved by poaching, canning, drying, or freezing, but there's nothing quite like a fresh juicy peach on a hot day.

- Peaches are best eaten fresh. When they're in season, enjoy them as often as you can for breakfast on your hot or cold cereal, in a protein shake, or added to your yogurt and fruit salad.
- Try peaches on the barbecue! Skewer half a fresh peach, brush with honey or maple syrup, grill for 2 or 3 minutes until browned, and enjoy.
- Frozen peach slices can be added to muffins, cakes, breads, and pancakes for a sweet treat. Be sure to thaw the peaches first so you don't affect the cooking time.

pears

There are thousands of different varieties of pears, each with their own flavour, shape, and colour, including yellow, green, brown, and red. Different varieties are popular in different countries, but in North America, the most common types are the Anjou, Bosc, Comice, and Bartlett pears.

Pears are nutritional winners as they offer many benefits such as an excellent source of fibre. Pears contain both soluble and insoluble fibre. The soluble fibre in pears is called pectin and dissolves into a gel-like substance in the intestinal tract. This gel-like substance binds with bile salts (made from cholesterol) and carries them out of the body. Thus, this process reduces both LDL (bad cholesterol) and total cholesterol without affecting HDL (good cholesterol) levels. The binding action can also slow the absorption of dietary carbohydrates after meals, which can be helpful in maintaining blood sugar control.

Pears are also rich in potassium, which is an important electrolyte needed for proper heart, nerve, and muscle function. Adequate potassium levels specifically are thought to be one reason for the low cardiovascular disease rates in vegetarians. Unfortunately North Americans consume double the sodium and about half the potassium recommended by current guidelines. Including more pears in your daily diet not only tastes great, but it can help reduce the risk of major cardiovascular disease in a number of ways.

nutritional breakdown
Suitable for weight loss: **yes ✓**
Calories per 1 raw, medium pear (178 g): **103**
Glycemic index rating: **33 (low)**
Glycemic load rating: **6 (low)**

Pears are an excellent source of fibre (24% of daily value) and good source of vitamins C (12% of daily value) and K (10% of daily value). They also offer beneficial amounts of copper (7% of daily value), potassium (6% of daily value), and magnesium (3% of daily value).

selection and storage

Pears are generally not allowed to ripen on the tree as this makes them coarse and mealy with a mushy centre. Instead, they're harvested when they reach full maturity and kept cold until they reach the stores. When choosing fresh pears, look for ones that are fresh looking with no bruises or external damage. Pears (other than Bartlett pears) do not dramatically change colour as they ripen. Test for ripeness by pressing gently near the stem—if the skin gives to gentle pressure, the pear is ready to eat.

Store unripe pears in a warm place outside the refrigerator in a fruit bowl or a paper bag. Check daily for ripeness, as there is a narrow window between too hard and overripe. To ripen pears quickly, put them in a paper bag with other ethylene gas–producing fruit such as an apple or banana. When pears are ripe, store them in the refrigerator, where they will last about three days.

preparation and recipe ideas

Pears require no preparation other than washing and coring if you're not eating them whole. There is no need to remove the skin as it is thin, edible, and a delicious source of fibre and phytonutrients.

- Add pears to your salads. Combine baby arugula, watercress, thinly sliced leeks, walnuts, pears, and a balsamic vinaigrette dressing for a nutritious lunch or side salad.
- Have pears for breakfast. Add chopped pears to your oatmeal, blend in your protein smoothie, or serve thinly sliced on pancakes drizzled with maple syrup.
- Warm up your pears. Cook pears in a saucepan with a little water for about 5 minutes or until soft. Being careful of the hot liquid, use an immersion blender to purée until smooth. Add cinnamon or other spices to taste. Serve warm over ice cream or spooned over a warm gingerbread cake.

DID YOU KNOW?

Pears are often recommended as one of the first foods for infants as they're considered to be hypoallergenic and less likely to produce an adverse response than other fruits.

pineapple

The pineapple is technically not a single fruit but the fruits of 100 or more separate flowers that fuse together to become the "fruit" around a central core. Each fruitlet can be identified as an "eye," the rough spiny marking on the pineapple's surface. This delightful tropical fruit is high in bromelain, vitamin C, and manganese, all of which contribute to its health benefits.

Bromelain is a proteolytic, or protein-digesting, enzyme found in both the fruit and stem of the pineapple. Pineapple has been used for centuries as a folk remedy, particularly for digestive problems because of its ability to digest proteins. Bromelain is typically extracted from pineapples and made into capsule or tablet form. When used as a digestive aid, it's taken with meals. Some bromelain appears to be absorbed by the body intact, so it's also thought to have effects outside the digestive tract. In fact, bromelain is often marketed as a natural anti-inflammatory for conditions such as arthritis. In Germany, bromelain is one of the most popular supplements and is approved by the *Commission E* for the treatment of inflammation and swelling due to injury or surgery, particularly of the nose and sinuses. (The *Commission E Monographs* is a therapeutic guide that evaluates the safety and efficacy of herbs for licensed prescribing in Germany.)

While many people often take extra vitamin C or drink extra orange juice when they have a cold, few consider eating pineapple or drinking pineapple juice. Pineapple contains large amounts of vitamin C, which boosts immune system function, while the bromelain is said to help suppress coughs and loosen mucus. In a study of 59 patients with acute or chronic sinusitis, 69 percent of those receiving bromelain had significant improvements in nasal discharge, inflammation, and breathing difficulties. Only 23 percent of the patients receiving a placebo found similar improvements.

nutritional breakdown
Suitable for weight loss: **yes** ✓
Calories per 1 cup (250 mL) raw, chunked pineapple (165 g): **82**
Glycemic index rating: **51 (low)**
Glycemic load rating: **6 (low)**

Pineapple is an excellent source of vitamin C (131% of daily value) and manganese (76% of daily value). It also contains beneficial amounts of B3 and B6 (both 9% of daily value), as well as copper (9% of daily value).

selection and storage

When choosing a fresh pineapple, do not judge its ripeness solely based on colour, as there are several varieties on the market ranging from green to golden yellow. The most important factor in determining ripeness is smell. Pineapple stops ripening as soon as it's picked, so choose fruit with a fragrant sweet smell and slight softness at the stem end. Avoid pineapples that smell musty, sour, or fermented. Look for ones that are heavy for their size and free of soft spots, bruises, and darkened "eyes," all of which may indicate that the pineapple is past its prime.

Pineapple can be stored at room temperature for a few days before eating. While this will not make the fruit any sweeter, it will become softer and juicier. If left on the counter for too long, pineapple will spoil, so it should be stored in the refrigerator if not being eaten within a few days. Pineapple that has been cut up should be stored in the refrigerator in an airtight container. It will stay fresher and juicier if you place some of the pineapple juice in the container. Pineapple does not freeze well and loses its flavour.

preparation and recipe ideas

To prepare pineapple, you need to peel it and remove the eyes and the fibrous centre. First, cut off the top and bottom of the pineapple with a sharp knife. Place the pineapple upright on a cutting board and carefully slice off the outer skin. With a sharp paring knife or the end of a vegetable peeler, remove the eyes. Don't cut too deeply, just enough to lift out the section that contains the eye. Then remove the fibrous core. Cut the pineapple lengthwise into four wedges (quarter it) and cut around the fibrous core. Pineapple can be enjoyed in the following ways.

- Escape to the tropics. Combine cut-up pineapple with other tropical fruits such as kiwi, mango, and papaya for a delicious fruit salad. Or throw everything into a blender with some ice for a tropical slushie.
- Spice up your pineapple into an easy salsa. Mix diced pineapple, tomatoes, chili peppers, and a touch of minced onion and cilantro. Toss with a bit of fresh lime juice and olive oil. This salsa complements most fish dishes.

plain yogurt

Yogurt is a highly predominant dairy food that we can't seem to get enough of. From plain yogurt to fruit-bottom yogurt and yogurt with friendly bacteria, the choices are endless.

Yogurt is made by adding bacterial culture to milk. Under the right conditions, these bacteria feed on the lactose (milk sugar) in milk and convert it to lactic acid, which gives yogurt its distinct tangy flavour. The strains of bacteria used to make yogurt are also responsible for its numerous health benefits. There are more than 500 different strains of bacteria that call our intestines home—some good, others bad. When we eat yogurt that contains good bacteria, or probiotics, they multiply and compete for food with the bad bacteria that are capable of causing problems such as diarrhea. There is mounting evidence that probiotics enhance the immune system, help alleviate the symptoms and incidence of irritable bowel syndrome, ulcerative colitis, and *Helicobacter pylori* (the bacterium responsible for most stomach ulcers), and even inhibit the growth of cancer-causing compounds in the gut.

According to a study published in the *Annals of Nutrition and Metabolism,* probiotics yogurt may also help to improve your cholesterol profile. Participants consumed either yogurt that contained active probiotics culture or yogurt that had no active bacteria for four weeks. Both groups ended the study with lower LDL (bad cholesterol), but the probiotics group also raised their HDL (good cholesterol) substantially, making yogurt not only a good choice for intestinal health but for heart health too.

Individuals who have difficulty digesting milk and milk sugars (lactose intolerance) may be in luck when eating probiotics yogurt. When consuming probiotics yogurt, the bacteria digest the lactose, alleviating symptoms and making this calcium- and mineral-rich food a great addition to the diet.

nutritional breakdown
Suitable for weight loss: **yes ✓**
Calories per 1 cup (250 mL) low-fat plain yogurt (245 g): 154
Glycemic index rating: **36 (low)**
Glycemic load rating: **10 (low)**

Low-fat plain yogurt is an excellent source of calcium (45% of daily value), phosphorus (35% of daily value), riboflavin (31% of daily value), and B12 (23% of daily value).

In terms of fat content in yogurt, consider the following nutritional values:
whole-fat yogurt = 7 g of fat per 8 oz serving
low-fat yogurt = 1 to 4 g of fat per 8 oz serving
non-fat yogurt = less than 0.5 g of fat per 8 oz serving

selection and storage
Most of the health benefits of yogurt come from the active bacteria they contain so be sure the ingredients label lists "active bacterial culture" or "live active cultures."

preparation and recipe ideas
- Yogurt is a classic breakfast food. Mix it with fresh fruit and nuts, stir it into muesli, add it to a smoothie for a creamier taste, or add a dollop on top of pancakes or waffles and sprinkle with cinnamon and brown sugar.
- Forget creamy commercial salad dressings. Yogurt is a great base for a homemade creamy dressing. Simply add 2 tbsp (25 mL) plain yogurt to 3 tbsp (50 mL) olive oil and 1 tbsp (15 mL) balsamic vinegar or fresh lemon juice. Mix well to emulsify and add different spices for different results: Dijon mustard, tamari sauce and grated ginger, pressed garlic, chopped basil and oregano, or chopped fresh dill (great on salmon).
- Yogurt-based sauces add a tangy note to many dishes, including Greek- and Indian-inspired ones. For any type of souvlaki, mix together 1 cup (250 mL) plain yogurt with 1 cup (250 mL) finely chopped cucumber, 2 minced garlic cloves, 2 tbsp (25 mL) fresh lemon juice, and sea salt and pepper to taste. Or mix 1 cup (250 mL) plain yogurt with 1 cup (250 mL) finely chopped tomato, 1 cup (250 mL) chopped onion, 1 tsp (5 mL) ground cumin seeds, 1 tsp (5 mL) ground coriander seeds, and 1 tsp (5 mL) minced medium to hot chili peppers.

DID YOU KNOW?
One of the friendly strains of bacteria used in yogurt, *Bacillus bulgaricus*, was named in honour of the long-lived Bulgarian peasants who ate quantities of yogurt.

quinoa

Quinoa (pronounced *keen*-wah), which many people think of as a type of grain, is actually a small seed. It is, however, used like a grain and substituted for grains in recipes because of its cooking characteristics. It is gluten free, easy to digest, and one of the least allergenic "grains."

Originating in the Andes Mountains of South America, quinoa was revered by the Incas, who called it "the mother grain" and used it to sustain their armies. In recent years quinoa has been rediscovered, brought to the North American market, and is now cultivated in parts of Canada and Colorado.

Cooked quinoa seeds have a delicate nutty flavour and are creamy and crunchy at the same time. The most popular type of quinoa is white or transparent yellow, but it can also run the spectrum from pink to red, purple, and black.

At 12 percent to 18 percent, quinoa has very high protein content—about twice that of rice. It contains all eight essential amino acids (the building blocks of proteins), making it a complete protein. Quinoa may be an especially good choice for vegetarians and vegans because it has particularly high levels of the essential amino acids lysine, cysteine, and methionine, which are typically lacking in most grains. It's also a good source of many minerals, such as magnesium, which is rapidly finding its way to the top of the most important minerals list. In fact, magnesium is needed for more than 300 biochemical reactions in the body, including those involved with insulin secretion and the body's use of glucose. A 2006 study in *Diabetes Care* showed that the risk of developing type 2 diabetes was 31 percent lower in the participants who frequently ate whole grains compared to those who ate the least amount of these magnesium-rich foods.

nutritional breakdown

Suitable for weight loss: **yes** ✓
Calories per 100 g cooked quinoa: **120**
Glycemic index rating: **53 (low)**
Glycemic load rating: **9 (low)**

Quinoa is also a good source of phosphorus (15% of daily value) and magnesium (16% of daily value) and a very good source of manganese (32% of daily value). As a rich source of fibre (11.5% of daily value), it also contributes to good bowel health.

selection and storage

Quinoa is available pre-packaged and in bulk in natural food stores and increasingly in supermarkets. When buying in bulk, make sure the store has high turnover and the bins are well covered and show no signs of moisture. Quinoa will keep in an airtight glass container for up to six months, or longer if you keep it in the fridge.

preparation and recipe ideas

Before harvesting, quinoa has a coating of bitter-tasting saponins that protect it from birds. Most commercially sold quinoa has had this coating removed, but as a first step in preparation, quinoa should be gently rubbed and rinsed in a fine mesh strainer under running water to remove any remaining powdery residue. The common cooking method is to treat quinoa like rice: bring 2 cups (500 mL) water or broth to a boil and add 1 cup (250 mL) quinoa, cover, and cook at a low simmer for 14 to 18 minutes. A rice cooker will work well too.

There are many ways to add quinoa to your diet.

- Quinoa can be substituted for rice in any recipe.
- Try it in soups, hot casseroles, and stir-fries during the colder months or serve it cold in salads in the summer.
- For a more nutty taste, dry-roast quinoa before cooking: place a skillet over medium-low heat and stir the seeds constantly for about 5 minutes.
- Mix quinoa with fresh fruit and nuts for a protein-packed, high-fibre breakfast.

DID YOU KNOW?

Because it is not a true grain, quinoa can be certified kosher for Passover, making it a good high-protein option for this holiday.

raspberries

Each single, sweet, delicious raspberry is actually dozens of tiny individual seeds containing fruits called drupelets that we think of as one whole fruit. Most raspberries are red, but you can now find other varieties in stores such as yellow, amber, purple, and black raspberries.

Raspberries are an outstanding source of ellagic acid, a phytonutrient compound with potent antioxidant properties. Plants produce many phytonutrients, including ellagic acid, for protection from microbiological infection and pests, but when we eat these compounds, they have health-promoting effects. Ellagic acid has the ability to block the cancer-causing actions of many carcinogens, including nitrosamines and polycyclic aromatic hydrocarbons, both of which are components of cigarette smoke.

Ellagic acid may also help promote cardiovascular health because as an antioxidant, it can reduce the oxidation of LDL (bad cholesterol) and help protect the blood vessels. Raspberries have many other nutrients that promote heart health, including vitamin C, manganese, and copper, all of which help protect the body from oxidative damage. Raspberries are also an excellent source of fibre, which is very effective at mopping up excess cholesterol in the body. In fact, 1 cup (250 mL) of raspberries is a delicious way to get 8 g (32% of daily value) of fibre.

nutritional breakdown

Suitable for weight loss: **yes** ✓
Calories per 1 cup (250 mL) raw raspberries (123 g): **64**
Glycemic index rating: There is no scientific study of the glycemic index of raspberries. Some sources have extrapolated from other similar foods that it would be around **40 (low)**.
Glycemic load rating: **3 (low)**

Raspberries are an excellent source of fibre (32% of daily value), vitamin C (54% of daily value), and manganese (41% of daily value). They also provide a good level of vitamin K (12% of daily value) and beneficial amounts of folate (65% of daily value) and magnesium (7% of daily value).

selection and storage

Prime raspberry season runs from mid-summer to early fall. Select plump, richly coloured raspberries that are dry and unblemished. Since raspberries don't continue to ripen after picking, avoid ones that still have the hull attached in the centre, as this is a sign they were picked before ripening fully. Also avoid juice in the package, as this means there are crushed berries, which increases the chance of mould. Raspberries are very delicate and perishable, so buy only what you're going to be able to use within two days. Store raspberries in the refrigerator right away after you bring them home and don't wash them until right before you're going to eat them.

If you want to have the fresh berry taste in the middle of winter, raspberries freeze well. Before freezing, gently wash the berries and pat dry. Spread them on a baking sheet in a single layer and place flat in the freezer. Once frozen, transfer the berries to freezer bags or containers. Prepared this way, frozen raspberries will keep for up to one year. Bear in mind that once thawed, the berries will be soft and tend to fall apart, so they may be best used for sauces. Raspberry purée also freezes well.

preparation and recipe ideas

Fresh raspberries only need to be washed before eating. Because they are so delicate, wash gently using light pressure with a sink sprayer. Avoid letting them soak in water, as they will become waterlogged and lose their flavour. Gently pat dry and enjoy. Here are some berrylicious ideas for you to try.

- Fresh is best. Add raspberries to fruit salad, yogurt, oatmeal, muesli, and, of course, breakfast smoothies (frozen ones are good for the smoothies too).
- Puréed raspberries make a great topping for pancakes, waffles, sponge cake, cheesecake, chocolate cake (any cake, really). Add a bit of lemon zest for more kick.
- Raspberry salad dressing is delicious. Please see page 260 for a homemade raspberry vinaigrette dressing.

DID YOU KNOW?

Raspberries are a member of the rose family and grow wild throughout North America.

sesame

Sesame is one of the oldest seeds known to humankind. Thought to have originated in India or Africa, sesame is grown primarily for its oil-rich seeds, which come in a variety of colours, from cream white to charcoal black. Sesame seeds possess a unique nutty taste, making them suitable for a variety of dishes from fish to chicken to baking options in cookies.

The minuscule size of sesame seeds hides their considerable health-promoting capacity. Of the nuts and seeds most commonly eaten in North America, sesame seeds have the highest total phytosterol content. Phytosterols (also called plant sterols) are naturally occurring compounds found in the cells and membranes of plants that reduce cholesterol levels in the blood by competing with the absorption of cholesterol in the intestine. Clinical trials indicate that adding 1 to 2 g of additional phytosterols to the diet can help reduce cholesterol levels (2 tbsp/25 mL of sesame seeds contains 200 mg of phytosterols).

Sesame seeds and sesame seed oil contain phytonutrients called lignans, which have antioxidant activity and protect the liver from oxidative damage. In early research, two of these lignans, sesamol and sesamin, demonstrated anti-inflammatory effects. In addition, sesame seeds are a very good source of copper, a trace mineral that is also important in a number of anti-inflammatory and antioxidant systems.

Sesame oil is rich in monounsaturated and polyunsaturated fats and is low in saturated fat.

nutritional breakdown

Suitable for weight loss: **yes** ✓
Calories per 1 oz (28 g), about 2 tbsp (25 mL) sesame seeds: **160**
Calories per 1 tbsp (15 mL) sesame oil (13.6 g): **120**
Glycemic index rating: **n/a**
Glycemic load rating: **n/a**

Sesame seeds are an excellent source of many minerals, including copper (57% of daily value), manganese (34% of daily value), calcium (27% of daily value), magnesium (25% of daily value), and iron (23% of daily value).

selection and storage

Sesame seeds are available pre-packaged and in bulk. Sesame seeds have high oil content so the seeds should smell sweet and not bitter or rancid. Because of the oil content, store sesame seeds in an airtight glass jar in the refrigerator for six months or the freezer for 12 months. Once you open a container of tahini or Asian sesame paste, it should be refrigerated.

Sesame oil comes in light and dark varieties. Light sesame oil has a nutty, rich distinctive taste that can enhance the flavour of many foods. The smoke point of light sesame oil is 400°F (200°C), making it suitable for sautéing, stir-fries, and grilling. It's also great in marinades, salad dressings, and sauces. Dark sesame oil has a stronger flavour and should only be used in small amounts and isn't suitable for cooking. The dark sesame oil can be added toward the end of cooking and is common in Asian cooking in hot dishes such as stir-fries or in cold noodle or salad recipes as part of a marinade or a dressing. Sesame oil should also be stored in the fridge.

preparation and recipe ideas

Sesame seeds and oil are extensively used in all types of Asian cuisine, in both sweet and savoury dishes. Use your imagination and some of the following tips to get more of these nutritious seeds in your diet.

- Liven up your cooked vegetables with a sprinkle of sesame seeds before serving.
- Top grilled fish, especially pan-seared tuna, with this mustard sauce and sprinkle liberally with black sesame seeds. Mix 1 tsp (5 mL) dry mustard powder, 1 tbsp (15 mL) water, and 1 tsp (5 mL) tamari sauce. Spread on cooked fish and top with seeds.
- Both whole and crushed sesame seeds make a healthy "breading" for chicken strips. Grind sesame seeds in a small coffee grinder and combine with sea salt, pepper, and your preference of spices. Dredge chicken strips in either milk or a beaten egg and dip or roll in sesame seeds. Bake at 400°F (200°C) for 25 to 30 minutes.

DID YOU KNOW?

"Open sesame," the famous phrase from the story of "Ali Baba and the Forty Thieves" in *1001 Arabian Nights*, reflects the way the sesame seed pod bursts open when it reaches maturity.

spelt

Spelt, an ancient cousin of wheat, may well be one of the earliest crops grown in the Western world. Archaeobotanists think that spelt's cultivation began between 6000 and 5000 BC in what historians call the Fertile Crescent, an area that spans parts of modern-day Iraq, Iran, and Jordan. Brought to North America in the 1890s, spelt was the primary grain used to produce flour until the 1920s, when wheat took over because of its lower processing cost.

While spelt can be used to produce bread and pasta with the familiar wheat-like taste and texture, its nutritional profile is superior to that of wheat. It contains more protein, is significantly higher in most of the B vitamins, and is naturally high in fibre. Although spelt contains gluten and is not suitable for those with celiac disease, many people with wheat sensitivities report that they can easily digest it without reaction.

Spelt also has a strong hull that protects the grain from pollutants and insects. This means that it's not normally treated with pesticides or other chemicals, making it a favourite with those who prefer organic foods.

This ancient grain is not only sweet and nutty tasting, it's a good source of niacin (B3), which helps reduce various risk factors associated with cardiovascular disease. Niacin can help reduce not only total cholesterol levels, but also LDL (bad cholesterol) and lipoprotein-a, which is called an independent risk factor for cardiovascular disease because it seems to increase the risk with or without other contributing factors.

nutritional breakdown

Suitable for weight loss: **yes** ✓
Calories: 100 g cooked spelt: **127**
Glycemic index rating: **63 (medium)**
Glycemic load rating: **11 (medium)**

Spelt offers an excellent source of manganese (55% of daily value) and is a good source of fibre (16% of daily value) and the B vitamins B2 (riboflavin) and B3 (niacin) (13% of daily value).

selection and storage

Spelt flour, pasta, and cereal can be found in most natural health food and grocery stores. Whole grain spelt (also called spelt berries) can also be found in bulk. When you purchase anything in bulk, make sure the bins are well covered and there are no signs of moisture, which may mean the product is mouldy. Store spelt berries in an airtight glass container away from air, moisture, and sunlight, which can make the oils go rancid. It should last this way for up to six months and longer if you store it in the fridge.

preparation and recipe ideas

As with any grain, rinse the spelt berries first to remove any grit and dirt, and then soak for about eight hours. For a richer, nuttier flavour, toast the spelt for a few minutes in a skillet before rinsing and soaking. Once soaked, bring 3 cups (750 mL) water or broth to a boil; stir in 1 cup (250 mL) spelt berries, and lower to a simmer for 1 hour. Let the berries rest for a bit after cooking as they will continue to soften and absorb liquid.

Here are some other ways to use spelt.

- Spelt flour can be substituted in any recipe with wheat flour, but it requires less liquid. Either reduce the amount of liquid called for by one-fourth or add one-fourth more spelt flour than the amount of wheat flour called for.
- Serve cooked spelt berries as a hot or cold breakfast cereal with some berries, nuts, and yogurt for a hearty start to the day.
- Because of its high protein content, spelt is a good choice for a one-dish meal. In summer, add chopped fresh seasonal vegetables and herbs to cooked spelt and drizzle with an olive oil dressing. On a wintry day, serve hot with roasted vegetables or add the cooked spelt to a favourite robust soup.

DID YOU KNOW?
Spelt's high levels of complex carbohydrates make it a good choice for "carbo-loading" before an athletic event and also for restoring glycogen levels in the muscles afterward.

spinach

It's not just Popeye's favourite food anymore! Low in calories, filled to the brim with minerals, vitamins, and phytonutrients, spinach has taken the nutritional limelight and is now considered a superfood because of its synergy of nutrients. It's time to get a little more green into your diet!

Spinach boasts excellent amounts of B vitamins, such as B6 and folate, which help promote cardiovascular health by keeping homocysteine levels in check. Homocysteine is an amino acid in the blood. Epidemiological studies have shown that too much homocysteine in the blood (plasma) is related to a higher risk of coronary heart disease, stroke, and peripheral vascular disease. Spinach also contains a rich supply of carotenoids (plant chemicals) that help protect artery walls from damage. Just 1 cup (250 mL) of cooked spinach provides almost 100 percent of a healthy daily intake of beta-carotene, the most abundant carotenoids in the North American diet.

Studies have also shown spinach eaters reduce their risk of a variety of cancers. It is thought that this antioxidant, anti-cancer effect may be largely due to the presence of phytonutrients, including glutathione and alpha-lipoic acid. Glutathione is the primary antioxidant in all cells and protects and repairs damaged DNA. Alpha-lipoic acid is both fat and water soluble, meaning it can protect the fatty part of the cell membranes and the water portions of the cells from oxidative damage, a contributing factor in aging, heart disease, and cancer. Spinach also contains an abundant amount of chlorophyll, which studies suggest has an antimutagenic effect against a wide range of potentially harmful carcinogens.

nutritional breakdown
Suitable for weight loss: **yes** ✓
Calories per 1 cup (250 mL) cooked spinach: **41**
Glycemic index rating: **n/a**
Glycemic load rating: **2 (low)**

Spinach is an excellent source of vitamins K (1111% of daily value), A (377% of daily value), and folate (66% of daily value), as well as a multitude of minerals, including manganese (84% of daily value), magnesium (39% of daily value), and iron (36% of daily value).

selection and storage

Available year-round, spinach is sold loose, bunched, in pre-packaged bags, and frozen. When selecting fresh spinach, look for bright green leaves with crisp stems. Avoid spinach that is yellowing, wilted, or bruised. A slimy coating indicates decay. The Environmental Working Group in the United States reports that spinach is one of the 12 most heavily pesticide-contaminated produce products available. Consider purchasing organic spinach.

Fresh spinach loses much of its nutritional value after about six days, so use it quickly. To keep your spinach crisp and fresh, store spinach wrapped in a damp paper towel in a plastic bag in the crisper drawer of the refrigerator. Wash the spinach just before using. Frozen spinach will keep for up to eight months.

preparation and recipe ideas

Bunched spinach generally has a lot of soil in it, so be sure to wash it thoroughly either under cool running water or by rinsing it in a sink full of water. Don't soak the spinach for too long, as it'll start to lose the water-soluble nutrients.

One of the best ways to cook spinach to maximize the nutrients is the "quick boil" method. Drop washed spinach into a large pot of boiling water for 1 minute; don't wait for the water to return to a boil. Drain the spinach in a colander and press out the excess water with a fork. Season to taste. This spinach will be tender, brightly coloured, and not mushy.

- Add chopped spinach to a hearty soup or pasta sauce.
- Make a meal of it. Toss some orange sections, walnuts, crumbled goat cheese, and chopped red peppers with fresh baby spinach leaves for a refreshing meal.
- Spinach is great for breakfast in scrambled eggs, a soufflé, an omelette, or a frittata.

DID YOU KNOW?

Florentine is a common name used for recipes in which spinach is a major ingredient. Florence, Italy, was the home of Catherine de Medici, who loved spinach so much that when she married the king of France, she brought along her own cooks to prepare her favourite spinach dishes.

squash

Squash is a native plant to Central America and is thought to have been consumed for more than 10,000 years. Originally squash was used only for its seeds because the flesh, which was limited, was bitter and unpalatable. Over time, cultivation spread throughout the Americas and Europe and resulted in the development of varieties of squash that had an abundance of sweeter-tasting flesh. Along with maize (corn) and beans, squash was one of the "Three Sisters," indigenous plants used by Native Americans for agriculture.

Squash is loosely grouped into two varieties: summer squash (zucchini, yellow crookneck, Patty pan) and winter squash (butternut, Hubbard, acorn, spaghetti, pumpkin). Despite its 95 percent water content, summer squash is an excellent source of vitamin C and has respectable amounts of folate, vitamin B6, beta-carotene, and fibre, making it a good dietary tool for the prevention of heart disease and cancer. Both types of squash contain the phytonutrients lutein and zeaxanthin. These carotenoids are potent antioxidants that protect the lens and the retina of the eye from light-induced oxidative damage. Research has noted that a higher dietary intake of both lutein and zeaxanthin is related to a decreased risk of cataracts and age-related macular degeneration.

One of the most abundant nutrients in winter squash is beta-carotene. This phytonutrient is an antioxidant with anti-inflammatory properties. Diets rich in carotenes offer protection against cancer, heart disease, and type 2 diabetes. Beta-carotene helps prevent the oxidation of cholesterol in the body. Oxidized cholesterol is the type that builds up on blood vessel walls and increases the risk of heart attack and stroke. The anti-inflammatory properties of beta-carotene may also help decrease the severity of conditions such as asthma, osteoarthritis, and rheumatoid arthritis, all of which involve inflammation. The seeds of one of the most popular winter squashes, pumpkin, have been shown to be helpful in reducing symptoms of benign prostatic hyperplasia (BPH) in men.

nutritional breakdown

Suitable for weight loss: **yes ✓ (summer squash is lower on the GI and lower in calories)**

Calories per 1 cup (250 mL) cooked: **36 (summer squash); 76 (winter squash)**

Glycemic index rating: **15 (low, summer squash); >70 (high, winter squash)**
Glycemic load rating: **3 (low, summer); 5 (low, winter)**

Winter squash is an excellent source of vitamin A (214% of daily value), vitamin C (33% of daily value), and fibre (23% of daily value). Summer squash is also a good source of vitamin C (16% of daily value), manganese (19% of daily value), and potassium (10% of daily value).

selection and storage

Summer squash has thin skin, so it bruises easily and should be handled with care. Look for small, firm squashes with glossy skin that are fairly heavy for their size. The skin should not be too hard, as this indicates overmaturity and the squash will most likely have hard seeds and stringy flesh. For winter squash, look for a deep-coloured rind that is free of blemishes, sunken spots, cuts, or slits, and that again is heavy for its size. Avoid a tender rind, as this indicates immaturity. Slight variations in the colour of the rind are fine and don't affect the flavour.

Store summer squash unwashed in a plastic bag in the crisper drawer of the refrigerator for up to one week. Wash just before use. Winter squash is much less perishable and can last from one to six months (depending on the variety) if stored in a dark, cool (about 50°F/10°C), well-ventilated place.

preparation and recipe ideas

Unlike winter squash, the entire summer squash can be eaten—the rind, seeds, and flesh—so make sure it's washed well. Boiling and steaming summer squash is not recommended, as it tends to absorb too much water, lose its flavour, and become mushy. Enjoy it raw, grilled, or sautéed.

Despite the hard rind, winter squash should be scrubbed thoroughly before using to avoid transferring bacteria and dirt to the interior flesh. The rind of most varieties is difficult to peel, so it's easier to cut the squash in half, scoop out the seeds and membrane, cook with the rind on, and then scoop out the cooked flesh. All varieties are great for steaming, puréeing, baking, and roasting.

- Raw summer squash is terrific sliced and served with your favourite dip.
- Grate zucchini into a crisp salad or add with other seasonal toppings to a hearty sandwich.
- You can eat the whole thing! Summer squash blossoms are edible and add a wonderful flair to a green salad. Winter squash seeds are delicious when they're cleaned, dried, tossed with olive oil and sea salt, and roasted or pan-fried.
- Brush summer squash with olive oil, season with sea salt and ground pepper, and grill on the barbecue for a great summer side dish or a healthy burger topping.
- Winter squash is very versatile and can be enjoyed as a traditional side dish, in soups and stews, and even added to breads, muffins, custards, and pies.

DID YOU KNOW?

Although we generally consider squash a vegetable, botanically speaking, it is a fruit, as it is the edible part of the plant that contains the seeds.

steel-cut oats

Oatmeal has long been considered a good way to start the day because it "sticks to your ribs." Steel-cut oats (also called coarse-cut oats, pinhead oats, Scotch oats, or Irish oats) have come a long way from being livestock feed to being one of the healthiest options for breakfast.

When the inedible outer husk, or chaff, of the oat is removed, the bran and germ stay intact and so do the fibre and other nutrients. These oat groats are then chopped a couple of times with steel blades—hence the name steel-cut oats. Rolled oats are whole groats that have been steamed and flattened between heavy rollers, and quick-cooking oats are similar to rolled oats except that after steaming they're cut finely before rolling. For instant oatmeal, the oats are partially cooked (rather than steamed) and then rolled very thinly. Oftentimes, sugars are added to instant oatmeal to enhance flavour, which thereby increases the glycemic index rating and potential of weight gain. Remember that with each bit of processing, there is a loss of nutrients that reduces the health benefits.

Steel-cut oats contain more soluble fibre than any other grain, so they move through the body slowly, keeping blood sugar stable and helping you feel full longer. Much of this soluble fibre is called beta-glucan. For the past 40 years, study after study has shown that eating just 3 g of this fibre a day can lower cholesterol by up to 23 percent, which helps decrease the risk of heart disease and stroke as well as lowering blood pressure.

Fibre isn't the only thing oats have going for them. They also have a unique blend of antioxidants, including ones called avenanthramides. These antioxidants have been shown to prevent LDL (bad cholesterol) from being converted into its oxidized form that damages arteries and can initiate the process of atherosclerosis (clogging of arteries).

nutritional breakdown

Suitable for weight loss: **yes** ✓
Calories per 1/2 cup (125 mL) cooked steel-cut oats (78 g): **303**
Glycemic index rating: **52 (moderate)**
Glycemic load rating: **17 (medium)**

Note: The glycemic index and load tend to be higher for instant oats than steel-cut oats.

Steel-cut oats provide an excellent source of zinc (21% of daily value), magnesium (35% of daily value), and acid tryptophan (52% of daily value). A bowl full of oatmeal is also a rich source of B1 or thiamin (39% of daily value) and phosphorus (40% of daily value), not to mention fibre (34% of daily value) and protein (26% of daily value).

selection and storage

Steel-cut oats are available pre-packaged and in bulk. If you buy oats in bulk, make sure the store has high turnover and the bins are well covered and show no signs of moisture. A slightly higher fat content than other grains means that oats can go rancid more quickly. As a result, purchasing small quantities at any given time is recommended. Oats can be kept for about two months if stored in an airtight container in a cool, dark, dry place.

preparation and recipe ideas

Depending on the degree of processing, different types of oats require different lengths of cooking time. Steel-cut oats generally need to cook for about 25 to 30 minutes. Oats don't need to be soaked and should be added to cold water and cooked at a simmer until they reach the desired consistency. Rolled oats will take a slightly shorter time (about 15 minutes), while oat groats may take up to 50 minutes.

- For a hearty, full-fibre breakfast, add fresh or dried fruit, chopped walnuts, some cinnamon, and a couple teaspoons (about 10 mL) of ground flaxseed to your oatmeal. Sweeten with some maple syrup or raw honey if desired.
- Oats aren't just for breakfast. Try whole oat groats as the starting point for your next turkey or chicken stuffing.
- Use whole oat groats instead of rice or barley for a tasty pilaf. Toast the oats in a skillet over medium heat for a few minutes; add vegetables such as onions, mushrooms, and peppers, and cook a few minutes longer. Add an appropriate amount of broth, cover, and let simmer for about 40 to 50 minutes, stirring occasionally. Remove from heat, add fresh herbs, and enjoy.

strawberries

Once reserved as a luxury food for royalty, the sweet, juicy strawberry is now enjoyed worldwide for its wonderful taste and considerable health benefits. Strawberries are one of nature's healthiest nutrient packages, containing an excellent source of vitamin C, fibre, and phytonutrients known as flavonoids.

In epidemiological studies (human population studies that attempt to link health effects to a specific cause), consumption of fruits and vegetables, particularly those high in flavonoids, has been associated with lower risk for heart disease as well as cancer. This effect in large part is due to the antioxidant capacity of the flavonoids. The flavonoids in strawberries contain unique anti-inflammatory properties that enable them to reduce the activity of the enzyme cyclooxygenase (COX). Many non-steroidal anti-inflammatory drugs such as aspirin and ibuprofen also block pain by blocking this enzyme, which is associated with inflammatory conditions such as asthma, osteoarthritis, and rheumatoid arthritis. Unlike strawberries that have no side effects, some of these COX-inhibitor drugs have been linked with heart disease and intestinal bleeding.

Strawberries also contain a variety of other health-promoting nutrients, including folate and vitamin B6—both of which promote heart health and may help prevent cognitive decline with aging.

nutritional breakdown
Suitable for weight loss: **yes ✓**
Calories per 1 cup (250 mL) raw, sliced strawberries (166 g): **53**
Glycemic index rating: **40 (low)**
Glycemic load rating: **3 (low)**

Strawberries are an excellent source of vitamin C (163% of daily value) and manganese (32% of daily value). They also contain beneficial amounts of fibre (13% of daily value), folate (10% of daily value), potassium (7% of daily value), and vitamin B6 (4% of daily value).

selection and storage
Strawberries are available year-round in North America, but the peak of the season is from April through July. Since strawberries don't continue to ripen once they've been picked, look for fresh strawberries that are plump and firm with a deep red colour,

attached green caps, and a wonderfully sweet aroma. Avoid ones with white, green, or yellow patches, as they aren't fully ripe and will be sour.

Refrigerate your strawberries as soon as you bring them home as they will spoil quickly at room temperature or in sunlight. To avoid mould and excess moisture, only wash strawberries right before you plan on eating them. Strawberries will stay fresh in the refrigerator for two to three days but are best eaten right away.

To freeze strawberries, wash them gently under running water and pat dry. Spread them out in a single layer on a baking sheet and put them flat in the freezer. When they are frozen, transfer to a freezer bag or container. They will keep well frozen for up to one year and will retain more of their vitamin C if they're frozen whole as opposed to sliced or crushed.

The Environmental Working Group in the United States reports that strawberries are among the 12 most heavily pesticide-contaminated produce products available. Consider purchasing organic strawberries.

preparation and recipe ideas

Like all berries, avoid letting strawberries soak as they'll absorb too much water, making them mushy and less flavourful. Wash them gently under cool running water and pat dry before you remove the stem and cap. Here are some palate-pleasing ways to add more of these sweet berries to your diet.

- Include strawberries, sliced or whole, in your next fruit salad. If you like a dollop of creamy topping on your fruit, purée fresh or frozen (and thawed) strawberries with plain or vanilla-flavoured yogurt and a touch of maple syrup, and top with chopped mint leaves.
- What's better than plain strawberries? Strawberries dipped in chocolate! In a double boiler, melt some bittersweet chocolate and dip. Eat right away or cool on a parchment-lined baking sheet in the refrigerator. To boost your heart-healthy capacity, use chocolate that contains more than 70 percent cocoa solids to maximize your flavonoid intake.

DID YOU KNOW?
The strawberry is the most popular type of berry fruit in the world.

sweet potatoes

Sweet potatoes belong to the tuber family and are always a huge hit at the dinner table. Whether in soups or side dishes, casseroles, and even baking, sweet potatoes are a highly versatile and nutritious spud-like vegetable.

While sweet potatoes and yams are technically not the same (true yams tend to contain more starch and less sugar than sweet potatoes), the terms are often used interchangeably.

The skin of sweet potatoes can be white, yellow, orange, red, or purple and their flesh can be white, yellow, or orange. In general, the deeper the colour of the skin and flesh of the sweet potato, the higher the concentration of health-promoting carotenoids.

Sweet potatoes boast impressive levels of antioxidants, specifically beta-carotene. They're also rich in vitamins A and C and manganese and copper. Unlike their distant cousin the white potato, sweet potatoes have been classified as an "anti-diabetic" food. A promising study in *Diabetes Care* showed that the nutraceutical caiapo, made from the extract of a variety of white sweet potato, had beneficial effects on the blood glucose and cholesterol levels of patients with type 2 diabetes. In addition, a study from Taiwan has found that the sweet potato has unique root storage proteins that also appear to scavenge free radicals. This helps to prevent cell and tissue damage associated with the development of conditions such as cancer and heart disease.

nutritional breakdown

Suitable for weight loss: **yes ✓, in moderation**
Calories per 1 cup (250 mL) baked-in-the-skin sweet potato (200 g): **180**
Glycemic index rating: **59 (moderate)**
Glycemic load rating: **17 (medium)**

Sweet potatoes offer an excellent source of vitamins A (769% of daily value) and C (65% of daily value) and are a very good source of most of the B vitamins, including B6 (29% of daily value). They also provide excellent amounts of manganese (50% of daily value) and potassium (27% of daily value).

selection and storage

Sweet potatoes are available year-round; however, the peak months when the concentration of nutrients is highest are November and December. Look for firm sweet potatoes without any cracks, bruising, or soft spots. Avoid leathery, wrinkled, and discoloured ones, especially those with a green tint, as this indicates that the toxic alkaloid solanine may be present.

This sturdy vegetable generally stores well, but it doesn't like the refrigerator. The cold temperature is fine, but the moisture can cause an increase in the conversion of starches to sugars and may cause them to sprout. Store sweet potatoes loose (not in a plastic bag) in a cool, well-ventilated place and they can keep for up to one month. Gently scrub sweet potatoes under cool running water before cooking. Keep the skin on for added fibre and nutrients.

preparation and recipe ideas

Sweet potatoes can be steamed for quick, healthy eating or baked for a sweeter, creamier treat. Boiling is not recommended because it increases water absorption and causes them to lose flavour as well as many of the water-soluble nutrients such as vitamin C and the B vitamins.

There are many ways to enjoy sweet potatoes.

- Sweet potatoes are a tasty, colourful, healthy substitution for potatoes, especially baked or mashed. When baking, be sure to pierce them with a fork or knife first to allow steam to escape and to prevent them from bursting.
- Thinly slice sweet potatoes and brush lightly with olive oil and a favourite seasoning. Bake until crispy for delicious sweet potato fries.
- Puréed sweet potatoes can be added to muffins, cakes, cookies, and pancakes. Try a sweet potato pie at your next family gathering.
- Sweet potatoes are delicious in savoury dishes such as curries and stir-fries, but they also go well in sweet dishes with the flavours of cinnamon, honey, lime, ginger, coconut, and nutmeg.

DID YOU KNOW?

It would take more than 20 cups (5 L) of broccoli to provide the same amount of beta-carotene as 1 cup (250 mL) of cooked sweet potato.

tomatoes

Tomatoes, which are actually a fruit, are members of the nightshade family. There are several types of tomatoes available, such as the Roma tomato (ideal for cooked dishes such as tomato sauce) and large beefsteak tomatoes, suitable for salads or slices on sandwiches.

Not only are tomatoes bursting with flavour, but they're also one of the healthiest foods on the planet. Tomatoes contain lycopene, one of a family of food pigments called carotenoids that occur naturally in fruits and vegetables. Carotenoids are antioxidants, which help fight off cellular damage and prevent and even reverse a variety of disease processes. In other words, free radicals in the body can be flushed out by consuming high levels of lycopene. While other fruits and vegetables do contain lycopene, none is as rich as the tomato. The human body cannot produce lycopene; therefore, it must be obtained from the diet.

One of the hottest areas of research has been the health benefits of lycopene, which has been demonstrated to be beneficial for heart disease, cataracts, high cholesterol, and a variety of cancers such as prostate, colorectal, stomach, cervical, breast, and pancreatic.

nutritional breakdown

Suitable for weight loss: **yes** ✓
Calories per 1 tomato: **30**
Glycemic index rating: **15 (low)**
Glycemic load rating: **2 (low)**

Tomatoes also offer an excellent source of vitamin C (40% of daily value) and are a good source of vitamin A (about 15% of daily value).

selection and storage

Although tomatoes are now available year-round, locally grown tomatoes are the sweetest from June to September. When choosing tomatoes, select those with the most vibrant hue of red. Typically, those are the tomatoes that contain the richest source of lycopene and beta-carotene.

Store tomatoes at room temperature and away from direct sunlight. Try not to store tomatoes in the fridge, as their flavour will dampen. Tomatoes will also keep longer if you store them stem down. If you need to ripen a tomato quickly, simply place it in a paper bag with a banana or apple. The ethylene gas released from these fruits will hasten the ripening process.

preparation and recipe ideas

Raw tomatoes are great for your health, but cooked tomatoes are even better. The red pigment lycopene is located in the cell wall of the tomato, so cooking the tomato with a bit of oil releases the compound fully. Thus, tomatoes and olive oil over whole grain pasta or vegetables offers a very strong nutritional punch!

Here are some other ways to enjoy the full benefits of tomatoes.

- Drink a glass of low-sodium tomato juice.
- Instead of snacking on calorie-laden crackers and cheese, try cherry tomatoes and a low-fat ranch dip.
- On a summer's night, enjoy a bowl of cool, refreshing gazpacho soup.
- Toss sun-dried tomatoes in your next salad or as a pizza topping on whole grain crust.
- During the fall and winter months, enjoy homemade tomato soup with some whole grain croutons on top (see page 268 for the recipe).
- Research has shown that when eaten together, tomatoes and broccoli have a powerful antioxidant effect. Enjoy a broccoli and tomato salad with goat cheese and balsamic vinaigrette.
- Serve bruschetta at your next dinner party (see page 232 for the recipe).
- Enjoy salsa (which has replaced ketchup as the top-selling condiment in the United States!) with baked nachos or on top of eggs.

DID YOU KNOW?

Organic ketchup offers three times as much lycopene as non-organic brands.

walnuts

About 20 years ago, all fats were given a bad rap and labelled as undesirable for your overall health and for your heart health. Unfortunately, when the media got hold of this and fat was considered the "evil" macronutrient, fat consumption dropped dramatically and a huge surge in low-fat diets started to take hold. It was estimated that nut consumption dropped by a full 40 percent.

As research in this area grew, scientists discovered a very important principle. When it comes to health, it's the *type* of fat that is more significant than the amount of fat you're consuming. As discussed in Chapter 4, there are good fats, which are critical to overall health, and there are bad fats, which are inflammatory and can lead to heart disease and high cholesterol, and can even be linked to a variety of cancers.

When it comes to nuts, the "king of all nuts" is truly the walnut. Not only do walnuts offer an abundant amount of nutrition such as protein, minerals, and vitamins, especially B6, but they also contain the greatest amount of the essential fat—omega-3 essential fatty acids.

There are several studies that demonstrate the cardio-protective effects of walnuts and omega-3 fats. A recent study in the *Journal of the American College of Cardiology* suggested that eating walnuts at the end of a meal helped to reduce unwanted inflammation that can lead to clogging of arteries and cardiac damage. Participants in the study were given two high-fat meals of salami and cheese, eaten one week apart. Following each meal, they were also given either 5 tsp (25 mL) of olive oil or eight shelled walnuts. Results showed that both the olive oil and the walnuts reduced the onset of harmful inflammation and oxidation that occurs after eating a meal high in saturated fat. Adding walnuts also helped preserve the elasticity and flexibility of the arteries, regardless of any changes in oxidation or inflammation. Arteries that are more elastic can expand when needed to increase blood flow and decrease blood pressure and adapt better to dietary changes.

Walnuts also have the highest overall antioxidant activity of any nut. They are an excellent source of copper and manganese, two minerals needed for the formation of superoxide dismutase, one of the most powerful antioxidant enzymes produced in the body. Walnuts are also a concentrated source of phytonutrients, including ellagic acid, which protects healthy cells from free radical damage and detoxifies potentially carcinogenic substances.

nutritional breakdown

Suitable for weight loss: **yes ✓, in moderation**
Calories per 1 oz (28 g/14 halves): **185**
Glycemic index rating: **n/a**
Glycemic load rating: **n/a**

Walnuts are an excellent source of manganese (48% of daily value) and copper (22% of daily value). They also supply beneficial amounts of magnesium (11% of daily value), vitamin B6 (8% of daily value), and folate (7% of daily value).

selection and storage

Unshelled and shelled walnuts are available pre-packaged or in bulk. If you're buying in bulk, make sure the store has high turnover and the bins are well covered and show no signs of moisture. If selecting unshelled walnuts, look for shells that are heavy for their size with no cracks or dark stains, which can often be a sign of mould on the nutmeat inside. Occasionally walnuts in the shells are bleached to make them look more attractive and uniform in colour, so if possible search out unbleached, unshelled walnuts.

Shelled walnuts should be uniform in colour without cracks, holes, or dark spots. Because of their high oil content, walnuts can turn rancid quickly. Make sure your walnuts smell sweet and nutty and not musty or bitter.

Store shelled walnuts in an airtight glass container in the refrigerator or freezer, where they will stay fresh for up to one year. Unshelled nuts will remain fresh for up to six months if stored in a cool, dry place, or longer if stored in the fridge. Don't shell the walnuts until they're ready to be used.

preparation and recipe ideas

The only tool you'll need to prepare walnuts is perhaps a nutcracker. As tasty as they are raw, there are many other ways to incorporate them into a healthy way of eating.

• Roasting your own is the healthiest way to enjoy roasted walnuts. Mix 2 tsp (10 mL) sea salt with enough water to cover 4 cups (1 L) of walnut halves. Let sit for 8 hours or overnight and then drain. Spread walnuts on a baking sheet and place in a 150°F to 170°F (65°C to 76°C) oven, turning often for 8 hours or until completely crisp. Eat as is or add your favourite combination of spices as follows: Melt 1/4 cup (50 mL) butter or use 1/4 cup (50 mL) olive oil and mix in 1/4 cup (50 mL) dried chopped rosemary, 1 tsp (5 mL) cayenne pepper, and a dash of sea salt. Toss with the prepared walnuts, spread on a baking sheet, and bake at 350°F (180°C) for 8 to 10 minutes. Try this with curry spices too.

- Try a lentil walnut dip with fresh raw veggies or baked pita crisps. Purée together 1 cup (250 mL) walnuts, 1 1/2 cups (375 mL) cooked lentils, 2 tsp (10 mL) Dijon mustard, 1 tbsp (15 mL) fresh lemon juice, and sea salt and ground pepper to taste. Add water or olive oil to reach desired consistency.
- Chopped walnuts are a great addition to muffins, cakes, brownies, and even pancakes.
- Sprinkle walnuts on your oatmeal, muesli, or fruit and yogurt for a healthy breakfast.
- Walnuts are a wonderful topper to any salad, including an update of a classic. Combine 1 cup (250 mL) walnut halves (raw or roasted), 4 cups (1 L) chopped romaine lettuce, 1 chopped radicchio head, 1 chopped apple each of Granny Smith, Red Delicious, and Yellow Delicious. Toss with a dressing of 1/2 cup (125 mL) walnut oil, 1 tsp (5 mL) Dijon mustard, 1 tbsp (15 mL) honey, 1/2 tsp (2 mL) grated orange or lemon rind, 1 tbsp (15 mL) fresh lemon juice, 2 tbsp (25 mL) apple cider vinegar, a dash of cayenne pepper, and a touch of sea salt if desired.

DID YOU KNOW?

The U.S. Food and Drug Administration (FDA) has endorsed the health benefits of walnuts by allowing the health claim that "eating 1.5 ounces of walnuts as part of a diet low in saturated fat and cholesterol may reduce the risk of heart disease."

wheat germ

The germ in wheat germ has nothing to do with viruses, bacteria, or getting sick. The germ is the reproductive part of the wheat kernel from which the seed germinates and forms the sprout that then becomes wheatgrass. Because of this reproductive role, wheat germ contains more nutrients per ounce than any other grain, making it one of the most nutritionally dense foods available.

A whole wheat kernel is made of three parts: the bran, the endosperm, and the germ. In order to make white refined flour, the bran and the germ are generally removed. If the flour is going to be whole grain wheat, then both the bran and the germ (and all their health-promoting benefits) are left intact.

Wheat germ is a great source of many vitamins, including vitamin E, most of the B vitamins group, folic acid, and a number of minerals such as iron, calcium, and zinc. Wheat germ contains a high amount of the antioxidant vitamin E, which not only helps protect the oils in the germ from becoming rancid but, when consumed, also helps protect fat-containing substances in our bodies such as cell membranes, brain cells, and cholesterol. Vitamin E has also been shown to be important in immune system function, Alzheimer's disease, and blood sugar control.

nutritional breakdown

Suitable for weight loss: **yes** ✓
Calories per 1 oz (28 g), about 2 tbsp (25 mL): **101**
Glycemic index rating: **whole grain, 41 (low)**
Glycemic load rating: **6 (low)**

Wheat germ is an excellent source of zinc (22% of daily value), vitamin E (24% of daily value), and the B vitamin thiamin (35% of daily value). It's also a good source of fibre (15% of daily value).

selection and storage

As wheat germ is a classic health food, it can be found in most grocery and health food stores. Because of its high unsaturated oil content, look for wheat germ that comes in vacuum-packed containers. This way, the oil is better protected from potential oxidation and rancidity. Wheat germ should always be stored in the refrigerator, where it can stay fresh for up to nine months.

preparation and recipe ideas

- To increase fibre and nutrients, wheat germ may be used to replace up to 1/2 cup (125 mL) to 1 cup (250 mL) of flour in most recipes. Because it tends to absorb moisture, you may need to add 1 to 2 tbsp (15 to 25 mL) of liquid for every 1/4 cup (50 mL) of wheat germ you add to a recipe.
- For a nutty taste, wheat germ can be sprinkled on salads. Simply dry-roast raw wheat germ in a skillet over medium-low heat for about 5 minutes, stirring constantly.
- Try wheat germ in place of bread crumbs in casseroles and burgers and as a coating for baked fish or chicken.
- Sprinkle a couple of tablespoons (25 to 50 mL) of wheat germ on your favourite yogurt or fruit or add it to your breakfast smoothie for an extra nutrient boost.

DID YOU KNOW?
The Mayo Clinic includes wheat germ in its "10 Great Health Foods for Eating Well."

wild salmon

Salmon varieties are usually classified by the ocean from which they come. There is only one species of wild Atlantic salmon, simply called Atlantic salmon, and five of Pacific: the Chinook (or king), sockeye (or red), Coho, pink, and chum. Each variety has different characteristics, including flesh colour, which can range from light pink through orange to red. Some species contain more fat than others, with the Chinook and sockeye generally having the most fat.

When consuming wild salmon, the predominant type of fat consumed is the essential fat: omega-3 essential fatty acid. The two important omega-3 fatty acids found in fish, particularly wild salmon, are called eicosapentaenoic acid (EPA) and docosahexaenoic acid (DHA). The type of fat we eat affects the body's production of compounds called eicosanoids that in turn have an effect on blood pressure, blood clotting, immune function, and inflammation. When we eat the omega-3 oils in wild salmon, certain eicosanoids are produced that may decrease LDL (bad cholesterol), increase relaxation in larger arteries (which can decrease blood pressure), and decrease inflammatory processes in the blood vessels, all of which serve to decrease our risk of heart disease.

Wild salmon and other coldwater fish are also often referred to as "brain food." The derivatives of omega-3 fat, EPA and DHA, are highly concentrated in the brain and are important for both cognitive and behavioural function. An increasing number of studies are linking low levels of omega-3 fats to various conditions, including depression, ADHD, hyperactivity, behavioural and learning disorders, and bipolar disorder. Still other studies are showing that an increased consumption of the omega-3 fats found in wild salmon can help stave off dementia and Alzheimer's disease, making these fats crucial to our diets throughout the lifespan.

nutritional breakdown

Suitable for weight loss: **yes** ✓
Calories per 100 g cooked (dry heat) salmon: about **150** (will vary depending on the variety)
Glycemic index rating: **n/a**
Glycemic load rating: **n/a**

Wild salmon is an excellent source of all the B vitamins, including B12 (51% to 83% of daily value) and B3 or niacin (40% to 50% of daily value). It's also an excellent source of many minerals, including selenium (54% to 67% of daily value) and phosphorus (26% to 32% of daily value).

selection and storage

When purchasing fresh wild salmon, ensure that the store has a reliable reputation and high turnover, and that the fish is fresh. Find out which day fresh fish is delivered and plan your shopping accordingly. Unfortunately, some stores will sell farmed salmon labelled as wild-caught salmon. Buy wild salmon displayed on crushed ice instead of pre-packaged. Smell it to make sure it isn't "fishy": fresh fish should smell more like sea water than fish. Take the wild salmon home right after purchasing or bring a cooler with ice if you're going to be at the market for a while. Fresh wild salmon will keep for a few days in the refrigerator, but it's best to cook it as soon as possible.

preparation and recipe ideas

Rinse the salmon under cold running water and pat dry before cooking. Most fish has been deboned, but it's always a good idea to double check. Lay salmon skin side down and run your fingers along the flesh in both directions to feel for bones. Remove any remaining bones with your fingers or tweezers.

As a general rule, salmon doesn't take long to cook, about 7 to 10 minutes per inch (2.5 cm) of thickness. If the fillet, steak, or whole fish is less than 1 inch (2.5 cm) thick, it will take half the time. Salmon is best grilled, broiled, or baked. Salmon skin is edible and should be left on during cooking. Remove the skin before serving if you aren't eating it.

- Grilled wild salmon can be topped with many different sauces so experiment with basil pesto, black olive tapenade, tamari, or teriyaki. Dill sauce is always a favourite: mix together 1 cup (250 mL) plain yogurt, 1 tsp (5 mL) minced garlic, 1 cup (250 mL) diced cucumber, 2 tbsp (25 mL) Dijon mustard, and 1 to 2 tbsp (15 to 25 mL) chopped fresh dillweed. Spoon over hot salmon and serve.
- Marinating salmon also adds delicious flavour. Combine 1/2 cup (125 mL) tamari sauce, 1/4 cup (50 mL) mirin (sweet Japanese cooking wine), 1/4 cup (50 mL) water, and 1 tbsp (15 mL) minced ginger. Place salmon in a plastic bag and pour

in the sauce. Squeeze out all the air, seal, and store in the refrigerator for at least 1 hour or overnight for a deeper flavour. Grill as usual but don't use the marinade on the cooked fish.

- Salmon cakes are always a hit, especially with kids. Place about 8 oz (225 g) cooked salmon in a bowl and flake with a fork. Add 2 cups (500 mL) mashed potatoes, 1/4 cup (50 mL) minced onions, 2 beaten eggs, 1/2 tsp (2 mL) lemon pepper, 2 tbsp (25 mL) minced parsley, and sea salt to taste. Mix all ingredients well and form into small patties. Bake or sauté patties until hot. Serve as is or with your favourite salmon sauce.

DID YOU KNOW?

The size of a salmon is usually related to its age. The Chinook is the largest of the Pacific species, with the world record catch of a 126 lb (57 kg) salmon.

101 *healthy sin foods* recipes

We combined my husband's love for cooking with my passion for eating well to develop a multitude of recipes not only loaded with tantalizing taste but packed with powerful nutrients. After a few years of testing recipes on our family, friends, and neighbours, we are thrilled to offer you our top 101 *Healthy Sin Foods* recipes.

These versatile meals fit into an array of lifestyles, tastes, and dietary restrictions. Some recipes are extremely simple and can be prepared in under 10 minutes (e.g., the power shakes or the authentic Mexican salsa). Others can be made in advance, then frozen and used for future grab-and-go meals (e.g., the hearty turkey chili). Entrees, salads, soups, and desserts round out the menu, whether it's just for you, for your family, or for larger dinner parties (impress your guests with a crustless quiche for brunch or wild salmon and dill-crusted fillets for dinner).

Why 101? We wanted to ensure that you had more than enough delicious and guilt-free daily meals to choose from in addition to healthy yet sinfully scrumptious options for holiday festivities or parties. We've gauged the recipes accordingly, from "über" healthy to "eat weekly" to more decadent "occasional" indulgences. All ingredients selected are healthier versions of their unhealthy counterparts (e.g., sweet potatoes instead of white potatoes, baked instead of fried, whole grain instead of refined grain). Antioxidant capacity, fibre content, saturated fat grams, and milligrams of sodium were carefully considered when developing the recipes.

To determine how often each meal, side dish, sauce, or dessert can be eaten, look at the end of each recipe for its nutritional breakdown and legend, which includes:

🍓🍓🍓 = SUPER SKINNY! 🍓🍓 = ENJOY ONCE A WEEK! 🍓 = SAVE FOR AN OCCASIONAL TREAT!

Note: If you're on a salt-restricted diet, omit the salt from the ingredients.

The 101 *Healthy Sin Foods* recipes also include nutrition and kitchen tips guaranteed to turn you into your own nutritional expert and top-notch chef.

We hope you enjoy preparing and eating these dishes as much as we have!

Bon appétit,
Joey and Randy

morning starters

goat cheese, dill, and asparagus omelette

This hefty omelette is filled with the creaminess of goat cheese and the tanginess of dill—a perfectly decadent way to start any morning. Use fresh dill instead of dried for maximum flavour in omelettes, salad dressings, and fish dishes.

3	asparagus, whole spears	3
1 tsp	butter	5 mL
3 tbsp	diced white onion	50 mL
1/2 tsp	minced garlic	2 mL
1/4 tsp	salt	1 mL
1/4 tsp	pepper	1 mL
1	omega-3 egg	1
4 tbsp	egg whites	60 mL
1 oz	goat cheese	28 g
1 tsp	fresh dill	5 mL

1. Wash asparagus spears and cut to 6-inch (15 cm) length.
2. Melt 1/2 tsp (2 mL) of the butter in nonstick skillet; add onion, garlic, salt, pepper, and asparagus. Cover and cook over medium-high heat for 5 minutes until tender; set aside.
3. Combine egg and egg whites and beat until fully mixed.
4. Melt remaining 1/2 tsp (2 mL) butter in nonstick skillet with an 8-inch (20 cm) base.
5. Pour egg mixture into pan and swirl back and forth until mixture begins to set (3 to 4 minutes over medium-high heat).
6. On one side of the egg mixture, place cooked asparagus and onion mixture. Top with goat cheese and fresh dill.
7. Fold open side over filling. Cook for 1 minute on each side.
8. Serve.

kitchen tip

Asparagus begins to lose its fresh flavour once it's picked, so try to use it as soon as possible after purchase. The bottoms of larger asparagus spears can be chewy and woody and should be snapped off. Simply bend the bottom portion until it breaks off easily. If you have to store asparagus in the refrigerator, place the cut ends in a bowl or tall glass (as you would cut flowers) to help prolong crispness until you're ready to cook.

health tip
Asparagus is a member of the lily family, which includes onions, leeks, and garlic. Low in calories and rich in folic acid, vitamin A, B vitamins, and vitamin C, this succulent and tender vegetable boasts numerous health benefits, from weight loss to healthy elimination and digestion. Pregnant women should eat asparagus regularly, as it's high in folic acid, which can help to prevent birth defects such as spina bifida.

Enjoy once a week!

makes: 1 serving
preparation time: 10 min
cooking time: 10 min
total time: 20 min

per serving: calories 234, protein 17 g, total fat 14 g, saturated fat 7 g, carbohydrate 9 g, fibre 0.75 g, sodium 611 mg, cholesterol 210 mg

cheesy omega-3 veggie omelette

If you have a few extra minutes in the morning for preparation, choose this satisfying and filling option for breakfast. In fact, the combination of fresh vegetables, cilantro, and spices will entice your palate for lunch or dinner too.

1 tsp	butter	5 mL
1/4 cup	diced red pepper	50 mL
1/4 cup	diced white onion	50 mL
3	large crimini mushrooms, thickly sliced	3
1/2 tsp	minced garlic	2 mL
1	omega-3 egg	1
4 tbsp	egg whites	60 mL
1/4 tsp	salt	1 mL
1/4 tsp	pepper	1 mL
2 tbsp	chopped fresh cilantro	25 mL
Pinch	cayenne pepper (optional)	Pinch
2 tbsp	shredded low-fat Cheddar cheese	25 mL
4	sliced tomatoes	4

1. Melt 1/2 tsp (2 mL) of the butter in nonstick skillet over medium-high heat. Sauté red pepper, onion, mushrooms, and garlic for 3 minutes. Set aside in bowl.
2. Combine egg and egg whites; whisk until blended. Add salt and pepper.
3. In a 9-inch (23 cm) nonstick skillet, melt remaining 1/2 tsp (2 mL) butter over medium-high heat. Once skillet is hot, pour in egg mixture evenly.
4. Reduce heat to medium, swirling egg mixture from side to side as it cooks.
5. Mix fresh cilantro with cooked vegetables.
6. Once the egg mixture is almost cooked completely through, spoon the vegetable mix onto half of the egg.
9. Sprinkle lightly with a pinch of cayenne pepper, if using.
10. Top the vegetables with cheese and fold open side over filling.
11. Cook on medium-high heat for 1 minute on each side.
12. Place on serving plate and top with sliced tomatoes lightly sprinkled with salt and pepper.

kitchen tip

To bring out more of the flavour and create a smoother consistency when cooking vegetable omelettes, always sauté your vegetables for 2 to 3 minutes on medium-high heat first in a separate skillet.

health tip

Cilantro, also called coriander, has long been known as a "healing spice." In addition to containing fibre, iron, and magnesium, cilantro helps lower blood sugar, helps reduce cholesterol, and has natural anti-inflammatory effects.

🍓🍓🍓 Super skinny!

makes: 1 serving
preparation time: 10 min
cooking time: 10 min
total time: 20 min

per serving: calories 211, protein 20 g, total fat 10 g, saturated fat 2 g, carbohydrates 8 g, fibre 0.75 g, sodium 339 mg, cholesterol 203 mg

opa! omelette

Now you can enjoy the delicious taste of Greek food without all the added calories. This appetizing Mediterranean recipe offers the savoury flavours of olives and feta with a boost of heart-healthy nutrients. Opa!

1 tsp	butter	5 mL
1/4 cup	diced red pepper	50 mL
1/4 cup	diced white onion	50 mL
1 tsp	minced garlic	5 mL
1/2 tsp	fresh oregano	2 mL
Pinch	salt	Pinch
1/4 tsp	black pepper	1 mL
1	egg	1
4 tbsp	egg whites	60 mL
2 tbsp	sliced black olives	25 mL
1 tbsp	feta cheese, crumbled	15 mL
2 tbsp	diced tomato	25 mL

1. Melt 1/2 tsp (2 mL) of the butter in nonstick skillet. Over medium-high heat, sauté pepper, onion, garlic, oregano, salt, and pepper for 3 minutes until tender.
2. Remove from heat and set aside.
3. Combine egg and egg whites and beat until fully mixed.
4. Melt remaining 1/2 tsp (2 mL) butter in separate nonstick pan with an 8-inch (20 cm) base.
5. Pour egg mixture into pan and swirl back and forth until mixture begins to set (3 to 4 minutes over medium-high heat).
6. On one side of the egg mixture, place sautéed vegetable mixture. Top with olives, feta cheese, and tomatoes.
7. Fold open side over filling. Cook for 1 minute on each side.
8. Serve.

kitchen tip

When dicing a tomato, be sure to remove the ends and leave as much of the flesh intact as possible. With a very sharp or serrated knife, cut the tomato into slices of equal thickness. Arrange the tomatoes next to each other or stacked on top of each other. Finally, turn your knife on a 90-degree angle and slice the tomato into chunks. If done correctly, there should be very little juice.

health tip
Research shows that individuals who follow a Mediterranean diet, which includes fruits, vegetables, healthy fats, moderate amounts of fish, dairy, and red wine, suffer from less heart attacks and cancers. One potential reason is the fact that the diet is so rich in olives and olive oil, which are loaded with heart-healthy monounsaturated fat and the antioxidant vitamin E.

🍓🍓🍓 Super skinny!

makes: 1 serving
preparation time: 10 min
cooking time: 10 min
total time: 20 min

per serving: calories 198, protein 15 g, total fat 10 g, saturated fat 3.5 g, carbohydrates 11 g, fibre 0.75 g, sodium 318 mg, cholesterol 203 mg

zesty asian omelette

Trying to lose a few pounds? This palate pleaser is low in calories and carbohydrates and high in lean proteins. It will fill you up and boost your metabolism at the same time.

1 tsp	butter	5 mL
1/8 cup	diced red pepper	25 mL
1/8 cup	diced yellow pepper	25 mL
1/8 cup	diced white onion	25 mL
2 tbsp	diced water chestnuts	25 mL
1/2 tsp	minced ginger	2 mL
1/4 cup	bean sprouts	50 mL
1 tsp	soy sauce	5 mL
1	omega-3 egg	1
4 tbsp	egg whites	60 mL
2 tbsp	shredded Swiss cheese	25 mL

1. Melt 1/2 tsp (2 mL) of the butter in nonstick pan. Over medium-high heat, sauté red and yellow pepper, onion, water chestnuts, and ginger for 3 minutes until tender. Add bean sprouts and soy sauce and continue to sauté for 1 minute. Do not overcook.
2. Combine egg and egg whites and beat until fully mixed.
3. Melt remaining 1/2 tsp butter in separate nonstick pan with an 8-inch (20 cm) base.
4. Pour egg mixture into pan and swirl back and forth until mixture begins to set (3 to 4 minutes over medium-high heat).
5. On one side of the cooked egg mixture, place sautéed vegetables. Top with Swiss cheese.
6. Fold open side over filling. Cook for 1 minute on each side.
7. Serve.

kitchen tip

Bean sprouts are widely available in most grocery stores. The most common sprouts are from the green mung bean, although certain Asian grocery stores may also stock yellow soybean sprouts (which are much larger). When buying bean sprouts, snap one in half to ensure they are crunchy. They will keep in your refrigerator for several days wrapped in a plastic bag and stored in the vegetable compartment. Whenever possible, try to use fresh bean sprouts as canned sprouts have been pre-cooked and are typically soggy, with less taste.

health tip

Bean sprouts are a good source of vitamin C, B complex, and protein. Bean sprouts are cholesterol free, low in calories, and perfect for the topping of any salad or sand-wich. One cup (250 mL) of bean sprouts contains 30 calories, 3 g of protein, 6 g of carbohydrates, and digestible fibre.

Super skinny!

makes: 1 serving
preparation time: 10 min
cooking time: 10 min
total time: 20 min

per serving: calories 170, protein 14 g, total fat 9 g, saturated fat 2.5 g, carbohydrates 6 g, fibre 0.5 g, sodium 317 mg, cholesterol 203 mg

peanut butter chocolate power smoothie

Peanut butter and chocolate—what could be bad about that? This creamy smoothie contains plenty of good monounsaturated fats from the ground flaxseed and also offers a whopping 7 g of fibre. If you're on a lower-carbohydrate weight-loss program, simply add half a banana (instead of a whole) to the shake. It will reduce your calories by 50 and reduce your carbohydrate intake by 10 to 15 g.

3/4 cup	soy milk (or 1% milk)	175 mL
1	banana, frozen	1
1 tsp	natural peanut butter	5 mL
1/4 cup	fat-free plain yogurt	50 mL
1 tbsp	chocolate sauce	15 mL
1 tbsp	cocoa powder	15 mL
1 tbsp	ground flaxseed	15 mL
1 cup	ice cubes	250 mL

Place ingredients in blender and liquefy for 2 minutes.

kitchen tip
The outer husk of flaxseed is very hard and difficult to crack when chewing. In order to properly digest flaxseed, grind it in a coffee grinder, food processor, or blender prior to using. After grinding, store flaxseed in an airtight, dark container. Ground flaxseed stays fresh and safe to eat for 90 days.

Enjoy once a week!

makes: 1 serving
yield: 16 oz (480 mL)
preparation time: 5 min
blender time: 2 min
total time: 7 min

per serving: calories 332, protein 11 g, total fat 7 g, saturated fat 0.5 g, carbohydrates 59 g, fibre 7 g, sodium 135 mg, cholesterol 0 mg

chocolate lover's smoothie delight

If you think you have to give up chocolate to lose weight and stay trim, think again! You can still enjoy the decadence of chocolate while staying in the health zone with lean proteins (such as yogurt) and essential fats (such as ground flaxseed). With any smoothie recipe, you can substitute 1% milk for soy milk if you prefer. Or if you wish to go dairy-free and don't want to drink soy, rice or almond milk are other options.

3/4 cup	soy milk (or 1% milk)	175 mL
1	banana, frozen	1
1/4 cup	plain yogurt	50 mL
1 tbsp	chocolate syrup	15 mL
1 tbsp	cocoa powder	15 mL
1 tbsp	ground flaxseed	15 mL
1 cup	ice cubes	250 mL

Place ingredients in blender and liquefy for 2 minutes.

kitchen tip

To make your morning smoothies creamier, use frozen bananas. Peel your bananas, wrap them with plastic wrap, and store in the freezer. They will last for at least six months.

health tip

Sweet and creamy, bananas are one of the best natural sources of potassium (an average banana contains 450 mg of potassium), which studies show may help to lower high blood pressure. Bananas also contain a soluble fibre called pectin, which helps promote regularity and ease constipation.

Enjoy once a week!

makes: 1 serving
yield: 16 oz (480 mL)
preparation time: 5 min
blender time: 2 min
total time: 7 min

per serving: calories 310, protein 11 g, total fat 5.5 g, saturated fat 0.5 g, carbohydrates 53 g, fibre 6.8 g, sodium 146 mg, cholesterol 1.33 mg

strawberry field smoothie

The perfect combination of juicy strawberries and creamy bananas satisfies your sweet tooth naturally while delivering a powerful boost of vitamin C and antioxidants.

1/2 cup	soy milk (or 1% milk)	125 mL
1/4 cup	orange juice	50 mL
1 cup	frozen strawberries	250 mL
1/2	banana, frozen	1/2
1/4 cup	plain yogurt	50 mL
1 cup	ice cubes	250 mL

Place ingredients in blender and liquefy for 2 minutes.

kitchen tip
Select strawberries that are bright red, firm, plump, and free of mould. Since strawberries are quite perishable, be sure to wash them right away (cut off tip and stem), spread them out on a plate or in Tupperware, and seal with plastic wrap or a lid. If freezing strawberries for smoothies or iced desserts, simply prepare and freeze in a plastic bag. All types of berries can be stored in the freezer for up to one year. Adding a few drops of lemon juice on the fruit prior to freezing will help to preserve their rich red colour.

health tip
Strawberries are an excellent daily source of vitamin C. Try to buy locally or opt for organic, as strawberries are among the 12 foods on which pesticide residues have been most frequently found, according to the Environmental Working Group's 2006 report *Shopper's Guide to Pesticides in Produce*.

 Super skinny!

makes: 1 serving
yield: 16 oz (480 mL)
preparation time: 5 min
blender time: 2 min
total time: 7 min

per serving: calories 264, protein 12.25 g, total fat 4 g, saturated fat 2 g, carbohydrates 45 g, fibre 4 g, sodium 46 mg, cholesterol 11 mg

creamy mango banana smoothie

Although a tropical fruit, mango is available year-round in the frozen fruit section of the grocery store. Not only is mango naturally sweet, but it contains a phenolic compound found to have antioxidant and anti-cancer properties. Remember that mango tends to be higher in calories than other fruits, so 1/4 cup (50 mL) in your morning shake will do the trick.

1 cup	soy milk (or 1% milk)	250 mL
1/4 cup	frozen mango	50 mL
1/2	banana, frozen	1/2
1/2 cup	low-fat plain yogurt	125 mL
2 scoops	vanilla protein powder*	2 scoops
1/2 cup	ice cubes	125 mL

* Please see the Product Resource Guide for protein powder recommendations.

Place ingredients in blender and liquefy for 2 minutes.

health tip

Mango is one of the most popular tropical fruits, with more than 400 varieties. Although slightly higher in sugar than other fruits (e.g., berries, pears, or apples), mangoes are rich in antioxidants, minerals, and vitamins. In fact, mangoes contain 20 percent more beta-carotene (a vitamin that acts as an antioxidant in the body and is converted to vitamin A) than cantaloupes and 50 percent more than apricots.

🍓🍓🍓 Super skinny!

makes: 1 serving
yield: 16 oz (480 mL)
preparation time: 5 min
blender time: 2 min
total time: 7 min

per serving: calories 369, protein 31 g, total fat 5.5 g, saturated fat 3 g, carbohydrates 47 g, fibre 2.5 g, sodium 232 mg, cholesterol 57 mg

pineapple burst smoothie

Tangy pineapple is perfect for that jump-start morning smoothie. Even though pineapple season is from March to June, they are available year-round in grocery stores. Whether fresh or frozen, be sure to blend pineapple well. It's also best to avoid canned pineapple, which is packed with preservatives and syrup.

1/4 cup	soy milk (or 1% milk)	50 mL
1/2 cup	orange juice	125 mL
1/2	banana, frozen	1/2
1/2 cup	chopped pineapple, fresh or frozen	125 mL
1/4 cup	plain yogurt	50 mL
1 scoop	vanilla protein powder*	1 scoop
1/2 cup	crushed ice	125 mL

* Please see the Product Resource Guide for protein powder recommendations.

Combine ingredients in blender and liquefy for 3 minutes.

health tip
Pineapples are chock full of vitamin C, beta-carotene, fibre, and antioxidants. Pineapple also contains a substance called bromelain, which has anti-inflammatory and digestive benefits. Digestive enzymes containing bromelain are very popular dietary supplements.

Enjoy once a week!

makes: 1 serving
yield: 16 oz (480 mL)
preparation time: 5 min
blender time: 3 min
total time: 8 min

per serving: calories 377, protein 24 g, total fat 3 g, saturated fat 1 g, carbohydrates 65 g, fibre 5 g, sodium 132 mg, cholesterol 36 mg

Source: www.genuinehealth.com

sweet creamy peach and flax shake

You'll think you're eating ice cream when you try this shake. In fact, turn this sweet and creamy blender drink into ice pops and satisfy those sugar cravings naturally.

1/2 cup	soy milk (or 1% milk)	125 mL
1/2 cup	orange juice	125 mL
1/2	banana, frozen	1/2
1/2 cup	peaches, fresh or frozen	125 mL
1 scoop	vanilla protein powder	1 scoop
1/2 cup	crushed ice	125 mL

Combine ingredients in blender and liquefy for 2 minutes.

kitchen tip

Food can often get trapped in a blender. To avoid potentially harmful bacteria, be sure to take apart your blender completely and always wash it with hot soapy water. If possible, run your blender through the dishwasher once a week for a deep clean.

health tip

Peaches are quite low in calories (1 medium peach = 40 calories), making them a perfect sweet treat for those who are trying to lose weight. These juicy fruits are also rich in vitamin C and can give your immune system some extra support through the cooler months.

🍓🍓🍓 Super skinny!

makes: 1 serving
yield: 16 oz (480 mL)
preparation time: 5 min
blender time: 2 min
total time: 7 min

per serving: calories 250, protein 19 g, total fat 3 g, saturated fat 1 g, carbohydrates 36 g, fibre 2 g, sodium 36 mg, cholesterol 30 mg

Source: www.genuinehealth.com

espresso coffee bean chocolate smoothie

Get your morning java jolt in this creamy smoothie. Not only is it quick and easy to make, but it's suitable for those trying to lose weight. Too good to be true?

1/4 cup	brewed espresso coffee	50 mL
1 cup	soy milk (or 1% milk)	250 mL
1/2	banana, frozen	1/2
1 tbsp	chocolate sauce	15 mL
2 scoops	chocolate protein powder	2 scoops
1/2 cup	crushed ice	125 mL

Combine ingredients in blender and liquefy for 2 minutes.

kitchen tip

A powerful blender is one of the most important kitchen tools you can have. From making morning smoothies to puréeing soups and blending homemade ice pops, you'll likely use your blender every day. When selecting a blender, choose a high-power glass one over a plastic model and make sure it comes apart easily for washing.

health tip

Keep a high-quality protein powder on hand to ensure you have easy-to-grab protein. Pre- or post-workout or as part of a weight-loss program, protein will fill you and stimulate the release of a hormone called glucagon, which helps to break down fat.

🍓🍓🍓 Super skinny!

makes: 1 serving
yield: 16 oz (480 mL)
preparation time: 5 min
blender time: 2 min
total time: 7 min

per serving: calories 363, protein 33 g, total fat 8.4 g, saturated fat 0 g, carbohydrates 38 g, fibre 2 g, sodium 23 mg, cholesterol 8 mg

Source: www.genuinehealth.com

old-fashioned cinnamon apple oatmeal

This is one of my favourite winter breakfasts when craving a stick to the ribs–type of meal. Oatmeal is high in fibre and low in fat, contains protein and iron, and has no cholesterol. In fact, oatmeal helps lower cholesterol levels. While steel-cut oats take more time to prepare than instant oatmeal, it's definitely worth the wait.

4 cups	water	1 L
1 cup	steel-cut oatmeal	250 mL
2	medium-sized apples	2
1 tbsp	brown sugar	15 mL
1 tsp	cinnamon	5 mL

1. In a medium-sized pot bring 4 cups (1 L) water to a boil.
2. Stir in the steel-cut oatmeal and cook at a medium boil for 5 minutes.
3. Reduce heat and simmer 10 minutes, stirring occasionally.
4. Meanwhile, peel and core apples and cut into 1-inch (2.5 cm) cubes.
5. Stir apples, brown sugar, and cinnamon into oatmeal. Simmer 20 minutes longer, stirring occasionally.

health tip

Steel-cut oats are whole grain oats that have been cut into smaller pieces, whereas rolled oats are oat groats that have been steamed, rolled, and flaked for easier cooking purposes. Quick-cooking oats have been chopped into even smaller pieces than rolled oats, and "instant" oats are basically powdered. Although steel-cut oats take longer to cook, their health advantages are enormous, in addition to having a lower glycemic index than instant oats (steel-cut oats have a GI rating of 42, whereas instant oatmeal has a GI rating of 65).

🍓🍓🍓 Super skinny!

makes: 4 servings
preparation time: 5 min
cooking time: 35 min
total time: 40 min

per serving: calories 201, protein 5 g, total fat 3 g, saturated fat 0 g, carbohydrates 40 g, fibre 5.5 g, sodium 0 mg, cholesterol 0 mg

high-protein walnut and banana oatmeal

Make this recipe ahead of time and reheat for a quick breakfast at home or at work. Filling, high in fibre and protein, and naturally sweet, it's a sure favourite.

4 cups	water	1 L
1 cup	steel-cut or Irish oatmeal	250 mL
1 tsp	vanilla	5 mL
1/4 cup	walnuts	50 mL
1/2 cup	mashed banana	125 mL
1 scoop	vanilla protein powder	1 scoop
1 tbsp	brown sugar	15 mL

1. In a medium-sized pot, bring 4 cups (1 L) water to a boil.
2. Stir in the steel-cut oatmeal.
3. Cook at a medium boil for 5 minutes.
4. Reduce heat and simmer for 30 minutes, stirring occasionally.
5. Add vanilla, walnuts, and mashed banana until desired consistency has been reached.
6. Add 1 scoop of vanilla protein powder and mix.
7. Top with brown sugar and add skim milk to taste (if desired).

health tip
To boost your "protein factor" and keep you fuller longer with lower insulin response, you can add a scoop of protein powder to your morning oats.

🍓🍓🍓 Super skinny!

makes: 4 servings
preparation time: 5 min
cooking time: 35 min
total time: 40 min

per serving: calories 276, protein 12 g, total fat 10 g, saturated fat 1.5 g, carbohydrates 33 g, fibre 5.5 g, sodium 16.5 mg, cholesterol 11.25 mg

Source: www.genuinehealth.com

good morning mixed berry parfait

Usually the words *parfait* and *healthy* don't go together—but not when it comes to this recipe. This is one of my favourite breakfast recipes because it's fast, steeped with nutritional benefits, and very appealing to the taste buds. It's also an efficient way to ensure that you're getting the fibre boost you need to keep regular. If you're looking for an "under 5 minutes" healthy option in the morning, this tempting delight is definitely for you.

1 cup	mixed berries	250 mL
1 cup	plain yogurt	250 mL
1/2 cup	bran flakes	125 mL
1/4 tsp	cocoa powder (optional)	1 mL

1. Spoon half of the mixed berries into the bottom of a parfait glass or other sundae-type dish. Top with half of the yogurt, and sprinkle with half of the cereal.
2. Repeat with remaining fruit and remaining yogurt.
3. For a finishing touch, decorate with a single sliced strawberry and sprinkle cocoa powder over top (if using). Enjoy!

health tip
Buying a healthy cereal can be quite confusing. To ensure that you're investing in the right fuel, follow these cereal standards.

- Try to maintain the "5 in 5" rule of cereal eating. Less than 5 g of sugar per serving, with at least 5 g of fibre per serving.
- Purchase cereals that list the top ingredients as whole grains, whole wheat, or wheat bran—not just wheat.
- The protein content should be a minimum of 3 g per serving. There are now several whole grain cereals available that are higher in fibre and protein.

Super skinny!

makes: 1 serving
preparation time: 5 min
total time: 5 min

per serving: calories 280, protein 15 g, total fat 2 g, saturated fat 0 g, carbohydrates 54 g, fibre 17 g, sodium 370 mg, cholesterol 10 mg

banana strawberry split

Banana splits for breakfast! Why not? With only 245 calories per serving, this scrumptious recipe is suitable for weight-loss or a weight-maintenance program. Or satisfy your sweet tooth and enjoy it after dinner for a treat.

1	banana	1
1/2 cup	low-fat strawberry yogurt	125 mL
1/2 cup	sliced strawberries	125 mL
2 tsp	toasted chopped almonds	10 mL

1. Peel and split banana.
2. Place banana halves in a serving bowl.
3. Top with strawberry yogurt, strawberries, and toasted almonds for added crunch.

health tip

When purchasing yogurt, be sure to read both the Nutrition Facts panel and the ingredients list. Avoid yogurts with added artificial sweeteners or stabilizers. As a general rule, the higher the protein and the lower the sugar content, the better it is for you. If you would like to enjoy a flavoured yogurt, select one that contains real fruit and offers natural sweetness. Keep in mind that yogurts offer a healthy dose of "friendly bacteria" called probiotics. These bacteria are beneficial to digestive function and overall health.

🍓🍓🍓 Super skinny!

makes: 1 serving
preparation time: 5 min
total time: 5 min

per serving: calories 218, protein 4 g, total fat 5 g, saturated fat 0.5 g, carbohydrates 41 g, fibre 3 g, sodium 33 mg, cholesterol 4 mg

spelt blueberry banana pancakes

These easy-to-make pancakes are a sure palate pleaser on a lazy weekend morning. Made with whole grain spelt flour, this delicious breakfast also offers a nutritional boost when it comes to fibre, vitamin B, and protein.

1	banana, mashed	1
1 cup	spelt pancake mix	250 mL
1	omega-3 egg	1
1/2 cup	soy milk (or 1% milk)	125 mL
1/4 cup	water	50 mL
1/2 cup	blueberries	125 mL

per serving

1/2 tsp	butter	2 mL
1 tbsp	light table syrup	15 mL

1. Combine banana, pancake mix, egg, soy milk, water, and blueberries.
2. Mix thoroughly.
3. Melt butter in nonstick 10-inch (25 cm) pan over medium heat.
4. Pour 1/2 cup (125 mL) mixture onto centre of the pan and rotate the pan to evenly spread mixture out.
5. Cook until bubbles appear over entire surface of pancake.
6. With spatula, turn and continue to cook for 1 to 2 minutes.
7. Plate, drizzle syrup over top, and serve.

kitchen tip

Looking to make your own pancake mix? It's healthier and can save you some money. Stored in a sealed container, a three-month supply of spelt pancake mix is an easy-to-make weekend treat for the entire family. Follow these directions and enjoy.

2 cups	spelt flour	500 mL
2 tbsp	baking powder	25 mL
1 tbsp	sugar	15 mL
1 tsp	salt	5 mL

1. Combine spelt flour with baking powder, sugar, and salt.
2. Mix thoroughly and store in sealed container.

health tip
Spelt's nutty flavour doesn't just taste good—it also offers myriad heath benefits. This ancient grain contains a significantly higher amount of protein than wheat and is also rich in B complex vitamins and fibre.

 Enjoy once a week!

makes: 6 servings
preparation time: 10 min
cooking time: 4–5 min (each pancake)
total time: 15 min

per serving (1 pancake with 1/2 tsp/2 mL butter and 1 tbsp/15 mL light syrup): calories 55, protein 2.2 g, total fat 1.5 g, saturated fat 0.5 g, carbohydrates 9.3 g, fibre 1 g, sodium 40 mg, cholesterol 36 mg

appetizers

hearty bruschetta

This heart-healthy and hearty bruschetta recipe is filled with "good fats" that have been shown to have cardio-protective benefits. The combination of olives, beans, fresh herbs, and tomatoes will make it hard to eat just once piece.

1/2 cup	diced white onion	125 mL
1/2 cup	sliced green olives	125 mL
2 cups	diced Roma tomatoes	500 mL
2 tbsp	finely chopped fresh oregano	25 mL
2 tbsp	finely chopped fresh basil	25 mL
1/2 cup	black beans	125 mL
2 tbsp	olive oil	25 mL
2 tbsp	tomato paste	25 mL
1 tbsp	minced garlic	15 mL
8	slices multigrain bread	8
2 tbsp	grated Parmesan cheese	25 mL

1. Combine onion, green olives, tomatoes, oregano, basil, black beans, olive oil, tomato paste, and minced garlic. Mix thoroughly.
2. Toast bread and top with bruschetta mix.
3. Sprinkle Parmesan cheese on top and serve.

health tip

Research in the *British Journal of Clinical Nutrition* demonstrated that simply replacing saturated fats with monounsaturated fats caused obese patients to lose a significant amount of weight. Even though the calories were exactly the same, monounsaturated fats found in olive oil appeared to have a positive fat-burning effect.

🍓🍓 Enjoy once a week!

makes: 8 servings
preparation time: 20 min
total time: 20 min

per serving (1 slice): calories 188, protein 7.3 g, total fat 7.5 g, saturated fat 0.8 g, carbohydrates 26 g, fibre 4.5 g, sodium 294 mg, cholesterol 0.75 mg

authentic mexican salsa

Low in cholesterol, fat, and calories, salsa is the healthy way to add depth and flavour to any dish. This recipe will tempt your taste buds with an authentic Mexican flair. Eaten on its own, with baked nachos, or on top of vegetables, fish, eggs, or brown rice, this tasty option is loaded with natural goodness.

3 cups	diced tomatoes	750 mL
1 cup	diced onion	250 mL
1/2 cup	finely chopped cilantro	125 mL
1	large jalapeño pepper, finely diced	1
1 tbsp	minced garlic	15 mL
1 tbsp	sugar	15 mL
2 tbsp	freshly squeezed lemon juice	25 mL
1 tbsp	olive oil	15 mL
1 tbsp	white vinegar	15 mL

1. Combine tomato, onion, cilantro, jalapeño pepper, garlic, sugar, lemon juice, olive oil, and white vinegar.
2. Mix thoroughly and refrigerate.
3. The salsa can be served immediately; however, allowing it to marinate in the refrigerator for 2 to 3 hours will improve the taste.

health tip
Eating just one jalapeño pepper provides about 10 percent of your necessary vitamin C intake for the day.

Note: If an extra zing in the recipe doesn't appeal to you, simply leave out the jalapeño peppers.

🍓🍓🍓 Super skinny!

makes: 16 servings (1/4 cup/50 mL each)
preparation time: 15 min
total time: 15 min

per serving: calories 36, protein 0.8 g, total fat 1.5 g, saturated fat 0 g, carbohydrates 5 g, fibre 2 g, sodium 8 mg, cholesterol 0 mg

healthy chicken wings

Chicken wings are one of the great sin foods—deep-fried and loaded with unwanted calories and fat. But now you can make them a great *healthy* sin food with this easy-to-follow recipe. You'll get all the taste without the guilt!

2	boneless chicken breasts (5 oz/142 g each)	2
1/2 cup	whole grain bread crumbs	125 mL
1 tsp	poultry seasoning	5 mL
2	omega-3 eggs	2
1 tsp	olive oil	5 mL
2 tbsp	chicken wing hot sauce	25 mL
1 tbsp	ketchup	15 mL
1 tbsp	honey	15 mL
1 tsp	white vinegar	5 mL

Note: You'll require ten 6-inch (15 cm) wooden meat skewers for this recipe. These can be purchased from any grocery store.

1. Cut chicken breasts into 1-inch-wide (2.5 cm wide) strips.
2. Thread each strip on one of the 6-inch (15 cm) skewers, pushing the skewer through the centre of the chicken strip lengthwise from one end to the other.
3. Place bread crumbs and poultry seasoning in a wide bowl and mix thoroughly.
4. Crack eggs in another bowl and whisk until completely mixed.
5. Lightly oil a baking sheet.
6. One at a time, dip chicken strips into egg mixture and then roll in bread crumb mixture. Repeat the process so that each strip is twice coated. Then space evenly on baking sheet.
7. Bake at 400°F (200°C) for 20 minutes, turning once after 10 minutes.
8. For dipping sauce, combine chicken wing hot sauce, ketchup, honey, and vinegar and mix thoroughly.
9. Remove chicken strips and brush liberally with sauce. Return to oven and continue cooking 10 minutes for regular, 15 minutes for crispy.
10. If you enjoy more of the taste of the dipping sauce, remove strips from oven, brush lightly with the remainder of the sauce, and serve.

To reduce the amount of saturated fat in your diet, try substituting chicken for red meat. The leanest part of the chicken is the chicken breast, which has less than half the fat of a trimmed, choice-grade T-bone steak. The fat in chicken is also less saturated than beef fat. However, it's important to note that eating chicken with the skin doubles the amount of fat and saturated fat. For this reason, chicken is best skinned before cooking.

health tip

Chicken provides an excellent source of protein and, if you're not vegetarian, should be a part of any healthy weight-maintenance plan. When choosing chicken, opt for organic. Organic chicken farmers provide the chickens with more humane and less crowded conditions, feed them a fully organic diet that hasn't been sprayed with artificial fertilizer or pesticides, and don't treat them with antibiotics. Lower toxicity, better for you, better for the chicken and the environment.

For interest's sake, 1 g of protein = 4 calories. The amount of protein grams in various cuts of chicken are:

- chicken breast: 30 g
- chicken thigh: 10 g (for average size)
- drumstick: 11 g
- wing: 6 g

Enjoy once a week!

makes: 2 servings
preparation time: 15 min
cooking time: 35 min
total time: 50 min

per serving: calories 396, protein 41.5 g, total fat 9.5 g, saturated fat 1.6 g, carbohydrates 31 g, fibre 1 g, sodium 690 mg, cholesterol 269 mg

crab-stuffed mushrooms

This mouth-watering appetizer is low on calories but loaded with decadence. Serve this appetizer piping hot from the oven either on its own or with a spicy Thai sauce or wasabi paste.

1	can (4 oz/113 g) crab meat, drained	1
1 tsp	butter	5 mL
1/2 cup	diced red pepper	125 mL
1/2 cup	diced white onion	125 mL
1/2 cup	whole grain bread crumbs	50 mL
1 tsp	minced garlic	5 mL
1/2 tsp	freshly squeezed lemon juice	2 mL
1/2 tsp	salt	2 mL
1/2 tsp	pepper	2 mL
1/4 tsp	cayenne pepper (optional)	1 mL
1	omega-3 egg	1
12	large white mushrooms	12

1. Empty drained crab meat into a large mixing bowl and break up with a fork until there are no clumps.
2. Melt 1/2 tsp (2 mL) of the butter in nonstick pan and sauté pepper and onion until tender. Do not allow to brown.
3. Toss sautéed pepper and onion, bread crumbs, garlic, lemon juice, salt, pepper, and cayenne pepper (if using) with the crab meat. Crack egg onto the top and mix until there is a standard consistency.
4. Remove stems from mushrooms and wash the tops lightly (do not get the underside wet).
5. Melt remaining 1/2 tsp (2 mL) butter and with a pastry brush coat the outside of the mushroom caps.
6. Spoon crab mixture evenly into the mushroom caps and place them on a nonstick baking pan. Bake at 400°F (200°C) for 20 minutes.
7. Prior to serving, broil on high for 3 minutes to brown the tops, being careful that they don't burn.
8. Serve immediately with spicy Thai sauce or wasabi paste.

kitchen tip

When preparing hot appetizers, timing is critical. A good rule of thumb is to establish your serving time (e.g., 6:30 p.m.) and then subtract the cooking time. This will help identify when the item should begin cooking. Always allow an extra 10 minutes to pre-heat your oven and to get your pots or pans ready. If boiling water is necessary prior to cooking, allow an additional 15 minutes.

health tip

To boost your health factor, use whole grain bread crumbs instead of white flour bread crumbs. Whole grain bread crumbs can be purchased at most bulk or health food stores. If you wish to make your own bread crumbs, pre-heat your oven to 375°F (190°C) and cover a baking sheet with foil. Cut whole grain bread into 1-inch (2.5 cm) cubes, place on baking sheet, and drizzle with olive oil. Place the baking sheet in the oven for about 10 to 12 minutes (or until bread is toasted). Put the bread in a bowl and firmly crush and mix until you get the desired bread crumb consistency.

Note: Crab meat is low in fat and calories, high in protein, and a good source of calcium. However, canned crab meat tends to be higher in sodium content, so if on a salt-restricted diet, enjoy this appetizer as an occasional treat.

🍓🍓 Enjoy once a week!

makes: 6 servings of 2 mushrooms per person
preparation time: 15 min
cooking time: 25 min
total time: 40 min

per serving: calories 60, protein 4.6 g, total fat 2 g, saturated fat 0.6 g, carbohydrates 5.6 g, fibre 0.5 g, sodium 525 mg, cholesterol 50 mg

endive tuna boats

Looking for an alternative to crackers or bread? Try endive. Endives are leafy salad vegetables that can be found in most grocery stores. Simply trim the end off the endive to use it as an elegant low-carb option for your next dinner party.

1	can (4 oz/113 g) tuna, drained	1
2 tbsp	diced onion	25 mL
2 tbsp	diced celery	25 mL
1 tbsp	light mayonnaise	15 mL
1 1/2 tsp	sweet chili sauce	7 mL
1/4 tsp	cumin	1 mL
Pinch	salt	Pinch
Pinch	pepper	Pinch
1	endive head	1
1/2 cup	diced tomato	125 mL

1. Combine tuna, onion, celery, mayonnaise, 1 tsp (5 mL) of the chili sauce, cumin, salt, and pepper.
2. Remove leaves from endive and wash.
3. Spoon 1 tbsp (15 mL) mixture into each leaf and spread out evenly.
4. Mix tomatoes with remaining 1/2 tsp (2 mL) chili sauce.
5. Spoon tomato mixture over tuna and serve.

health tip
Endives are extremely low in calories. One cup of endives contains only 7.5 calories. Endives are very water dense (95 percent water) and also offer a good source of vitamins A and C and fibre.

🍓🍓🍓 Super skinny!

makes: 4 servings
preparation time: 15 min
total time: 15 min

per serving (1 boat): calories 79, protein 9 g, total fat 2 g, saturated fat 0.3 g, carbohydrates 7 g, fibre 4 g, sodium 423 mg, cholesterol 9 mg

salmon spa cakes

Loaded with protein and omega-3 fats and with a low glycemic index, this savoury appetizer is a perfect choice to serve your guests—the health benefits and taste cannot be beat.

4	slices whole grain bread*	4
2	cans (each 4 oz/113 g) salmon, drained	2
2	green onions, minced	2
1	egg white, beaten lightly	1
1 tbsp	finely chopped fresh mint	15 mL
1 tbsp	finely chopped fresh dill	15 mL
1 tsp	lemon zest	5 mL
1 tbsp	freshly squeezed lemon juice	15 mL
3/4 tsp	black pepper	4 mL

* See Product Resource Guide for recommendations.

1. Break bread into rough pieces and put into food processor; pulse until mixture resembles coarse crumbs.
2. In bowl, mix together salmon, green onion, egg white, mint, dill, lemon zest, lemon juice, pepper, and 1/2 cup (125 mL) of the bread crumbs until well combined.
3. Place remaining crumbs in a shallow dish or pie plate. Form the salmon mixture into 12 patties. Lightly press the patties into the crumb mixture, turning to coat evenly.
4. Arrange salmon cakes in a large nonstick skillet lightly sprayed with non-hydrogenated olive oil cooking spray. Cook over medium-high heat, just until browned, about 3 minutes per side. Serve warm, at room temperature, or cold with low-fat plain yogurt on the side.

kitchen tip

When selecting bread, don't be fooled by the words *fortified with*. Fortification typically occurs with refined grains. Precious nutrients that have been stripped away during the refining process are added back in. Manufacturers are sometimes required by law to fortify refined grain products to make up for the loss of vitamins and minerals. While this may add back some of the lost nutrients, it can never reproduce the original whole grain benefits.

health tip
Turn this appetizer into a main course by making your salmon cakes twice as large. Enjoy with a side salad for dinner for the perfect way to stay full and lose weight.

🍓🍓🍓 Super skinny!

makes: 12 servings
preparation time: 5 min
cooking time: 10 min
total time: 15 min

per serving (1 salmon cake): calories 65, protein 7 g, total fat 2 g, saturated fat 0.5 g, carbohydrates 4 g, fibre 1 g, sodium 62 mg, cholesterol 15 mg

Source: www.stonemillbakehouse.com

pizza bites

As an appetizer or lunch, pizza bites are a healthier version of your classic pizza. If serving them at a dinner party, simply slice pieces of bread into halves.

4	slices whole grain bread*	4
4 tbsp	pizza sauce (see page 258)	60 mL
8	thin slices tomato	8
2 tbsp	diced green pepper	25 mL
1/4 cup	shredded light mozzarella cheese	50 mL

* See Product Resource Guide for recommendations.

1. Toast whole grain bread.
2. Spread 1 tbsp (15 mL) pizza sauce on each slice.
3. Top with sliced tomatoes and green pepper.
4. Sprinkle shredded cheese over top.
5. Bake at 425°F (220°C) for 5 to 7 minutes or until cheese melts.
6. Cut each slice into 4 and serve.

kitchen tip
When storing cheese, the softer the cheese, the shorter the amount of time it will keep fresh. As a general rule, firm and semi-firm cheeses will keep for two weeks, while soft cheeses (e.g., blue cheese) will keep for one week.

health tip
It's always best to purchase cheese made from part-skim milk. One ounce of part-skim mozzarella contains 72 calories, 183 mg of calcium, 5 g of fat (3 g are saturated), 7 g of protein, and 1 g of carbohydrates.

🍓🍓🍓 Super skinny!

makes: 4 servings
preparation time: 10 min
cooking time: 10 min
total time: 20 min

per serving (1 slice of bread and toppings): calories 119, protein 7.5 g, total fat 3.5 g, saturated fat 1.5 g, carbohydrates 15 g, fibre 2.5 g, sodium 235 mg, cholesterol 9 mg

sweet martini mashed potatoes

This elegant mashed potato dish will impress with its look and taste—and it's healthier, too. Simply spoon the sweet potatoes into a martini glass and add your favourite topping, such as the delicious creamy mushroom sauce on page 259.

2 1/2 lb	sweet potatoes	1.14 kg
12 tbsp	creamy mushroom sauce	200 mL

1. Peel and dice sweet potatoes.
2. Place in steam basket over a pot of boiling water. Cover and cook for 20 to 25 minutes.
3. Transfer to a large bowl and mash thoroughly (for a creamy consistency, use an electric hand blender).
4. Spoon into martini glasses.
5. Heat creamy mushroom sauce.
6. Top each serving with 2 tbsp (25 mL) mushroom sauce and serve.

health tip

Among the root vegetables, sweet potatoes offer the lowest glycemic index rating. And they contain almost twice the recommended daily allowance (RDA) of vitamin A, 42 percent of the RDA of vitamin C, four times the RDA of beta-carotene, and, when eaten with the skin, more fibre than oatmeal. The average sweet potato contains between 130 and 160 calories.

🍓🍓 Enjoy once a week!

makes: 6 servings
preparation time: 10 min
cooking time: 25 min
total time: 35 min

per serving: calories 259, protein 5 g, total fat 1 g, saturated fat 0.5 g, carbohydrates 57 g, fibre 8 g, sodium 86 mg, cholesterol 3.5 mg

lox-wrapped scallops

If you're a seafood lover, this classic match of dill, capers, and smoked salmon is sure to please—and it's also high in protein, leaving you satiated.

12	large scallops	12
4 oz	low-sodium lox (smoked salmon)	113 g
3 tsp	freshly squeezed lemon juice	15 mL
1 tbsp	finely chopped fresh dill	15 mL
2 tbsp	capers	25 mL

Note: You'll need 12 wooden toothpicks for this recipe.

1. Rinse scallops in cold water and pat dry with paper towel.
2. Separate lox slices and cut into 12 strips.
3. Wrap each scallop with a strip of lox and secure it in place with a toothpick.
4. Place on nonstick baking sheet.
5. Top each scallop with 1/4 tsp (1 mL) lemon juice; sprinkle with dill and capers.
6. Place in oven, 4 to 5 inches (10 to 12 cm) below boiler, and broil on high for 8 to 10 minutes, until scallops appear opaque.
7. Serve.

kitchen tip

When buying fish and seafood, follow these few basic rules to ensure you're purchasing the freshest products possible.

- There should be absolutely no "fishy smell." Fresh fish don't smell.
- If the eye is still in the fish, it should be clear and should bulge slightly.
- There should be no discolouration or darkening around the edges of the fish.
- The fish or seafood should be refrigerated or properly packed on ice.
- Don't buy cooked seafood, such as shrimp, crab, or smoked fish, if it's displayed in the same case as raw fish. Cross-contamination can occur.

health tip

When buying smoked salmon (lox) or other salmon sources, purchase wild salmon. Not only is the taste far superior, but wild salmon tends to be higher in omega-3 essential fatty acids and significantly lower in chemical pollutants such as PCBs and other contaminants. In fact, research has demonstrated that farmed salmon can have as much as 16 times higher amounts of chemical pollutants than wild salmon.

Save for an occasional treat!

makes: 6 servings
preparation time: 15 min
cooking time: 10 min
total time: 25 min

per serving (2 per person): calories 92, protein 16 g, total fat 1.5 g, saturated fat 0 g, carbohydrates 3 g, fibre 0 g, sodium 608 mg, cholesterol 29 mg

veggie wontons

Instead of filling your wontons with meats high in saturated fats and calories, opt for these veggie wontons, which are a tasty "pop in your mouth" healthy treat. These delicious dumplings tend to go very quickly, so be sure to prepare enough if guests are coming by.

1 tbsp	olive oil	15 mL
1/2 cup	finely chopped cabbage	125 mL
1/4 cup	diced celery	50 mL
1/4 cup	diced red pepper	50 mL
1/2 cup	chopped green onion tops	125 mL
2 tbsp	sweet chili sauce	25 mL
1 tsp	sesame oil	5 mL
1 tsp	low-sodium soy sauce	5 mL
1 tsp	grated ginger	5 mL
12	wonton wraps	12

1. In nonstick skillet, heat olive oil and sauté cabbage, celery, and red pepper for 3 to 4 minutes (vegetables should remain crispy).
2. Remove from heat and in a mixing bowl combine the sautéed vegetables with the green onions, sweet chili sauce, sesame oil, soy sauce, and ginger.
3. Separate the wonton sheets and place on a dry surface.
4. Spoon 1 tsp (5 mL) of filling mixture into the centre of each wrap.
5. With your finger or a small pastry brush, wet the edges of the wonton.
6. Fold over from one corner to the other, creating a triangle.
7. Firmly press sides together (to ensure a more secure fit, press down with the tines of a fork around the edges of the wonton where the sides meet).
8. Bring a large pot of water to a boil. Gently place wontons in the water and cook for 3 to 5 minutes or until they begin to float.
9. Drain and serve with your favourite dipping sauce.

kitchen tip

There are three main types of cabbage: green, red, and Savoy. Bok choy is also a cabbage variety that is mild in flavour and matches any dish. Keeping cabbage cold will keep it fresh and help retain its vitamin C content. Place the whole head of cabbage in a plastic bag in the crisper of your refrigerator. Red and green cabbage will keep this way for about two weeks, while Savoy cabbage will keep for about one week.

health tip
When buying soy sauce, always select the low-sodium option. There is absolutely no difference in taste, yet it contains half the sodium. In fact, traditional soy sauce has about 1100 mg of sodium per 1 tbsp (15 mL), while low-sodium soy sauce contains about 550 mg of sodium per 1 tbsp (15 mL).

🍓🍓🍓 Super skinny!

makes: 20
preparation time: 30 min
cooking time: 10 min
total time: 40 min

per serving (2 wontons): calories 59, protein 1 g, total fat 3 g, saturated fat 0.5 g, carbohydrates 7 g, fibre 0.5 g, sodium 171 mg, cholesterol 0.5 mg

gourmet egg bake

Why not serve eggs as an appetizer? Guests will love nibbling on their own individual egg bake—served warm out of the oven—at your next brunch.

1 tsp	butter	5 mL
1 cup	diced onion	250 mL
1 cup	thinly sliced mushrooms	250 mL
1/4 tsp	dried thyme	1 mL
	Salt and pepper to taste	
6	slices sprouted grain bread*	6
1 cup	shredded low-fat mozzarella cheese	250 mL
6	eggs	6
	Chopped parsley for garnish	

* See Product Resource Guide for recommendations.

1. Heat butter in a nonstick skillet over medium-high heat; add onion and mushrooms. Season with thyme, salt, and pepper; cook, stirring, until onions are soft and liquid has been released and absorbed from mushrooms, about 5 minutes. Set aside.
2. Grease a 6-cup muffin tray.
3. With a cup whose opening is the same size as the bottom of the muffin cups, cut bread into rounds. Place a bread round in the bottom of each muffin cup and divide cooked onion mixture evenly among the 6 cups.
4. Sprinkle half of the cheese over the onion mixture. With fingers, gently press down on cheese.
5. Crack 1 egg into each cup. Bake at 375ºF (190ºC) for 15 minutes. Remove from oven, scatter remainder of shredded cheese on top of each egg, and continue baking for 3 minutes.
6. Sprinkle with chopped parsley and serve immediately.

kitchen tip

This appetizer can also be made into a delicious dinner. Simply enjoy one or two gourmet egg bakes with a side salad.

health tip

If you wish to lower the fat content of this appetizer, replace the cheese with a vegetable mixture of your choice.

🍓🍓🍓 Super skinny!

makes: 6 servings
preparation time: 5 min
cooking time: 20 min
total time: 25 min

per serving: calories 197, protein 15 g, total fat 8 g, saturated fat 3 g, carbohydrates 15 g, fibre 2.5 g, sodium 406 mg, cholesterol 194 mg

Source: www.stonemillbakehouse.com

dips, sauces, and dressings

sweet mango and pear salsa

The sweet taste of mango and pear mixed with cilantro is a complementary salsa over meat, poultry, or fish. This salsa can also be puréed with a hand blender and spooned over your favourite dish. The jalapeño pepper adds a spicy hot element to the recipe.

3	mangoes	3
2	pears	2
1	jalapeño pepper	1
2 cups	finely diced white onion	500 mL
1 cup	finely diced red pepper	250 mL
1 1/2 cups	finely chopped cilantro	375 mL
1/4 cup	freshly squeezed lemon juice	50 mL
1 tsp	black pepper	5 mL

1. Peel mangoes and pears, remove pits from mango, and finely dice both fruits.
2. Remove pulp and stem from jalapeño pepper and finely dice.
3. In a medium mixing bowl, combine mango, pears, jalapeño pepper, onion, red pepper, cilantro, lemon juice, and black pepper; mix thoroughly.
4. Remove one-third of the mixture and roughly chop with an electric hand blender. Return chopped mixture to bowl and mix thoroughly.
5. Cover and refrigerate for 2 hours prior to serving.

Note: The salsa can be refrigerated for up to 4 days.

health tip
Mangoes are naturally sweet and are rich in vitamins, minerals, and antioxidants. This delectable fruit is also high in fibre and low in calories, and offers a burst of vitamins A, B, and C.

Super skinny!

makes: 8 servings (4 cups/1 L in total: 1/2 cup/125 mL for each serving over meat or poultry dish)
preparation time: 15 min
total time: 15 min

per serving (1/2 cup): calories 79, protein 1 g, total fat 0.3 g, saturated fat 0.1 g, carbohydrates 20 g, fibre 2.5 g, sodium 7 mg, cholesterol 0 mg

guacamole and pepper dip

If company is dropping by last minute and you have ripe avocados on hand, you're in luck. Guacamole's creamy texture and health benefits make it a nutritional superstar—as a dip for veggies, a topping for baked nachos, or a spread on a wrap or sandwich.

2	large avocados	2
1/4 cup	diced white onion	50 mL
1/4 cup	diced red pepper	50 mL
2 tbsp	freshly squeezed lemon juice	25 mL
1/2 tsp	salt	2 mL
1/2 tsp	pepper	2 mL

1. Slice avocados in half from stem to top point and remove pit.
2. Spoon out avocado flesh into medium-sized mixing bowl and mash with a potato masher.
3. Add onion, red pepper, lemon juice, salt, and pepper.
4. Mash again to thoroughly mix all ingredients.
5. Cover and refrigerate for 2 hours prior to serving.

health tip

Although avocados contain heart-healthy monounsaturated fat, they are higher in calories. While you don't want to avoid these fats because of their enormous health benefits, it is wise to watch portion size in an effort to maintain a proper body weight. As a general rule, the following serving sizes are recommended:

- average amount for wraps or sandwiches = 1 to 2 tbsp (15 to 25 mL)
- average amount to eat as a dip = 3 tbsp (50 mL)

Super skinny! (with proper portion size in mind)

makes: 2 cups/500 mL
preparation time: 10 min
total time: 10 min

per serving (1 tsp): calories 21, protein 0 g, total fat 2 g, saturated fat 3 g, carbohydrates 1 g, fibre 6 g, sodium 23 mg, cholesterol 0 mg

horseradish hummus

Hummus (a.k.a. chickpea dip) is quickly becoming one of North America's favourite (and healthiest) dips. Enjoyed with flatbread or vegetables, this delicious horseradish version can be served for guests or on a sandwich instead of mustard. Easy to make and easy to eat—what could be better?

1	can (19 oz/540 mL) chickpeas	1
1/4 cup	tahini	50 mL
4 tbsp	olive oil	60 mL
3 tbsp	water	50 mL
3 tbsp	horseradish	50 mL
2 tbsp	freshly squeezed lemon juice	25 mL
1 tsp	minced garlic	5 mL
1/2 tsp	cumin	2 mL
1/2 tsp	paprika	2 mL

1. Empty can of chickpeas into a strainer and rinse with cold water.
2. In a medium mixing bowl, combine chickpeas, tahini, olive oil, water, horseradish, lemon juice, garlic, cumin, and paprika.
3. With an electric hand mixer, blend thoroughly.
4. Chill and serve.

health tip
Hummus is a nutritional winner. High in iron and vitamin C and rich in dietary fibre, protein, and monounsaturated fat, this recipe offers a multitude of heart-healthy benefits in addition to great taste.

🍓🍓🍓 Super skinny! (with proper portion size in mind)

makes: 2 cups (500 mL)
preparation time: 10 min
total time: 10 min

per serving (2 tbsp/25 mL): calories 84, protein 2 g, total fat 6 g, saturated fat 1 g, carbohydrates 5 g, fibre 1 g, sodium 111 mg, cholesterol 0 mg

black bean and lime dip

Filled with cilantro, high-fibre black beans, and tangy lime, this Mexican-flavoured dip is the perfect complement to any wrap, baked nacho chip, or vegetable.

1	can (19 oz/540 mL) black beans	1
3 tbsp	diced onion	50 mL
3 tbsp	chopped cilantro	50 mL
1	lime, juiced	1
1 tbsp	white vinegar	15 mL
1/2 tsp	cumin	2 mL
1/4 tsp	black pepper	1 mL
Pinch	cayenne pepper	Pinch

1. Empty black beans into strainer and rinse thoroughly with cold water to reduce sodium levels.
2. Combine black beans, onion, cilantro, lime juice, white vinegar, cumin, black pepper, and cayenne pepper in a food processor (or in a medium-sized mixing bowl if using an electric hand blender).
3. Blend thoroughly until consistency of dip is achieved.
4. Refrigerate.

health tip
Australian researchers demonstrated that as lemons and limes ripen, their antioxidant capacity actually increases.

🍓🍓🍓 Super skinny!

makes: 2 1/4 cups (550 mL)
preparation time: 15 min
total time: 15 min

per serving (2 tbsp/25 mL): calories 31, protein 2 g, total fat 0.5 g, saturated fat 0 g, carbohydrates 5 g, fibre 2 g, sodium 92 mg, cholesterol 0 mg

curried bean dip

This heart-healthy bean dip is a must for curry lovers. Served with whole grain crackers or cut-up vegetables, this creamy dip offers the perfect blend of smooth and spicy.

1	can (19 oz/540 mL) pinto beans	1
5 tbsp	plain yogurt (2%)	75 mL
2 tbsp	tahini	25 mL
1 tbsp	yellow curry powder	15 mL
1 tsp	sesame oil	5 mL
1/2 tsp	minced garlic	2 mL
1/2 tsp	onion powder	2 mL

1. Empty beans into strainer and rinse thoroughly with cold water.
2. Combine beans, yogurt, tahini, yellow curry powder, sesame oil, garlic, and onion powder in food processor (or medium-sized mixing bowl if using an electric hand blender).
3. Blend until fully mixed and with the smooth consistency of a dip.
4. Refrigerate.

kitchen tip

Tahini is a thick Middle Eastern paste made from ground sesame seeds. It can be found in health food stores and the ethnic section of most grocery stores. Tahini is often used by people following a raw foods diet as it can be used as a dip with vegetables or as a spread on whole grain bread.

🍓🍓🍓 Super skinny!

makes: 2 cups (500 mL)
preparation time: 10 min
total time: 10 min

per serving (2 tbsp/25 mL): calories 47, protein 2 g, total fat 1.5 g, saturated fat 0 g, carbohydrates 5.5 g, fibre 2 g, sodium 8 mg, cholesterol 0 mg

creamy dill sauce

This easy-to-make sauce offers the subtle but creamy taste of dill as an enhanced flavour to salmon, potatoes, and steamed or grilled vegetables.

1 tbsp	butter	15 mL
1 tbsp	flour	15 mL
3/4 cup	1% milk	175 mL
3 tbsp	chopped fresh dill	50 mL
Pinch	salt	Pinch
Pinch	pepper	Pinch

1. Melt butter in nonstick skillet over high heat.
2. Reduce heat to medium and sprinkle flour over melted butter. Mix in flour with a small whisk; continue cooking for 1 to 2 minutes.
3. Slowly pour in milk while continuing to whisk.
4. Add chopped dill, salt, and pepper to mixture; continue to whisk until sauce thickens.
5. Remove from heat and spoon over desired dish.

kitchen tip
Whenever possible, choose fresh dill over dried dill as it's superior in flavour. The leaves of fresh dill should look feathery and be a rich green colour. Dill leaves that are a little wilted can still be used, since they usually droop very quickly after being picked.

health tip
Did you know that dill is a good source of iron? Add dill to your regular seasoning to help strengthen your bones.

🍓🍓🍓 Super skinny! (watch portion size)

makes: 3/4 cup (175 mL)
preparation time: 5 min
cooking time: 5 min
total time: 10 min

per serving (2 tbsp/25 mL): calories 40 g, protein 1 g, total fat 3 g, saturated fat 2 g, carbohydrates 3 g, fibre 0 g, sodium 134 mg, cholesterol 8 mg

pesto sauce

Pesto sauce is an all-time favourite over pasta, tossed with vegetables, or spread onto whole grain bread. Yet many tend to avoid pesto because it's high in fat. The *Healthy Sin Foods* pesto sauce has replaced pine nuts with some fibre-rich, low glycemic index chickpeas. Your guests won't even notice the difference!

2 cups	tightly packed fresh basil	500 mL
1	can (14 oz/398 mL) chickpeas, drained and rinsed	1
1/2 cup	grated Parmesan cheese	125 mL
4 tbsp	olive oil	60 mL
3 tbsp	water	50 mL
2 tbsp	minced garlic	25 mL
2 tsp	white vinegar	10 mL
1/4 tsp	salt	1 mL
1/4 tsp	black pepper	1 mL

1. Place fresh basil in food processor and pulse until finely chopped. (*Note:* Electric hand blender can be used.)
2. Add chickpeas, Parmesan cheese, olive oil, water, garlic, vinegar, salt, and pepper.
3. Again with food processor or electric hand blender, blend until well mixed.
4. May be used immediately or stored in refrigerator for up to 1 week.

kitchen tip

Parmesan is a hard cheese that tends to last longer than soft cheeses. Fresh wedge Parmesan wrapped carefully in foil and kept in an airtight plastic container in the refrigerator should last for about eight to 10 weeks. If purchasing bags of pre-shredded cheese, check the best-before date.

🍓🍓 Enjoy once a week!

makes: 1 1/4 cups (300 mL)
preparation time: 15 min
total time: 15 min

per serving (2 tbsp/25 mL): calories 115 g, protein 5 g, total fat 8.5 g, saturated fat 2 g, carbohydrates 4 g, fibre 1 g, sodium 257 mg, cholesterol 7 mg

zesty cheese sauce

Jazz up vegetables such as broccoli, spinach, or kale with this zesty cheese sauce.

1 tbsp	butter	15 mL
1 tbsp	flour	15 mL
1 cup	1% milk	250 mL
1/2 cup	shredded low-fat Cheddar cheese	125 mL
1/2 tsp	salt	2 mL
1/4 tsp	white pepper	1 mL
1/4 tsp	onion powder	1 mL
1/4 tsp	cayenne pepper	1 mL

1. Melt butter in nonstick skillet.
2. When it begins to bubble, sprinkle flour over top and stir in with a whisk.
3. Once all the flour has been absorbed, slowly pour the milk in while continuing to stir with your whisk.
4. Add Cheddar cheese, salt, pepper, onion powder, and cayenne pepper.
5. Continue to stir until the cheese is melted and the sauce thickens.
6. Serve or store in refrigerator (will last 4 to 5 days).

kitchen tip
Want a healthier alternative to the processed mac and cheese found at your grocery store? Buy whole grain or spelt pasta rotini noodles and top with this recipe.

health tip
As a general rule, choose cheese options that have 3 g of fat or less per 1 oz.

Enjoy once a week! (with portion size in mind)

makes: 1 1/2 cups (375 mL, just over 12 servings total)
preparation time: 5 min
cooking time: 5 min
total time: 10 min

per serving (1 tbsp/15 mL): calories 16, protein 1.25 g, total fat 0.8 g, saturated fat 0.5 g, carbohydrates 1 g, fibre 0 g, sodium 45 mg, cholesterol 2.5 mg

world famous pizza sauce

Okay ... so maybe not "world" famous, but this pizza sauce has become such a hit with our friends, family, and guests that we had to share it. Made with tasty oregano, basil, and garlic, this savoury pizza sauce makes any pizza dish pop.

1	can (14 oz/398 mL) low-sodium tomato sauce	1
1	can (5.5 oz/156 mL) tomato paste	1
1 tbsp	sugar	15 mL
1 1/2 tsp	dry basil	7 mL
1 tsp	dry oregano	5 mL
1/2 tsp	garlic powder	2 mL
1/4 tsp	black pepper	1 mL

1. Combine tomato sauce and tomato paste in mixing bowl.
2. Add sugar, basil, oregano, garlic powder, and black pepper.
3. Mix thoroughly and refrigerate if not using right away.

kitchen tip

The zesty pizza sauce will last in your refrigerator for four to five days.

health tip

Lycopene, the powerful phytonutrient found in tomatoes, is absorbed better in the presence of fat. To boost your lycopene intake, add a dash of olive oil to your tomato sauce or tomato paste.

🍓🍓🍓 Super skinny!

makes: 2 1/4 cups (550 mL)
preparation time: 10 min
total time: 10 min
Use approximately 1/2 cup per 8-slice pizza

per serving (2 tbsp/25 mL): calories 18, protein 0.5 g, total fat 0.1 g, saturated fat 0 g, carbohydrates 0.5 g, fibre 0.5 g, sodium 77 mg, cholesterol 0 mg

creamy mushroom sauce

It *is* possible to make cream sauces without the cream! Made with 1% milk and low-calorie crimini mushrooms, this rich mushroom sauce is the perfect addition to meats, over eggs, or on top of mashed sweet potatoes.

1 tbsp	butter	15 mL
1 1/2 cups	diced crimini mushrooms	375 mL
1/2 cup	diced white onion	125 mL
1 tbsp	flour	15 mL
1 cup	1% milk	250 mL
1 1/2 tsp	minced garlic	7 mL
1/4 tsp	salt	1 mL
1/4 tsp	white pepper	1 mL

1. Melt 1 tsp (5 mL) of the butter in nonstick skillet over medium-high heat.
2. Sauté mushrooms and onion until they begin to turn golden brown.
3. Push mushrooms and onion to outside edges of skillet.
4. Melt remaining butter in the centre of the same skillet.
5. When butter begins to bubble, sprinkle the flour over the melted butter and whisk until completely combined.
6. Pour milk in slowly, whisking constantly.
7. Stir in the mushrooms and onion.
8. Add garlic, salt, and pepper; continue to whisk until mixture thickens.
9. Serve.

health tip
Mushrooms are low in calories, saturated fat, cholesterol, and sodium.

🍓🍓🍓 Super skinny! (with portion size in mind)

makes: 1 1/2 cups (375 mL)
preparation time: 10 min
cooking time: 10 min
total time: 20 min

per serving (2 tbsp/25 mL): calories 25, protein 1 g, total fat 1 g, saturated fat 0.5 g, carbohydrates 2 g, fibre 0 g, sodium 62 mg, cholesterol 3.5 mg

homemade raspberry vinaigrette

Many people shy away from making their own salad dressing, believing it will take too much time and effort. Well, fear not, novices! This delicious homemade dressing could not be easier and provides the fresh-bursting taste of raspberries loaded with natural sweetness and antioxidants.

2 cups	fresh raspberries	500 mL
1/2 cup	red wine vinegar	125 mL
1/4 cup	olive oil	50 mL
1 tbsp	sugar	15 mL
1/2 tsp	onion powder	2 mL

1. In a blender, combine raspberries, red wine vinegar, olive oil, sugar, and onion powder. Blend on high for 1 minute.
2. Bottle and refrigerate.

kitchen tip
Unlike bottled salad dressings that have a long shelf life, homemade salad dressing will typically last for 1 week in the refrigerator. Store in glass bottles and shake prior to use. Wash and save up your old jam jars with a tight lid for future salad dressings.

Note: This salad dressing is so low in calories and fat, you can allow yourself 2 tbsp (25 mL) per serving and still stay in the "super skinny" mode!

🍓🍓🍓 Super skinny!

makes: 1 3/4 cups (425 mL)
preparation time: 5 min
total time: 5 min

per serving (2 tbsp/25 mL): calories 38, protein 0.15 g, total fat 3 g, saturated fat 0.5 g, carbohydrates 3 g, fibre 0 g, sodium 0 mg, cholesterol 0 mg

ginger and mandarin orange salad dressing

Filled with vitamin C, antioxidants, and natural sweetness, this tangy salad dressing over spinach salad and chicken is a true crowd pleaser. Your friends and family will be asking for more.

1 cup	mandarin orange sections	250 mL
1/2 cup	orange juice	125 mL
1/4 cup	diced white onion	50 mL
2 tbsp	olive oil	25 mL
1 tbsp	red wine vinegar	15 mL
2 tsp	minced ginger	10 mL
2 tsp	sesame oil	10 mL

1. In a blender, combine orange sections, orange juice, onion, olive oil, red wine vinegar, ginger, and sesame oil. Blend on high for 2 minutes.
2. Bottle and refrigerate.

health tip

In addition to being rich in monounsaturated fats, polyunsaturated fats, and vitamin E and low in saturated fats, sesame oil contains two powerful antioxidants called sesamol and sesamin. Research conducted and presented at the American Heart Association's 2003 annual meeting showed that study participants supplementing with sesame oil had a reduction in overall blood pressure.

🍓🍓🍓 Super skinny!

makes: 1 1/2 cups (375 mL)
preparation time: 10 min
total time: 10 min

per serving (2 tbsp/25 mL): calories 42, protein 0.2 g, total fat 3 g, saturated fat 0.5 g, carbohydrates 4 g, fibre 0.5 g, sodium 0 mg, cholesterol 0 mg

mixed-herb red wine vinaigrette

This lovely vinaigrette tastes as though it has come directly from the garden. Whenever possible, try to use fresh herbs. Not only do they offer an abundant amount of antioxidants, minerals, and vitamins, but they're much more flavourful than the dried and powdered versions.

1/2 cup	red wine vinegar	125 mL
1/2 cup	olive oil	125 mL
1 tbsp	sugar	15 mL
1 tbsp	chopped fresh basil	15 mL
1 tbsp	chopped fresh oregano	15 mL
1 tsp	minced garlic	5 mL
1/4 tsp	onion powder	1 mL

1. Combine red wine vinegar, olive oil, sugar, basil, oregano, garlic, and onion powder in a large jar with a lid.
2. Shake to mix thoroughly.
3. Refrigerate.

health tip
Loaded with antibacterial properties and antioxidant effects, oregano (and oregano oil) is a nutritional superstar. According to the *Journal of Agricultural and Food Chemistry*, ground cloves, cinnamon, and oregano top the antioxidant chart for herbs and spices.

Super skinny!

makes: 1 cup (250 mL)
preparation time: 5 min
total time: 5 min

per serving (2 tbsp/25 mL): calories 99, protein 0 g, total fat 10 g, saturated fat 1.5 g, carbohydrates 1 g, fibre 0 g, sodium 0 mg, cholesterol 0 mg

spicy mango mint salad dressing

Filled with succulent mangoes, fiery jalapeño peppers, and cool and refreshing mint, this spicy and sweet sensation is the ideal topping over fish, vegetables, chicken, or your favourite salad.

1/2	jalapeño pepper	1/2
2 cups	diced mango*	500 mL
1 cup	orange juice	250 mL
2 tbsp	chopped fresh mint	25 mL
1/4 cup	olive oil	50 mL

* 1 mango = 1 cup (250 mL) diced

1. Remove stem and pulp from jalapeño pepper and finely dice.
2. Combine jalapeño pepper, mango, orange juice, mint, and olive oil in blender and liquefy for 1 to 2 minutes.
3. Refrigerate.

health tip
Mint is known as a general pick-me-up food that offers numerous health benefits such as its antibacterial and antifungal properties. One of its best-known medicinal effects is its ability to soothe an ailing digestive system.

Note: This salad dressing is so low in calories, you can allow yourself 2 tablespoons (25 mL) per serving and still stay in the "super skinny" mode!

♡♡♡ Super skinny!

makes: 2 1/2 cups (625 mL)
preparation time: 15 min
total time: 15 min

per serving (2 tbsp/25 mL): calories 35, protein 0.1 g, total fat 3 g, saturated fat 0.5 g, carbohydrates 3 g, fibre 0.3 g, sodium 3 mg, cholesterol 0 mg

creamy dill salad dressing

This easy-to-make recipe is wonderful as a salad dressing, over steamed vegetables, with fish, or mixed with whole grain pasta. Lower in fat than typical cream dressing (plain yogurt is a main ingredient), it should be your "dressing of choice" if weight loss or weight maintenance is one of your health goals.

1 cup	low-fat plain yogurt	250 mL
1/4 cup	chopped fresh dill	50 mL
1 tbsp	chopped capers	15 mL
1 tbsp	freshly squeezed lemon juice	15 mL
1 tsp	sugar	5 mL
1/4 tsp	black pepper	1 mL

1. In a medium-sized bowl, combine yogurt, dill, capers, lemon juice, sugar, and black pepper.
2. Mix thoroughly with a wooden spoon.
3. Refrigerate.

kitchen tip

Many salad dressing recipes call for the ingredients to be mixed in a blender. For dressings made with yogurt, however, avoid using a blender, as your dressing will become overly watery. It's better to mix by hand.

health tip

Dill's medicinal abilities have been touted for centuries and include aiding the digestive system, providing relief from insomnia, being a natural breath freshener, and even helping to cure a case of the hiccups.

🍓🍓🍓 Super skinny!

makes: 1 cup (250 mL)
preparation time: 5 min
total time: 5 min

per serving (2 tbsp/25 mL): calories 18, protein 1.5 g, total fat 0.5 g, saturated fat 0 g, carbohydrates 2.5 g, fibre 0 g, sodium 55 mg, cholesterol 0 mg

orange sesame salad dressing

Light, sweet, and distinctive best describe this out-of-the-ordinary salad dressing. Many dressings rely heavily on a cream or oil base, but this recipe explodes with flavour without the added fat and calories.

2 tbsp	sesame seeds	25 mL
1/2 cup	orange juice	125 mL
1/4 cup	low-sodium soy sauce	50 mL
1 tbsp	sesame oil	15 mL
1 tbsp	freshly squeezed lemon juice	15 mL
1 tsp	sugar	5 mL

1. Toast sesame seeds in nonstick pan for 2 to 3 minutes (seeds are dry roasted, not in oil).
2. Combine sesame seeds, orange juice, soy sauce, sesame oil, lemon juice, and sugar in a mixing bowl and whisk until thoroughly blended.
3. Refrigerate.

kitchen tip
Sesame seeds can be roasted by pan frying on medium-high heat and stirring occasionally to ensure they don't burn. You can also spread the sesame seeds on a baking sheet and roast them in an oven for 10 minutes or until they are lightly brown.

health tip
In addition to adding a nutty taste and crunch to dressings, salads, and dishes, sesame seeds are loaded with nutritional benefits: 100 g of sesame seeds contains 26.4 g protein, 12.6 mg vitamin B3, 7.8 mg iron, 131 mg calcium, 10.3 mg zinc, and dietary fibre.

Super skinny!

makes: 1 cup (250 mL)
preparation time: 5 min
cooking time: 5 min
total time: 10 min

per serving (2 tbsp/25 mL): calories 20, protein 0.4 g, total fat 1.3 g, saturated fat 0.125 g, carbohydrates 1.5 g, fibre 0 g, sodium 135 mg, cholesterol 0 mg

soups and salads

quick-and-easy tomato basil soup

Enjoy the warm flavour of this no-fuss, low-calorie homemade tomato soup with a slice of whole grain bread and feel satisfied and slim (!) at the same time.

1 tbsp	butter	15 mL
1/2 cup	diced onion	125 mL
1/2 cup	diced celery	125 mL
1 tbsp	flour	15 mL
2 cups	low-sodium chicken broth	500 mL
2	cans (each 28 oz/796 mL) crushed tomatoes	2
2 tbsp	chopped fresh basil	25 mL
1/2 tsp	salt	2 mL
1/2 tsp	pepper	2 mL

1. Melt butter in a nonstick skillet over medium-high heat. Sauté onion and celery until tender (about 3 minutes).
2. Add flour and continue to cook, stirring, for 1 minute.
3. Slowly pour in chicken broth and whisk until completely blended.
4. Empty crushed tomatoes into 4-quart (3.75 L) pot.
5. Add contents of skillet along with basil, salt, and pepper.
6. Bring to a boil, reduce heat, and simmer for 20 minutes.
7. Allow to cool and purée in blender to create a smooth texture.
8. Reheat and serve.

kitchen tip

Although slightly more time-consuming, making this soup with fresh tomatoes will reduce its sodium content significantly. Prior to using fresh tomatoes, it's best to remove the skin through a process called blanching. Bring a medium-sized pot of water to a boil and place your tomatoes (very ripe is best) in the water for 2 to 3 minutes. Remove from heat and run cold water over them to allow for handling. Peel off skins and discard. Dice tomatoes and add to your recipe.

health tip

According to the U.S.-based Institute of Medicine, surpassing the recommended upper limit of 2300 mg of sodium daily for people over the age of 14 can lead to health problems, including hypertension. Unfortunately, salt is easy to accumulate in the diet if an excess of fast, processed, or canned food is consumed. When preparing soup with vegetable or chicken broth, always opt for the low-sodium version, which contains 140 mg of salt or less per serving.

🍓🍓🍓 Super skinny!

makes: 8 servings
preparation time: 10 min
cooking time: 25 min
total time: 35 min

per serving: calories 97.5, protein 4 g, total fat 1.75 g, saturated fat 0 g, carbohydrates 16.5 g, fibre 3.6 g, sodium 450 mg, cholesterol 3.75 mg

red pepper potato soup

This is a favourite "cold winter's day" soup. Its creamy texture, distinctive red pepper zing, and subtle bite of cayenne pepper create the perfect storm of flavour. Consider preparing a double batch and freezing it in individual containers for some grab-and-go lunch options at the office or for quick and easy dinners.

2 lb	white potatoes	1 kg
3	large red peppers	3
2	cartons (each 32 oz/900 mL) low-sodium chicken broth	2
1 cup	diced onion	250 mL
2 tbsp	butter	25 mL
1/2 tsp	cayenne pepper	2 mL
1/2 tsp	black pepper	2 mL
1 cup	1% milk	250 mL

1. Peel potatoes and dice into cubes no larger than 1 inch (2.5 cm).
2. Remove stem and core contents of peppers. Dice.
3. Pour chicken broth into medium-sized, heavy-bottom pot.
4. Add potatoes, red pepper, onion, butter, cayenne pepper, and black pepper.
5. Bring to a boil and cook over medium heat for 25 minutes or until potatoes and peppers are soft and can be pierced easily with a fork.
6. Pour in milk and stir.
7. Allow to cool to lukewarm.
8. Purée in blender.
9. Return to cooking pot, reheat, and serve.

kitchen tip

No cook really likes to spend time peeling potatoes, so keep these two key points in mind to improve efficiency:

1. If you're planning on peeling your potatoes in advance and not using them right away, they will brown in colour. Cover them in water with a small amount of salt mixed in.
2. Using a potato peeler will likely cut the peeling time in half and will cut waste by almost 50 percent.

health tip

If you enjoy a bit of hot and spicy in your meals, cayenne pepper is one of the health-iest additions to any dish. As a member of the chili pepper family, cayenne peppers have been used for hundreds of years for their medicinal properties. The ingredient in cayenne pepper responsible for that heat or zip to its taste is called capsaicin. Capsaicin has been widely studied for its pain-reducing effects, its cardiovascular benefits, and its ability to help prevent ulcers.

🍓🍓🍓 Super skinny!

makes: 6 servings
preparation time: 15 min
cooking time: 25 min
total time: 40 min

per serving: calories 146, protein 7 g, total fat 4 g, saturated fat 0 g, carbohydrates 18 g, fibre 6 g, sodium 123 mg, cholesterol 11 mg

savoury mushroom soup

This homemade soup offers the delicious taste of crimini mushrooms without the added cream and calories. Crimini mushrooms—a type of Portobello mushroom that has been harvested while young—are brown in colour and are far meatier in taste with a firm texture.

1 tbsp	butter	15 mL
3 cups	thickly sliced crimini mushrooms	750 mL
1 cup	halved, thinly sliced white onion	250 mL
4 cups	low-sodium chicken broth	1 L
1 tsp	pepper	5 mL
1/2 tsp	salt	2 mL
1/4 tsp	cayenne pepper	1 mL

1. Melt 1/2 tsp (2 mL) of the butter in nonstick skillet over medium-high heat. Sweat the mushrooms and onion for 6 to 8 minutes, until the mushrooms are partially cooked and onion is translucent. Do not allow the onion to brown.
2. Add chicken broth, remainder of butter, black pepper, salt, and cayenne pepper.
3. Bring to a boil, reduce heat, and simmer for 20 minutes.

health tip
In addition to being low in calories, fat, and salt, mushrooms contain protein that will help fill you up throughout your day. Mushroom protein is superior to many other types of vegetable protein because of its essential amino acid content. Between 70 percent and 90 percent of the vegetable protein in mushrooms can be easily digested.

🍓🍓🍓 Super skinny!

makes: 4 servings
preparation time: 10 min
cooking time: 30 min
total time: 40 min

per serving: calories 78, protein 2.5 g, total fat 4.5 g, saturated fat 1.75 g, carbohydrates 7.75 g, fibre 0.25 g, sodium 271 mg, cholesterol 7.5 mg

egg drop soup

Keep plenty of this tasty, low-calorie soup (suitable for any weight-loss or weight-maintenance plan) on hand during the winter months. It's sure to hit the spot.

4 cups	low-sodium chicken broth	1 L
1 tsp	sesame oil	5 mL
1 cup	diced celery	250 mL
2	omega-3 eggs	2
1/2 cup	diced green onion	125 mL
2 cups	bean sprouts	500 mL

1. In a heavy-bottom pot, bring chicken broth and sesame oil to a boil over medium-high heat.
2. Add celery and simmer for 15 minutes.
3. Crack eggs into bowl and beat only lightly.
4. Stir eggs into soup mixture; continue cooking for 5 minutes.
5. Add green onion and bean sprouts; continue cooking for 2 minutes.
6. Serve.

kitchen tip

One of the often overlooked keys to improving your skills in the kitchen is the sharpness of the knives you use. Learning how to sharpen your own knives can save you time and money and improve your recipes. Here are some basic points (pun intended!) to sharpening your kitchen knives.

- Hold the sharpening steel handle side up and rest the tip on a counter.
- Hold the knife as you would to carve a turkey and slice against the steel at a 20-degree angle.
- Make sure to apply even but light pressure as you sweep across the entire blade surface on your way down toward the counter.
- Repeat on the other side of the blade and alternate on each side several times. If you want to know if you are doing it correctly, you can listen for a light ringing sound as the blade moves across the steel.

health tip

In addition to being rich in vitamins K and C, celery contains the minerals potassium and sodium, which stimulate urine production and help to rid the body of excess fluid. For weight-loss or night-time munching, snack on cut-up celery as a "free food" to eat.

🍓🍓🍓 Super skinny!

makes: 4 servings
preparation time: 10 min
cooking time: 20 min
total time: 30 min

per serving: calories 75, protein 8.5 g, total fat 2.5 g, saturated fat 0.6 g, carbohydrates 2.6 g, fibre 1.2 g, sodium 222 mg, cholesterol 53 mg

decadent squash apple soup

Who doesn't love the taste of a warm harvest soup on a cool autumn day? When preparing this creamy, sweet soup, make a double batch and freeze in small containers so you'll have some healthy grab-and-go options.

4 cups	low-sodium chicken broth	1 L
4 cups	diced butternut squash	1 L
2 cups	diced apple	500 mL
1 cup	diced onion	250 mL
1/4 cup	diced celery	50 mL

1. Heat chicken broth in medium-sized pot over medium heat.
2. Add squash, apple, onion, and celery and simmer for 50 minutes or until ingredients can be pierced easily with a fork.
3. Remove from heat and allow to cool.
4. Purée in a blender on high for 2 minutes. Depending on the size of the blender, you may have to purée in batches.
5. Reheat and serve with whole grain toast or a salad.

health tip

Winter squash is typically bright orange or yellow and includes pumpkin, acorn, butternut, and spaghetti squash. The colour of the squash indicates the amount of carotene (a precursor to vitamin A) it provides. Winter squash offers an excellent source of vitamin A and a very good source of vitamin C, fibre, magnesium, and potassium. Summer squash comes in many shapes and varieties.

🍓🍓🍓 Super skinny!

makes: 8 servings
preparation time: 20 min
cooking time: 50 min
total time: 1 hr 10 min

per serving: calories 73, protein 3.5 g, total fat 0 g, saturated fat 0 g, carbohydrates 14 g, fibre 1.6 g, sodium 91 mg, cholesterol 0 mg

winterlicious hearty vegetable soup

This homemade vegetable soup isn't just satisfying, it's healthy too. Easy to make, it's a tasty starter or a savoury full dinner with a hearty piece of whole grain bread.

4 cups	low-sodium chicken broth	1 L
1/2 cup	thinly sliced carrots	125 mL
1/2 cup	diced white onion	125 mL
1/2 cup	extra firm tofu, cut in 1-inch (2.5 cm) cubes	125 mL
1/2 tsp	minced garlic	2 mL
1/2 tsp	dried basil	2 m
1/4 tsp	black pepper	1 mL
1 cup	broccoli, cut in florets	250 mL
1 cup	diced tomato	250 mL
1 cup	sliced crimini mushrooms	250 mL
1/2 cup	thinly sliced celery	125 mL
1/2 cup	diced red pepper	125 mL
1 tbsp	butter	15 mL

1. Bring broth to a boil and add carrots, onion, tofu, garlic, basil, and black pepper; cook over medium heat for 30 minutes.
2. Stir in broccoli, tomato, mushrooms, celery, red pepper, and butter; simmer over low heat for 20 minutes.
3. Serve.

kitchen tip
A stainless-steel or enamel-coated heavy-bottom soup pot is best for soups. Aluminum and cast iron can react to acidic ingredients and alter a soup's flavour and colour.

🍓🍓🍓 Super skinny!

makes: 6 servings
preparation time: 20 min
cooking time: 50 min
total time: 1 hr 10 min

per serving: calories 67, protein 3.5 g, total fat 2.5 g, saturated fat 1.5 g, carbohydrates 7.5 g, fibre 1.5 g, sodium 146 mg, cholesterol 5 mg

whole grain chicken noodle soup

Filled with vegetables, whole grains, and protein-rich chicken, this hearty and soothing soup will be a commonly requested meal in your household.

1 tsp	olive oil	5 mL
5 oz	boneless, skinless chicken breast	142 g
4 cups	low-sodium chicken broth	1 L
1/2 cup	diced onion	125 mL
1/2 cup	diced celery	125 mL
1/2 cup	diced carrots	125 mL
1/2 cup	thinly sliced mushrooms	125 mL
1 tsp	basil	15 mL
1 tsp	thyme	15 mL
2 oz	whole grain spelt egg noodles	57 g

1. Heat oil in nonstick skillet over medium-high heat.
2. Place chicken breast in skillet and cover. Cook on each side for 5 minutes.
3. Dice cooked chicken breast into 1/2-inch (1 cm) cubes.
4. Heat chicken broth in large pot over medium heat. Add chicken, onion, celery, carrots, mushrooms, basil, and thyme.
5. Simmer for 20 minutes.
6. Stir in noodles and continue to cook for 5 minutes.
7. Serve.

kitchen tip

Most Italian cooks will agree that pasta interacts better with a sauce when it's cooked al dente (undercooked by 1 to 2 minutes for a chewier texture). In addition, pasta that is cooked al dente breaks down more slowly into glucose (the sugar derived from carbohydrates) and is therefore lower on the glycemic index. Lower glycemic index carbohydrates have been shown to be beneficial for prevention of type 2 diabetes and for weight loss.

health tip

Whole grain pasta offers higher amounts of fibre, B vitamins, antioxidants, and trace minerals than refined grains. Available in kamut, spelt, 100 percent whole wheat, and whole grain mix, whole grain pastas are in most supermarkets in a variety of options such as penne, linguini, or rotini.

🍓🍓🍓 Super skinny!

makes: 6 servings
preparation time: 10 min
cooking time: 35 min
total time: 45 min

per serving: calories 109, protein 12 g, total fat 2.5 g, saturated fat 0.5 g, carbohydrates 10 g, fibre 1.5 g, sodium 125 mg, cholesterol 0 mg

tasty pea soup

Looking to fill up but not on calories? Having a bowl of this tasty and nutritious pea soup with whole grain bread or a protein selection at lunch or dinner will keep blood sugar stabilized and energy up throughout your day.

8 cups	low-sodium chicken broth	2 L
2 cups	water	500 mL
2 cups	dry yellow peas	500 mL
1 cup	diced celery	250 mL
1 cup	diced carrots	250 mL
1 cup	diced onion	250 mL
3 tsp	minced garlic	15 mL
1/2 tsp	salt	2 mL
1/2 tsp	white pepper	2 mL
1 tsp	poultry seasoning	5 mL

1. In large soup pot over high heat, combine broth, water, and peas.
2. Bring to a boil, cover, and reduce heat to medium.
3. Cook for 1 1/2 hours.
4. Stir in celery, carrots, onion, garlic, salt, pepper, and poultry seasoning. Simmer for 30 minutes uncovered.
5. For a creamier consistency, remove approximately one-third of the soup and purée in a blender. Return puréed soup to the pot and mix thoroughly.
6. Serve.

Note: Although this soup takes time to make, it doesn't require much work while it's cooking. Once the vegetables are diced and the peas are simmering, you can leave it to cook, checking on it occasionally.

kitchen tip
When selecting a soup pot, choose one with a heavy bottom to avoid burning.

health tip
In addition to being loaded with fibre, peas offer slow-burning carbohydrates and protein, making them an excellent choice for a weight-loss or weight-maintenance program.

🍓🍓🍓 Super skinny!

makes: 10 servings
preparation time: 15 min
cooking time: 2 hrs
total time: 2 hrs 15 min

per serving: calories 188, protein 13 g, total fat 1 g, saturated fat 0.5 g, carbohydrates 30 g, fibre 1 g, sodium 245 mg, cholesterol 4 mg

warm mushroom salad

Quick and easy to make, this salad can be used as an appetizer or eaten as a light meal for dinner or lunch. The mushrooms offer a "meaty" and flavour-filled texture that balances nicely with the fresh spinach and crunchy walnuts.

1 tbsp	olive oil	15 mL
1 tsp	minced garlic	5 mL
4	large Portobello mushrooms, thickly sliced	4
3 tbsp	balsamic vinegar	50 mL
1 tsp	sugar	5 mL
2 cups	baby spinach leaves	500 mL
4 tbsp	walnuts	60 mL

1. Heat oil in nonstick skillet over high heat.
2. Add garlic and mushrooms, spreading mushrooms out to allow them to cook evenly. Cook for 2 minutes on each side.
3. Stir in balsamic vinegar and sugar. Continue to cook, covered, for 2 minutes over medium-low heat.
4. Allow to cool for a couple of minutes to avoid wilting the spinach leaves.
5. Place spinach on plates and top with mushrooms and walnuts; drizzle with remaining sauce from the skillet.

kitchen tip

Portobello mushrooms are available and sold year-round. It's best to use them promptly or store them in a brown paper bag in the refrigerator, where they will last from seven to 10 days. To clean, gently wipe with a damp cloth or soft brush. If you need to rinse them, do not do so until you're ready to use them. Rinse with cold water and pat dry with paper towel.

health tip

There are more than 14,000 types of mushrooms, with only about 3000 edible varieties and about 700 varieties with known medicinal properties. Crimini and

Portobello mushrooms are the same type of mushroom, with the Portobellos being left to grow much larger. Portobellos are rich in a variety of B vitamins such as riboflavin (vitamin B2) and niacin (vitamin B3).

🍓🍓🍓 Super skinny!

makes: 2 servings
preparation time: 5 min
cooking time: 5 min
total time: 10 min

per serving: calories 246, protein 7 g, total fat 16 g, saturated fat 2 g, carbohydrates 18 g, fibre 5 g, sodium 57 mg, cholesterol 0 mg

crumbled goat cheese, apple, and pear salad

Lower in fat, rich in antioxidants and protein, this salad is still big on taste: the creamy, earthy flavour of the goat cheese is a rich complement to the sweet fruit and crunchy nuts.

2 cups	spring salad mix	500 mL
1/2 cup	peeled, sliced Royal Gala apple	125 mL
1/2 cup	peeled, sliced Bosc pear	125 mL
1/2 cup	cherry tomatoes	125 mL
2 oz	crumbled goat cheese	57 g
4 tbsp	walnuts	60 mL
4 tbsp	raspberry vinaigrette	60 mL

1. In medium-sized mixing bowl, combine spring salad mix, apple, pear, cherry tomatoes, crumbled goat cheese, and walnuts; toss.
2. Drizzle salad dressing over top and serve.

Note: For a delicious *Healthy Sin Foods* homemade raspberry vinaigrette, see page 260.

health tip

While regular Cheddar cheese has about 9 g of fat per 1 oz, with 6 g being saturated fat, goat cheese tends to be lower in calories and fat: 1 oz of goat cheese contains about 4 to 5 g of fat. Goat cheese is also rich in protein and contains potassium, vitamin A, thiamin, and niacin. Because cheese overall tends to be slightly higher in fat, it is ideal to use it as a flavouring agent and not the main ingredient of your recipe.

Goat cheese is often used by those who have a low tolerance to cow's milk, as it is far more easily digested.

🍓🍓🍓 Super skinny!

makes: 2 servings
preparation time: 15 min
total time: 15 min

per serving: calories 243, protein 9 g, total fat 17 g, saturated fat 5 g, carbohydrates 16 g, fibre 4 g, sodium 121 mg, cholesterol 13 mg

whole grain rotini, vegetable, and goat cheese salad

When it comes to guilt-free flavour, this salad offers it all: healthy pasta, crispy vegetables, and creamy lower-fat goat cheese. Indulge in some pasta without worrying about gaining weight!

2 cups	cooked (al dente) whole grain rotini	500 mL
1/4 cup	diced celery	50 mL
1/4 cup	diced red pepper	50 mL
1/4 cup	diced green onion	50 mL
1/2 cup	finely chopped cilantro	125 mL
3 oz	goat cheese	85 g
2 tbsp	olive oil	25 mL
2 tbsp	white vinegar	25 mL
1 tsp	minced garlic	5 mL
1 tsp	finely diced jalapeño pepper	5 mL

1. In a large bowl, combine rotini, celery, red pepper, green onion, cilantro, and goat cheese; mix thoroughly.
2. In a small bowl, whisk oil, vinegar, garlic, and jalapeño pepper. Pour over salad and mix thoroughly.
3. Refrigerate for 2 hours and serve.

kitchen tip

Do you think you have to give up pasta altogether to lose weight and be healthy? Not necessarily so. A small serving of whole grain pasta offers fibre, selenium, potassium, and magnesium.

health tip

A 2008 study in the *American Journal of Clinical Nutrition* demonstrated that whole grains help to reduce body weight, cardiovascular risk factor, abdominal fat, and an inflammatory marker called C-reactive protein. Here are some whole grain options:

WHOLE GRAINS	REFINED GRAINS
Barley	Corn flakes
Brown rice	Couscous
Buckwheat	Enriched macaroni or spaghetti
Bulgur (cracked wheat)	Grits
Kamut	Pretzels
Millet	White bread (refined)
Oatmeal	White rice
Popcorn	
Spelt	
Whole wheat bread, pasta, or crackers	
Wild rice	

 Super skinny!

makes: 8 servings (1/2 cup/125 mL each)
preparation time: 15 min
cooking time: 10 min
total time: 25 min

per serving (1/2 cup/125 mL): calories 107, protein 4 g, total fat 6 g, saturated fat 2 g, carbohydrates 10 g, fibre 1 g, sodium 43 mg, cholesterol 5 mg

quinoa curry salad

Curry powder adds a punch of flavour to salads, stews, chilies, and meat or poultry dishes. Your family and guests will be quite impressed when they discover you've made your own curry sauce too. (Just don't tell them how easy it was!) Combined with high-protein quinoa, juicy tomatoes, asparagus, and naturally sweet mangoes, this recipe offers the triple threat of flavour: sweet, tangy, and satisfying.

4 cups	quinoa	1 L
1 cup	asparagus, cut in 1/2-inch (1 cm) pieces	250 mL
1 1/2 cups	chopped mango	375 mL
1 1/2 cups	cherry tomatoes	375 mL
1 cup	finely chopped green onion tops	250 mL
1	can (19 oz/540 mL) chickpeas, drained and rinsed	1
1/3 cup	olive oil	75 mL
1/3 cup	orange juice with pulp	75 mL
3 tbsp	vinegar	50 mL
4 tbsp	sugar	60 mL
4 tbsp	curry powder	60 mL

1. Soak quinoa in cold water for 5 minutes, drain, and rinse thoroughly.
2. Bring 8 cups (2 L) of water to a boil in a wide-bottomed pot with a lid.
3. Add a pinch of salt and stir in quinoa.
4. Reduce heat to a simmer, cover, and cook until all the water is absorbed (about 25 to 30 minutes).
5. Bring a small pot of water to a boil. Add asparagus and cook for 3 minutes. Drain, rinse in cold water, and allow to cool.
6. In a large bowl, combine quinoa, asparagus, mango, cherry tomatoes, green onion, and chickpeas.
7. In a small bowl, whisk olive oil, orange juice, vinegar, sugar, and curry powder until fully blended.
8. Drizzle curry sauce over quinoa mixture and toss well.
9. Serve.

kitchen tip

When cooking quinoa, you can cook any amount you like as long as you keep the 2:1 ratio of liquid to grain. You can also experiment with cooking quinoa in vegetable or chicken stock or coconut milk for extra flavour. Quinoa can be added to a chili, eaten with a stir-fry, or served as a side dish or on its own.

health tip

Quinoa is a grain that is gaining enormous popularity. It is light and easily digested and has the most complete nutrition and highest protein content of any grain.

🍓🍓🍓 Super skinny! (with proper portion size in mind)

makes: 8 servings (1 cup/250 mL each)
preparation time: 20 min
cooking time: 40 min
total time: 60 min

per serving (1 cup/250 mL): calories 171, protein 5 g, total fat 5 g, saturated fat 0.5 g, carbohydrates 28 g, fibre 4 g, sodium 185 mg, cholesterol 0 mg

sweet red pepper and mango salad

Loaded with vitamin C, this colourful and antioxidant-rich salad offers a powerful nutritional punch that satisfies your sweet tooth naturally.

2 cups	mesclun salad mix	500 mL
1	mango, peeled and sliced	1
1	jalapeño pepper, finely diced	1
1	red pepper, thinly sliced	1
2 tbsp	chopped almonds	25 mL
4 tbsp	salad dressing	60 mL

For the perfect homemade dressing for this salad, see page 263. A basic balsamic vinaigrette would also be suitable.

1. In a large bowl, combine mesclun salad mix, mango, jalapeño pepper, red pepper, and almonds; toss.
2. Serve and top with dressing.

kitchen tip

Since almonds have a high fat content (72 percent is monounsaturated fat, 21 percent is polyunsaturated fat, and only 7 percent is saturated fat), it's important to store them properly to protect them from becoming rancid. Raw almonds will last about four to six months in the refrigerator and about nine to 12 months in the freezer.

🍓🍓🍓 Super skinny!

makes: 2 servings (1 cup/250 mL each)
preparation time: 10 min
total time: 10 min

per serving (1 cup/250 mL): calories 154, protein 3.5 g, total fat 5 g, saturated fat 0.3 g, carbohydrates 24 g, fibre 4.5 g, sodium 63 mg, cholesterol 0 mg

strawberry, walnut, and spinach salad

Crunchy, heart-healthy walnuts add not only a twist to this classic strawberry spinach salad but also an omega-3 boost. Drizzled with homemade raspberry vinaigrette and topped with green onions, this is the ideal salad for any season.

2 cups	baby spinach leaves	500 mL
1 cup	sliced strawberries	250 mL
4 tbsp	chopped walnuts	60 mL
1/4 cup	finely chopped green onion tops	50 mL
4 tbsp	raspberry vinaigrette	60 mL

See page 260 for a homemade raspberry vinaigrette. A perfect blend with this salad.

1. In a large bowl, combine baby spinach leaves, strawberries, walnuts, and chopped green onion; toss.
2. Drizzle with vinaigrette and serve.

kitchen tip
Prior to preparing this salad, sort through the strawberries and separate the soft ones from the firm, fully ripe berries. Discard any mushy or spoiled berries.

health tip
Walnuts far outweigh any other nut when it comes to omega-3 essential fatty acids. Unfortunately, the typical American diet tends to consume 11 to 30 times more omega-6 fatty acids than omega-3 fatty acids. Many researchers believe this imbalance is a significant factor in the rising rate of inflammatory disorders.

🍓🍓🍓 Super skinny!

makes: 2 servings (1 cup/250 mL each)
preparation time: 10 min
total time: 10 min

per serving (1 cup/250): calories 173, protein 3.5 g, total fat 13 g, saturated fat, 1 g, carbohydrates 15 g, fibre 4 g, sodium 40 mg, cholesterol 0 mg

wraps and sandwiches

egg foo young wrap

Filled with crunchy bean sprouts, water chestnuts, and onions, this tasty, low-calorie wrap is a fast and easy low glycemic option for lunch or dinner.

1 tsp	butter	5 mL
2 tbsp	diced onion	25 mL
2 tbsp	diced celery	25 mL
1 tbsp	diced water chestnuts	15 mL
1/2 cup	bean sprouts	125 mL
1 tsp	soy sauce	5 mL
1	omega-3 egg	1
4 tbsp	egg whites	60 mL
1	whole grain wrap (10 in/25 cm)	1
2 tbsp	chopped green onion tops	25 mL

1. Melt butter in a 10-inch nonstick skillet over medium-high heat.
2. Sauté onion, celery, and water chestnuts for 3 minutes.
3. Add bean sprouts and soy sauce, and continue to sauté for 1 minute. Don't overcook.
4. In a small bowl, combine egg and egg whites and beat until fully mixed.
5. Add eggs to sautéed vegetables and cook over medium-high heat until eggs are set (approximately 4 to 5 minutes), stirring with a wooden spoon.
6. Brown whole grain tortilla. On an electric stove, turn an element on medium heat and place wrap directly on the element, for 10 to 15 seconds each side. On a gas stove, follow the same directions (results are better on a gas stove). Or, heat in microwave.
7. Place egg mixture in the centre of the wrap.
8. Top with green onions.
9. Fold and serve.

kitchen tip

Bean sprouts add a great crunch and taste to all recipes. It's important to note that the shelf life of bean sprouts from grocer to table is quite short, so try to purchase your bean sprouts within a day or two of use. When purchased, they should be dry and crispy. Cook bean sprouts for only a short period of time, as they will lose their crunch if cooked for more than a minute or two.

health tip

When a seed is sprouted, the "nutrition factor" tends to increase. The sprouting process increases the vitamins and minerals and decreases the calorie and carbohydrate content. Bean sprouts, also called mung bean sprouts, contain vitamins A, B, C, and E and an assortment of minerals, including calcium, iron, and potassium.

🍓🍓🍓 Super skinny!

makes: 1 serving
preparation time: 10 min
cooking time: 5 min
total time: 15 min

per serving: calories 248, protein 12 g, total fat 11 g, saturated fat 2.5 g, carbohydrates 8 g, fibre 2.5 g, sodium 240 mg, cholesterol 200 mg

veggie rice wraps

One of the challenges many families face is getting more fresh vegetables into their diets. According to a study in the *American Journal of Preventative Medicine*, less than 12 percent of American children are eating the recommended amount of fruits and vegetables.

This easy-to-make recipe offers the entire family a one-two punch of vegetables likely missing in the daily diet. Filled with low glycemic index and nutrient-packed vegetables and healthy protein, it's a quick option for dinner or lunch.

6	rice paper wraps	6
4 oz	extra firm tofu	113 g
3/4 cup	bean sprouts	175 mL
1/2 cup	seedless sliced cucumber	125 mL
1/2	red pepper, thinly sliced	1/2
1/2	avocado, sliced	1/2
4 tbsp	chopped green onion tops	60 mL
1 cup	thinly sliced romaine lettuce	250 mL
3 tsp	hoisin sauce	15 mL
2 tbsp	sweet chili sauce	25 mL

1. Slice firm tofu into long strips
2. Place rice wraps one at a time in warm water for no more than 5 seconds.
3. Remove from water and place flat on wet paper towel.
4. On one-half of the wrap, place tofu, bean sprouts, cucumber, red pepper, avocado, and green onion; top with lettuce. Leave a 2-inch (5 cm) border around the filling.
5. Spread 1/2 tsp (2 mL) hoisin sauce across each wrap in front of filling.
6. Beginning with the side with the filling, roll wrap one full turn and fold in outside edges. Continue to roll until tightly wrapped.
7. Repeat the process for each wrap, and serve with 1 tbsp (15 mL) sweet chili sauce for dipping.

Note: The tofu can be replaced with thin slices of cooked chicken breast if desired.

kitchen tip

Avocados are the perfect addition to many recipes, offering a creamy, smooth texture. If you're planning to use avocados within a day or so, select ones that are dark-skinned and a bit soft to the touch. Brighter and greener avocados are for later use, as they take two to four days to ripen on your counter.

In order to achieve the greatest yield when slicing avocados, simply cut from stem to tip. To remove the pit, hold the avocado in one hand and with a firm stroke hit the pit with a sharp knife. Twist the knife and pull. The pit should come out easily. If half of the avocado is not going to be used, leave the pit in the side, wrap, and put in the refrigerator.

health tip

Did you know avocados are one of the first fresh fruits a baby can enjoy? Low in sodium, creamy in texture, and loaded with fats that support brain function, avocados should be included in a baby's diet. If your baby is at first a fussy eater, feel free to mash a little sweet, ripe banana with the avocado.

🍓🍓🍓 Super skinny!

makes: 3 servings (2 rice wraps each)
preparation time: 20 min
total time: 20 min

per serving (2 rice wraps): calories 110, protein 4.6 g, total fat 4 g, saturated fat 0.3 g, carbohydrates 14 g, fibre 2 g, sodium 263 mg, cholesterol 0 mg

hearty pizza wrap

Instead of ordering in a pizza for dinner, why not make the family a slightly different version? These mouth-watering pizza wraps are filled with heart-healthy tomatoes, sweet and tasty tomato sauce, lean protein (egg whites), and savoury cheese.

1 tsp	butter	5 mL
2 tbsp	chopped onion	25 mL
2 tbsp	sliced mushrooms	25 mL
1	omega-3 egg	1
4 tbsp	egg whites	60 mL
2 tbsp	pizza sauce (see page 258)	25 mL
1 tsp	basil	5 mL
1 tsp	oregano	5 mL
1 tsp	sugar	5 mL
1	whole grain wrap (10 in/25 cm)	1
2 tbsp	chopped tomatoes	25 mL
2 tbsp	shredded mozzarella cheese	25 mL

1. Melt butter in a 10-inch nonstick skillet over medium-high heat.
2. Sauté onion and mushrooms for 2 to 3 minutes.
3. In a small bowl, combine egg and egg whites and beat until blended.
4. Add eggs to sautéed vegetables and cook over medium-high heat for 2 to 3 minutes, continuing to stir.
5. Mix pizza sauce, basil, oregano, and sugar in separate dish and heat in microwave for 20 seconds.
6. Brown whole grain wrap. On an electric stove, turn element on medium heat and place wrap directly on the element, for 10 to 15 seconds each side. On a gas stove, follow the same directions (results are better on a gas stove).
7. Place egg mixture in the centre of the wrap.
8. Pour sauce mix over egg mixture.
9. Top with tomatoes and cheese.
10. Fold and serve.

kitchen tip
Smooth out the taste of spaghetti and pizza sauces by adding 1 tsp (5 mL) of sugar to the sauce.

health tip
Want to make this recipe even more heart healthy? Replace the 1 egg with 2 extra tsp (10 mL) of egg white. You'll reduce your total fat intake by 4 g and your saturated fat intake by 2 g.

🍓🍓 Enjoy once a week!

makes: 1 serving
preparation time: 10 min
cooking time: 5 min
total time: 15 min

per serving: calories 319, protein 19 g, total fat 13 g, saturated fat 6.5 g, carbohydrates 28 g, fibre 2.4 g, sodium 463 mg, cholesterol 207 mg

grilled salmon and dill wrap

Salmon lovers, rejoice! This grilled, dill-flavoured salmon wrap is loaded with anti-inflammatory omega-3 essential fats and tons of flavour. It's also high in fibre, filling, and can be part of any weight-loss program.

2	boneless salmon fillets (3 oz/75 g)	2
1 tbsp	freshly squeezed lemon juice	15 mL
1 tsp	finely chopped fresh dill	5 mL
Pinch	salt and pepper	Pinch
1 tsp	butter	5 mL
2	whole grain wraps (each 10 in/25 cm)	2
1 tbsp	dill sauce (see page 255)	15 mL
4	slices tomato	4
1/4 cup	shredded romaine lettuce	50 mL

1. Season salmon fillets with lemon juice, dill, salt, and pepper.
2. Melt butter in nonstick skillet over medium-high heat.
3. Place fillets in skillet and cover. Cook for 4 minutes.
4. Pour 2 tbsp (25 mL) water into skillet, turn fillets over, and return the cover. Cook for 4 minutes.
5. For added flavour, brown the wraps. With either a gas or electric stove, turn burner on medium-high and place the wrap directly on the element for 10 to 15 seconds each side.
6. Spread dill sauce equally in the centre of each wrap.
7. Slice salmon fillets into long strips.
8. Fill wrap with sliced salmon fillet, tomato, and lettuce.
9. Roll and serve.

kitchen tip

Although butter is higher in saturated fat, it offers considerable nutritional benefits—it's high in an absorbable form of vitamin A and rich in vitamins E and K. Butter also contains lauric acid, which offers potent antifungal and antibacterial properties. Lastly, butter contains vitamin D, which is essential for the absorption of calcium. The take-home point: eat butter in moderation.

health tip

Recent studies have demonstrated the importance of omega-3 for pregnant and breastfeeding mothers. Omega-3s have been shown to be a vital part of cardiac and respiratory development, in addition to supporting both eye and brain function. In fact, omega-3s improve both cognitive and motor skills in young children.

🍓🍓🍓 Super skinny!

makes: 2 servings
preparation time: 15 min
cooking time: 10 min
total time: 25 min

per serving: calories 188, protein 11.5 g, total fat 6 g, saturated fat 2 g, carbohydrates 21 g, fibre 2.5 g, sodium 371 mg, cholesterol 27 mg

open-faced poached eggs supreme

Popeye would love this open-faced sandwich filled with muscle-building spinach, poached omega-3 eggs, and wild smoked salmon. Poached eggs are healthier than scrambled or fried eggs because poaching doesn't require any extra oil or butter.

4	omega-3 eggs	4
1 tsp	butter	5 mL
1 tsp	minced garlic	5 mL
4 cups	baby spinach	1 L
4	slices whole grain toast	4
4 oz	wild smoked salmon (lox)	113 g
Pinch	black pepper	Pinch

1. In a large nonstick skillet, bring 2 inches (5 cm) water to a boil.
2. Reduce heat to low and wait until the boiling action stops.
3. Gently crack eggs into the water and do not disturb. Increase heat to medium-high and cook 5 minutes.
4. While the eggs are cooking, in a separate nonstick skillet, melt butter and stir in garlic. Add spinach and cook until spinach wilts. Turn off heat, cover, and leave in the pan.
5. After eggs have cooked for 5 minutes, gently spoon water overtop until whites are cooked.
6. Plate the toast, top each slice with lox, then cooked spinach, and one egg. Sprinkle with pepper.
7. Serve.

kitchen tip

Though poached eggs may seem difficult to make, they're actually quite easy once you get the hang of it. In order to prevent the egg from separating, bring the water to a full boil, then reduce the heat until all the bubbles and boiling action have stopped. Gently crack and add the egg and increase to medium-high heat. Be sure that each egg has sufficient space in the pan and doesn't crowd its neighbours.

health tip

Of all the superfoods, spinach gets the gold medal. Dark leafy greens such as spinach, kale, and collards are loaded with calcium, folic acid, vitamin K, and iron. Spinach is also rich in vitamin C, fibre, and carotenoids. Eating spinach regularly will help to keep the body's pH (potential of hydrogen) in an alkaline rather than an acidic state. For more information on alkaline and acidic foods, see page 18.

🍓 Save for an occasional treat!

makes: 2 servings
preparation time: 10 min
cooking time: 10 min
total time: 20 min

per serving: calories 427, protein 35 g, total fat 17 g, saturated fat 5 g, carbohydrates 30 g, fibre 6 g, sodium 469 mg, cholesterol 467 mg

roasted red pepper and pesto sandwich

Roasted red pepper, Swiss cheese, and pesto is a winning combination when it comes to taste. To boost the nutritional makeup of this savoury sandwich, prepare on whole grain bread and opt for low-fat Swiss cheese.

2	medium red peppers	2
1 tsp	olive oil	5 mL
4	slices whole grain toast	4
2 tbsp	pesto sauce	25 mL
2	slices light Swiss cheese	2
4	slices tomato	4
1/3 cup	shredded lettuce	75 mL
Pinch	salt and pepper	Pinch

1. Cut peppers in half; remove stems and pulp.
2. Brush with olive oil and set skin side up in pan lined with foil. Place the pan 5 inches (12 cm) below the broiling element.
3. Broil until the skin has blackened. Remove from oven.
4. Turn off broiler and allow to cool. Place towel over peppers and allow to steam for 10 minutes.
5. Remove towel and allow to cool for a few more minutes.
6. Peel the skin from the peppers.
7. Spread pesto sauce on 2 slices of toast (for a homemade pesto sauce, see page 256).
8. Top each with 2 slices of roasted pepper, 1 slice of Swiss cheese, 2 tomato slices, and lettuce.
9. Sprinkle with salt and pepper.
10. Top each with with toast slice, cut in half, and serve.

kitchen tip
When storing your olive oil, keep it in a dark bottle away from light. Air, heat, and light cause olive oil to turn rancid. If your oil has a buttery taste, chances are it has gone rancid.

health tip

A regular intake of whole grains in the form of bread and pasta has been associated with a decrease in weight, reduced cardiovascular risk, and improved digestive health.

🍓🍓 Enjoy once a week!

makes: 2 servings
preparation time: 20 min
cooking time: 20 min
total time: 40 min

per serving: calories 291, protein 13 g, total fat 11.5 g, saturated fat 3 g, carbohydrates 34 g, fibre 8 g, sodium 660 mg, cholesterol 10 mg

portobello swiss sandwich

This delicious mushroom sandwich offers a meaty taste without the unwanted saturated fat found in hamburgers. The Portobello mushroom stands out as the "nutritional winner" of all mushrooms, as it's rich in minerals, vitamins (such as B vitamins), and protein.

1	Portobello mushroom, stem removed	1
1/2 tsp	butter	2 mL
1/2 tsp	minced garlic	2 mL
1	slice light Swiss cheese	1
1 tsp	light mayonnaise	5 mL
1 tsp	horseradish	5 mL
2	slices whole grain toast	2
1/4 cup	finely chopped romaine lettuce	50 mL
2	slices tomato	2

1. Spread butter and garlic on underside of mushroom.
2. Place under broiler and broil for 6 to 7 minutes or until tender.
3. Top with Swiss cheese slice.
4. Broil for another 1 to 2 minutes until cheese is melted.
5. In a small bowl, mix mayonnaise and horseradish.
6. Spread evenly on a slice of toast.
7. Top with mushroom, lettuce, tomato, and remaining toast slice.
8. Cut in half and serve.

health tip
When buying whole grain bread, ensure that you're purchasing a loaf made with the entire grain. This includes the bran, the germ, and the endosperm.

🍓🍓 Enjoy once a week!

makes: 1 serving
preparation time: 10 min
cooking time: 10 min
total time: 20 min

per serving: calories 238, protein 10 g, total fat 9 g, saturated fat 3 g, carbohydrates 26 g, fibre 5 g, sodium 663 mg, cholesterol 20 mg

gourmet grilled cheese

This tweak to a classic favourite is a huge winner with our family. Served at lunch or cut up into mini appetizers at a party, all that's left of this sandwich is a few crumbs on the plate.

1 tsp	butter	5 mL
3	medium mushrooms, sliced	3
1/4 tsp	minced garlic	1 mL
2	slices whole grain bread	2
1 oz	sliced light Cheddar cheese	28 g
1 tsp	chopped cilantro	5 mL
2	slices tomato	2

1. Melt 1/4 tsp (1 mL) of the butter in a skillet. Sauté mushrooms and garlic for 2 to 3 minutes.
2. Lightly butter a slice of bread on one side (outer side facing pan).
3. Layer with cheese, mushroom mixture, cilantro, and tomato.
4. Top with other slice of bread and spread with remaining butter.
5. Heat nonstick skillet over medium-high and cook sandwich on each side for 2 to 3 minutes or until golden brown. (To get cheese to melt easier in sandwich, cover pan while cooking.)
6. Slice in half and serve.

kitchen tip

As part of a well-stocked kitchen, you'll need a decent set of pots and pans. A set of pots and pans can run the gamut, ranging from two hundred dollars to thousands of dollars. Prior to investing, ask yourself the following questions to help determine what you are looking for.

- How many people do you cook for? This will determine how many pots and pans you require.
- What type of cooking do you do? For example, if you are a soup maker, you will need a large stockpot.

- How important is ease of cleanup to you? If it's of utmost importance, you may want to consider purchasing nonstick cookware.
- Do you require cookware that can go in the dishwasher? For example, hard-anodized aluminum cookware is popular, but if put in the dishwasher it will change colour and darken.

health tip

Are you looking to increase your child's intake of high-fibre, nutrient-dense foods in a kid-friendly way? Simply use whole grain bread with the usual peanut butter and jam, French toast and maple syrup, and grilled cheese.

🍓🍓 Enjoy once a week!

makes: 1 serving
preparation time: 10 min
cooking time: 5 min
total time: 15 min

per serving: calories 256, protein 15 g, total fat 10 g, saturated fat 5 g, carbohydrates 25 g, fibre 4.5 g, sodium 418 mg, cholesterol 25 mg

vegetabagel

Loaded with red peppers, sweet carrots, whole grain flax bread, and low-fat cream cheese, this tasty, lunchbox-friendly sandwich will fill you up without crashing energy levels.

1	flax and honey bagel*	1
1 tbsp	low-fat cream cheese with chives or onions	15 mL
6	thin slices cucumber	6
2	thin red pepper rings	2
1/4 cup	shredded carrot	50 mL

* See Product Resource Guide for recommendations.

1. Slice bagel and lightly toast.
2. Spread cream cheese and chives onto one half of sliced bagel.
3. Layer with cucumber, pepper rings, and shredded carrots.
4. Top with other half of bagel and enjoy.

health tip
When shopping for healthy bread, choose one that contains ground flaxseed—you'll bump up your daily intake of omega-3 and fibre in a tasty and delicious way.

🍓🍓 Enjoy once a week!

makes: 1 serving
preparation time: 5 min
total time: 5 min

per serving (1 bagel): calories 350, protein 14 g, total fat 4.5 g, saturated fat 1 g, carbohydrates 65 g, fibre 6 g, sodium 552 mg, cholesterol 5 mg

Source: www.stonemillbakehouse.com

chickwich

The chickwich provides high protein and low glycemic index carbohydrates for stamina, as well as slow-burning fuel that will keep you satiated throughout the day.

1/2 cup	chopped cooked chicken breast	125 mL
1/4 cup	finely chopped red pepper, cucumber, mango	50 mL
2 tbsp	sliced green onion	25 mL
1/4 cup	low-fat plain yogurt	50 mL
1 tbsp	lime juice	15 mL
1/4 tsp	salt	1 mL
1/4 tsp	fresh cracked pepper	1 mL
1 tbsp	chopped fresh cilantro	15 mL
1	sprouted grain bagel*	1
1	lettuce leaf	1

* See Product Resource Guide for recommendations.

1. In a medium-sized bowl, combine chicken, red pepper, cucumber, mango, and green onion.
2. Stir in yogurt, lime juice, salt, and pepper until well combined. Sprinkle with cilantro and toss to combine.
3. Slice bagel in half horizontally. Arrange lettuce over cut side of bottom half. Top with chicken mixture. Cover with top half of bagel.

health tip
Use plain yogurt as an alternative to mayonnaise and sour cream in dips, sauces, dressings, and more. If the tangy flavour of yogurt is too much for a full substitution, start with a half-and-half mixture (e.g., half yogurt, half mayonnaise in a tuna salad).

Enjoy once a week!

makes: 1 serving
preparation time: 5 min
total time: 5 min

per serving: calories 450, protein 38 g, total fat 7.5 g, saturated fat 1.3 g, carbohydrates 58 g, fibre 7 g, sodium 1100 mg, cholesterol 65 mg

Source: www.stonemillbakehouse.com

open-faced asian chicken sandwich

Thai condiments and vibrant fresh mint and coriander take this open-faced feast to another level. Sitting atop whole grain bread, the mixture of spicy and sweet makes this an extraordinary chicken sandwich.

Dressing

1/4 cup	lime juice	50 mL
1 tbsp	low-sodium soy sauce	15 mL
1 tbsp	sugar	15 mL
1 1/2 tsp	red pepper flakes	7 mL
3 tbsp	canola oil	50 mL
1/2 tsp	toasted sesame oil (optional)	2 mL

Sandwich

2 cups	shredded cooked chicken breast	500 mL
1 cup	shredded carrots	250 mL
1/2 cup	bean sprouts	125 mL
1/4 cup	sliced radishes	50 mL
1/4 cup	sliced chopped green onions	50 mL
2 tbsp	each chopped fresh mint and coriander	25 mL
4	slices whole grain bread	4
2 tbsp	chopped roasted peanuts	25 mL

1. In measuring cup, whisk together lime juice, soy sauce, sugar, red pepper flakes, canola oil, and sesame oil (if using). Set aside.
2. In bowl, combine chicken, carrot, bean sprouts, radish, green onion, mint, and coriander. Pour dressing overtop and gently stir to combine (this can be made up to a day ahead).
3. Arrange bread slices on four plates. Divide chicken mixture evenly between bread slices. Top with peanuts. Serve immediately.

kitchen tip
To retain the freshness and crunchiness of radishes, store them in water in the fridge.

health tip

Radishes are members of the cruciferous family (cabbage, kale, broccoli, and brussels sprouts) that are rich in vitamin C, potassium, and folic acid. Vitamin C in raw radishes is significantly higher than in cooked radishes.

🥕🥕🥕 Super skinny!

makes: 4 servings
preparation time: 10 min
total time: 10 min

per serving: calories 353, protein 28 g, total fat 17 g, saturated fat 2 g, carbohydrates 21 g, fibre 3.5 g, sodium 318 mg, cholesterol 59 mg

Source: www.stonemillbakehouse.com

skinny tuna on sprouted grain bread

Flavoured with fennel and lemon juice and garnished with pea sprouts and fresh cucumber, this savoury sandwich is proof that dieting doesn't have to result in tasteless food and no carbohydrates.

1	can (4 oz/113 g) white tuna, packed in water, drained	1
1/4 cup	finely diced fennel bulb	50 mL
1 tbsp	freshly squeezed lemon juice	15 mL
2 tsp	minced fennel fronds	10 mL
1 tsp	lemon zest	5 mL
1/4 tsp	each, salt and pepper	1 mL
6	thin cucumber slices	6
2	slices sprouted grain bread*	2
1/4 cup	pea or radish sprouts	50 mL

* See Product Resource Guide for recommendations.

1. In a medium-sized bowl, combine tuna, fennel bulb, lemon juice, fennel fronds, lemon zest, salt, and pepper.
2. Using a fork, stir to combine, breaking up any large chunks of tuna.
3. Arrange cucumber slices on a slice of bread. Spread half the tuna mixture over the cucumber and save the other half in an airtight container for another sandwich (will keep in the refrigerator for up to 3 days).
4. Top with sprouts and cover with the remaining slice of bread.

kitchen tip

Lemon zest refers to the yellow part on the outside of the peel. It has a very intense lemon flavour and adds wonderful taste to a variety of dishes. To make lemon zest, remove the yellow outer skin of the lemon with a grater. Try to avoid removing too much of the skin, as the pith (the white underpart of the yellow skin) has a bitter taste that won't complement your dishes. Lemon zest is best when grated and used immediately. One lemon yields approximately 1 tbsp (15 mL) of zest.

health tip

Fennel is a vegetable with a white or pale green bulb and green feathery stalks and leaves, which grow to produce the fennel seeds. Fennel is beneficial for a range of digestive complaints. Fennel leaves offer an excellent source of iron and a very high source of calcium. Fennel fronds are the tender, wispy green fronds that can be chopped finely and used in dishes.

🍓🍓🍓 Super skinny!

makes: 1 serving (1 sandwich)
preparation time: 5 min
total time: 5 min

per serving: calories 240, protein 29 g, total fat 3 g, saturated fat 0.3 g, carbohydrates 26 g, fibre 4 g, sodium 540 mg, cholesterol 25 mg

Source: www.stonemillbakehouse.com

smoked salmon on sprouted grain bagel with japanese mayo

This spicier variation of bagels and lox is a dieter's dream. Prepped in less than 5 minutes, this elegant-looking sandwich makes a great brunch or luncheon item, and you don't have to worry about counting calories.

1	prebiotic bagel*	1
3/4 tsp	non-fat mayonnaise	4 mL
1/4 tsp	wasabi paste	1 mL
4	slices of wild smoked salmon	4
6	slices of cucumber	6
2	thin slices of red onion rounds	2
1 tbsp	capers	15 mL
	Pepper to taste	

* See Product Resource Guide for recommendations.

1. Slice bagel in half.
2. In a small bowl, combine mayonnaise and wasabi paste; mix well, then spread on one-half of the bagel.
3. Layer the smoked salmon, cucumber, onion, and capers on top of the mayonnaise and season with pepper.
4. Close sandwich with the other bagel half.
5. Slice and serve.

kitchen tip
Wasabi paste can be found in the fresh sushi section at most supermarkets.

health tip
Prebiotics are indigestible carbohydrates such as inulin fibre that promote and stimulate the growth of beneficial bacteria in the intestinal flora. Prebiotics are also

heat resistant, which enables them to stay intact during the baking process. Additional benefits include:

- inhibiting the growth of harmful bacteria
- boosting immune system function
- rebalancing intestinal micro-flora after a round of antibiotics
- producing of digestive enzymes

🍓🍓 Enjoy once a week!

makes: 1 serving (1 sandwich)
preparation time: 5 min
total time: 5 min

per serving: calories 297, protein 22 g, total fat 6.5 g, saturated fat 1 g, carbohydrates 41 g, fibre 7 g, sodium 1175 mg, cholesterol 19 mg

Source: www.stonemillbakehouse.com

entrees

dill-crusted wild salmon fillets

This salmon dish is so crispy and decadent, it's hard to believe it's good for you. Made with whole grain bread crumbs, wild salmon, and omega-3 eggs, it offers the nutritional benefits of essential fats, lean protein, and fibre.

2	wild salmon fillets (5 oz/142 g)	2
1	omega-3 egg	1
1 tsp	freshly squeezed lemon juice	15 mL
1/2 cup	whole grain bread crumbs	125 mL
2 tbsp	finely chopped fresh dill	25 mL
1 tsp	butter	5 mL

1. Unwrap salmon fillets, draining off excess liquid.
2. Crack egg into wide serving bowl, add lemon juice, and beat until fully blended.
3. In another bowl, combine whole grain bread crumbs and dill.
4. Dip salmon fillets in egg mixture, then roll in bread crumb mix. Expect to discard half of the egg and bread crumb mixtures. The extra is needed to ensure that the fillets are fully coated.
5. Heat nonstick skillet on medium-high heat, and melt butter.
6. Sear fillets on one side for 3 minutes. Turn and cook on other side for 5 minutes.

kitchen tip

When preparing, first dip the fillets into the egg mixture and then into the bread crumbs. In order to avoid a mess, use your right hand to dip each fillet into the egg mixture and then set it on the bread crumbs. With the opposite hand, cover the fillet with bread crumbs and roll until fully coated. Again, with the hand used for the bread crumb coating, remove the fillet from the bread crumbs and place in the pre-heated pan. Repeat the process until all fillets are breaded.

health tip

Wild salmon offers an excellent nutrient profile: it's high in protein and rich in nutrients, such as vitamins D, B6, and B12. Salmon is also an excellent source of omega-3 essential fats, which have been shown to reduce inflammation, improve brain function, decrease cholesterol levels, and help alleviate and heal bowel diseases such as Crohn's disease and colitis. Salmon also contains far less saturated fat than other protein sources, such as chicken and red meat. Poached, baked, or barbecued, wild salmon is a wonderful addition to the diet.

When eating salmon, choose wild sources rather than farmed. Wild salmon is a "cleaner" fish and can be consumed without concern of eating excess contaminants such as mercury or PCBs (polychlorinated biphenyls are chemicals that have been banned in the United States since 1979, but they persist in the environment and end up in animal fat).

🍓🍓🍓 Super skinny!

makes: 2 servings
preparation time: 10 min
cooking time: 10 min
total time: 20 min

per serving: calories 331, protein 34 g, total fat 11.5 g, saturated fat 1.5 g, carbohydrates 19.5 g, fibre 1 g, sodium 308 mg, cholesterol 104 mg

california walnut-stuffed salmon

This entree packs a "mega punch," with California walnuts and salmon both being rich in omega-3 fatty acids. The addition of brown rice and spinach rounds out the nutritional balance and boasts delectable flavour.

2 tsp	olive oil	10 mL
1/4 cup	minced onion	50 mL
4 cups	chopped spinach	1 L
1	clove garlic, minced	1
1/2 tsp	each, salt and pepper	2 mL
1 cup	cooked brown rice	250 mL
2 tsp	lemon zest	10 mL
1 lb	salmon fillet, skinned and pin bones removed	500 g
1/4 cup	shredded old Cheddar cheese	50 mL
1/2 cup	chopped walnuts	125 mL

1. In large nonstick skillet, heat oil over medium heat. Add onions; cook until tender but not browned, about 5 minutes. Stir in spinach, garlic, salt, and pepper.
2. Cook just until spinach starts to wilt, about 3 minutes. Remove from heat.
3. Add cooked rice to spinach and stir in lemon zest until well combined.
4. Spread spinach mixture evenly over salmon; sprinkle with cheese and walnuts.
5. Roll up gently using toothpicks or butcher's twine to secure.
6. Place salmon on a parchment-lined rimmed baking sheet and bake in 375ºF (190ºC) oven until fish is cooked through, about 15 to 20 minutes.
7. Transfer to cutting board and let rest 10 minutes before slicing.
8. Serve with steamed seasonal vegetables or green salad.

kitchen tip
Shelled walnuts should be kept in an odour-free environment, away from excessive heat, moisture, light, and air, to ensure maximum shelf life.

health tip

California has the perfect conditions for growing walnuts. The result? Walnuts that are sweet, plump, large, and tan in colour. Chop these tasty walnuts up and sprinkle over salads, muffins, or chicken or fish for a boost of omega-3 essential fat.

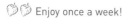 Enjoy once a week!

makes: 4 servings
preparation time: 10 min
cooking time: 30 min
total time: 40 min

per serving: calories 378, protein 24 g, total fat 24 g, saturated fat 5 g, carbohydrates 17 g, fibre 4 g, sodium 419 mg, cholesterol 57 mg

Source: www.walnutinfo.com

blackened tilapia on greens

Tilapia is a lean white fish with a mild taste, making it adaptable to a variety of recipes. While tilapia is low in calories and fat, it's also a protein powerhouse, containing 21 g of protein per 3.5 oz! Easy to make, low in calories, and rich in dark leafy greens, this delicious recipe is perfect for weight loss or weight maintenance.

2	tilapia fillets (5 oz/142 g)	2
2 tsp	blackening spice	10 mL
1 lb	asparagus	500 g
1 tsp	butter	5 mL
1 cup	diced onion	250 mL
6 cups	fresh spinach	1.5 L

1. Generously coat tilapia fillets in blackening spice.
2. Thoroughly wash asparagus and break off woody bottom portion of each stalk.
3. Melt butter in nonstick pan and cook onion over high heat for 3 to 4 minutes.
4. In large heavy-bottom pot, boil 2 to 3 inches (5 to 8 cm) of water. Place asparagus evenly across the bottom. Cover and cook over high heat for 3 minutes.
5. Add spinach to pot and continue cooking, covered, for 3 minutes.
6. Push cooked onions off to one side of the pan. Over high heat, sear tilapia fillets for 1 minute on each side.
7. Cover pan with lid and reduce heat to medium.
8. Cook on each side for 3 minutes.
9. Pour 1/3 cup (75 mL) water into pan, replace the lid, and increase heat to high for 2 minutes. (This will force steam into the tilapia, making it moist.)
10. Arrange asparagus, topped with spinach, evenly in the centre of each plate. Top with the tilapia fillets, and spoon sautéed onions evenly over the fillets.
11. Serve.

Note: To make your own blackening spice, see page 329 for the Cajun blackened chicken breast recipe. If you are on a salt-restricted diet, please reduce the blackening spice by half.

kitchen tip

For serving and measuring purposes, 1 pound (500 g) fresh spinach leaves will cook down to about 1 cup (250 mL) cooked spinach. For a side dish of cooked spinach, figure 8 oz (225 g) raw spinach per serving. Spinach should be washed thoroughly, as it can be very gritty because of the sandy soil it grows in. The quickest and easiest method to wash loose spinach is to cut off the stems, put it into a large container of cold water, let the dirt soak to the bottom, and remove. Dry by using a salad spinner or patting down with paper towel.

health tip

Spinach is a leafy green considered a superfood because of its high concentration of nutrients. To name just a few, spinach is an excellent source of vitamins K, A, C, calcium, and iron. The more spinach you can add to your daily diet, the more likely you'll benefit from its anti-aging effects and enjoy optimal health.

🍎🍎🍎 Super skinny!

makes: 2 servings
preparation time: 10 min
cooking time: 20 min
total time: 30 min

per serving: calories 272, protein 36 g, total fat 5 g, saturated fat 2 g, carbohydrates 26 g, fibre 10 g, sodium 600 mg, cholesterol 76 mg

sautéed chicken in a creamy mushroom sauce

Looking for a high-protein dish that will fill you up for the night? Try this easy-to-make chicken recipe that boasts a rich and buttery flavour the entire family will rave about.

1	boneless, skinless chicken breast (5 oz/142 g)	1
2	boneless, skinless chicken thighs (3 oz/85 g each)	2
1 tsp	poultry seasoning	5 mL
1/4 tsp	black pepper	1 mL
1 tsp	olive oil	5 mL
2 tsp	butter	10 mL
1 cup	sliced mushrooms	250 mL
2 tsp	flour	10 mL
1/2 cup	1% milk	125 mL

1. Cut chicken breast in half. Sprinkle chicken breast and thighs with poultry seasoning and pepper.
2. Heat olive oil in nonstick skillet on medium-high.
3. Add chicken, cover, and cook for 15 minutes, turning occasionally. Check chicken with a knife to ensure it is fully cooked.
4. Melt 1 tsp (5 mL) of the butter in nonstick skillet and sauté mushrooms for 4 minutes over medium-high heat.
5. In another nonstick skillet, melt remaining 1 tsp (5 mL) butter. Once it begins to bubble, whisk in flour until cooked. (Don't allow it to brown.)
6. Slowly pour the milk into the flour/butter mixture, whisking constantly.
7. Add sautéed mushrooms and cooked chicken; cover.
8. Simmer for 10 minutes and serve.

🍓🍓 Enjoy once a week!

makes: 2 servings
preparation time: 15 min
cooking time: 30 min
total time: 45 min

per serving: calories 307, protein 30 g, total fat 17 g, saturated fat 6 g, carbohydrates 14 g, fibre 1 g, sodium 640 mg, cholesterol 113 mg

orange and ginger chicken scallops

Tangy and sweet, this high-protein recipe is the ideal meal for dinner (and leftovers the next day).

2	boneless, skinless chicken breasts (5 oz/142 g)	2
1/4 tsp	sage	1 mL
Pinch	salt and pepper	Pinch
1 tsp	olive oil	5 mL
1/2 cup	orange juice	125 mL
1/2 cup	low-sodium chicken broth	125 mL
1 tsp	brown sugar	5mL
2 tsp	minced ginger	10 mL
1 tbsp	butter	15 mL
1 tbsp	flour	15 mL

1. Slice chicken breasts horizontally into 1-inch (2.5 cm) slices.
2. With a meat tenderizer, pound the slices on a cutting board to 1/2-inch (1 cm) thickness.
3. Season chicken scallops with sage, salt, and pepper.
4. Place oil in nonstick pan, cover, and sear the chicken scallops on both sides (about 4 minutes each side).
5. Remove chicken from pan when cooked.
6. In a medium-sized mixing bowl, combine orange juice, chicken broth, brown sugar, and ginger; mix thoroughly.
7. In the nonstick pan, melt butter until bubbling.
8. Whisk in flour until fully blended.
9. Slowly pour in orange juice mixture, whisking until thickened.
10. Return chicken to pan.
11. Simmer, covered, for 15 minutes.
12. Serve over brown rice or quinoa.

kitchen tip
Fresh sage is always best for flavour; however, this recipe can incorporate dried or fresh sage.

health tip

Sage, a member of the mint family, has long been used for its health properties, which include reducing hot flashes and inflammation of the gums and improving cognitive function.

🍓🍓🍓 Super skinny!

makes: 2 servings
preparation time: 15 min
cooking time: 25 min
total time: 40 min

per serving: calories 293, protein 34 g, total fat 10 g, saturated fat 4.5 g, carbohydrates 13 g, fibre 0.5 g, sodium 249 mg, cholesterol 99 mg

chicken breast stuffed with asparagus

High in protein and low in fat, this mouth-watering chicken dish is lightly coated with whole bread crumbs, making it both deliciously creamy and satisfyingly crunchy.

2	butterflied boneless, skinless chicken breasts (4 oz/113 g)	2
1/2 tsp	poultry seasoning	2 mL
1/2 tsp	minced garlic	2 mL
Pinch	black pepper	Pinch
6	asparagus spears	6
1 oz	goat cheese	25 g
1	large egg	1
2	egg whites	2
1/2 cup	whole grain bread crumbs	125 mL

Note: You'll need 4 wooden toothpicks for this recipe.

1. Lay each chicken breast on a cutting board. With a very sharp knife, slice it horizontally three-quarters of the way through.
2. Rub with poultry seasoning, garlic, and pepper.
3. Wash asparagus and remove woody ends.
4. Divide the goat cheese into two and spread over the inside of the chicken breasts.
5. Lay 3 asparagus spears inside each chicken breast.
6. Close breast and secure with toothpicks.
7. In a small bowl, beat egg with egg whites.
8. Place bread crumbs in separate mixing bowl.
9. Dip each breast first in egg mixture and then gently roll in bread crumbs.
10. Place in nonstick baking pan and cover top of pan with foil. (To ensure they turn out moist, place 3 tbsp/50 mL of water in bottom of baking pan.)
11. Cook at 400°F (200°C) for 50 minutes.
12. Uncover for last 10 minutes to allow chicken to brown.
13. Serve.

kitchen tip

To butterfly your chicken breast, lay the breast on a cutting board, take a chef's knife, and cut down the centre of the breast. Put your hand on top of the chicken breast to hold it still and run knife horizontally through the breast. Be sure not to cut the chicken breast all the way through so that it holds together properly.

health tip

A daily dose of garlic in the wintertime (whether in your meals or in pill form) will help to ward off infections, coughs, and colds. If purchasing garlic pills from the health food store, ensure they are odourless.

🍓🍓🍓 Super skinny!

makes: 2 servings
preparation time: 15 min
cooking time: 50 min
total time: 1 hr 5 min

per serving: calories 286, protein 38 g, total fat 7.5 g, saturated fat 3 g, carbohydrates 13 g, fibre 1.5 g, sodium 312 mg, cholesterol 180 mg

hearty turkey chili

This delicious and filling chili recipe is perfect to prepare in advance and have ready for cool evenings in the fall or winter. If you're not a spice fan, remove or reduce the amount of chili powder.

1 cup	diced onion	250 mL
1	can (12 oz/340 g) turkey	1
6 cups	diced tomatoes	1.5 L
1 cup	sliced carrots	250 mL
1/2 cup	diced celery	125 mL
1/2 cup	diced red pepper	125 mL
1	can (14 oz/398 mL) low-sodium tomato sauce	1
1	can (5.5 oz/156 mL) low-sodium tomato paste	1
1	can (19 oz/540 mL) red kidney beans	1
1	can (19 oz/540 mL) black beans	1
1 tbsp	chili powder	15 mL
1 tbsp	sugar	15 mL
2 tsp	minced garlic	10 mL
1 tsp	salt	5 mL
1 tsp	oregano	5 mL
1 tsp	basil	5 mL

1. In a nonstick pan, sauté onion for 3 minutes. Add turkey and continue cooking on high until turkey is no longer pink (about 5 minutes).
2. In a 6-quart (5.7 L) pot, combine onion, turkey, tomatoes, carrots, celery, red pepper, tomato sauce, tomato paste, rinsed kidney beans and black beans, chili powder, sugar, garlic, salt, oregano, and basil.
3. Bring to a boil, then reduce heat to medium simmer.
4. Simmer for 40 minutes, stirring often.

kitchen tip

Chili is an incredibly versatile dish that can be great as an entree, served overtop a crisp bed of lettuce; as a healthy sloppy joe on whole grain toast; or over whole grain pasta topped with shredded cheese.

health tip

Research published in the *Journal of Agriculture and Food Chemistry* indicates that red kidney beans are extremely rich in disease-fighting antioxidant compounds. The top 10 antioxidant foods (from most to least) are:

1. small red beans (dried)
2. blueberries (wild)
3. red kidney beans
4. pinto beans
5. blueberries (cultivated)
6. cranberries
7. artichokes (cooked)
8. blackberries
9. prunes
10. raspberries

🍓🍓🍓 Super skinny!

makes: 6 servings
preparation time: 15 min
cooking time: 50 min
total time: 65 min

per serving: calories 277, protein 22 g, total fat 1.5 g, saturated fat 0 g, carbohydrates 42 g, fibre 17 g, sodium 582 mg, cholesterol 0 mg

cajun blackened chicken breast

Add a little New Orleans flair to your food with this versatile blackening spice—a zesty seasoning for roasts, stews, and pan-blackened chicken or fish.

Blackening spice

1 tbsp	paprika	15 mL
1 tsp	salt	5 mL
1 tsp	garlic powder	5 mL
1 tsp	onion powder	5 mL
1/4 tsp	cayenne pepper	1 mL
2 tsp	black pepper	10 mL
1/2 tsp	thyme	2 mL
1/2 tsp	oregano	2 mL
1 tsp	white pepper	5 mL

Note: The blackening spice increases the sodium content of this recipe. For those on a salt-restricted diet, reduce the blackening spice by half.

Blackened chicken breast

2	boneless, skinless chicken breasts (5 oz/142 g)	2
1 tsp	butter	5 mL

1. Mix ingredients for blackening spice thoroughly and place in a shaker.
2. With a sharp French knife, fillet each breast in half.
3. In nonstick pan, heat butter on high.
4. Liberally coat each piece of chicken with blackening spice.
5. With pan very hot, sear each side for 2 minutes.
6. Cover and reduce heat to medium. Cook for 5 minutes.
7. Serve with salad or vegetable side dish.

kitchen tip

When preparing any meat, chicken, or fish, make sure the dish doesn't dry out by adding 2 to 3 tbsp (25 to 50 mL) of water into the hot pan and covering it immediately.

The water will steam quickly, forcing the steam into the meat and creating a juicy texture.

health tip
When purchasing chicken breasts, find a local organic farmer or butcher and buy in large quantities to freeze. Certified organic meat and poultry means no pesticides or chemical fertilizers were permitted *on* the animals' feed, no antibiotics or genetically modified organisms (GMOs) were permitted *in* the feed, and the crops that they fed on weren't sprayed for a minimum of three years.

🍓🍓🍓 Super skinny!

makes: 2 servings
preparation time: 10 min
cooking time: 10 min
total time: 20 min

per serving (1 chicken breast): calories 185, protein 30 g, total fat 6 g, saturated fat 2 g, carbohydrates 6 g, fibre 2.5 g, sodium 1401 mg, cholesterol 86 mg

creamy lasagna

Filled with healthy fats, whole grain carbohydrate, and lean proteins, this recipe represents the true concept of *Healthy Sin Foods*: it fully delivers on taste while offering the nutritional benefits of a balanced meal. Healthy eating never came with such little guilt!

3 cups	cauliflower florets	750 mL
1 cup	diced onion	250 mL
2 cups	diced crimini mushrooms	500 mL
1 tbsp	olive oil	15 mL
3 cups	diced fresh tomatoes	750 mL
1	can (10 oz/284 mL) low-sodium tomato sauce	1
1	can (5.5 oz/156 mL) tomato paste	1
2 tbsp	dry oregano	25 mL
2 tbsp	dry basil	25 mL
1 tbsp	sugar	15 mL
1/2 tsp	cayenne pepper	2 mL
1 cup	1% cottage cheese	250 mL
4 tbsp	egg whites	60 mL
2 tbsp	light cream cheese	25 mL
3	large Portobello mushrooms	3
1 tsp	butter	5 mL
5 1/2	sheets whole grain lasagna noodles	5 1/2
1/2 cup	shredded light mozzarella cheese	125 mL

1. Steam cauliflower for 15 minutes.
2. Sauté onions and mushrooms in olive oil for 3 minutes until tender.
3. In separate pot, bring 6 cups (1.5 L) of water to a boil and place fresh tomatoes in for 2 to 3 minutes until skins are loosened.
4. Remove tomatoes and cover with cold water for 5 minutes.
5. Remove skins and dice tomatoes.

6. In a large pot, combine diced tomatoes, onions, mushrooms, tomato sauce, tomato paste, oregano, basil, sugar, and cayenne pepper. Stir and cook over medium heat for 10 minutes.
7. Roughly chop cauliflower and combine with cottage cheese, egg whites, and cream cheese. Mix thoroughly.
8. Slice Portobello mushrooms 1-inch (2.5 cm) thick. Sauté mushrooms in butter over high heat until both sides are browned.
9. Lightly oil 9- x 11-inch (23 x 27 cm) glass baking pan.
10. Spread 1/2 cup (125 mL) tomato sauce mixture onto bottom of pan.
11. Layer with 2 whole grain pasta sheets. Cut to fit pan size.
12. Spread 1 1/2 cups (375 mL) tomato sauce mixture over top of pasta noodles.
13. Spread half of the cauliflower/cheese mixture overtop of tomato sauce.
14. Distribute half of cooked Portobello mushrooms on top of cauliflower/cheese mixture.
15. Top with next layer of lasagna noodles and repeat the process of steps 12 to 15.
16. Top this layer with another 2 sheets of lasagna noodles.
17. Spread remaining 1/2 cup (125 mL) tomato sauce and top with shredded mozzarella cheese.
18. Cover with foil and bake at 375°F (190°C) for 1 hour.
19. Remove foil and continue to cook for 10 more minutes.
20. Remove from oven and allow to cool for 10 minutes prior to serving.
21. Cut into 6 sections and serve.

Note: This recipe uses fresh lasagna sheets. If using dry noodles, cook in boiling water for 8 to 10 minutes prior to use.

kitchen tip

Add some extra taste to your lasagna by sprinkling some cinnamon into the cream cheese/cottage cheese mixture. It's an old Italian trick that provides great flavour!

health tip

If a sculpted body and a flat tummy is what you are looking for, then including cottage cheese in your diet is a great nutritional choice! Cottage cheese is a low-carbohydrate food that is high in protein and rich in calcium and iron. A typical 1/2 cup (125 mL) of cottage cheese has:

- 80 calories
- 1 g of fat
- 0.5 g of saturated fat
- 10 mg of cholesterol
- 380 mg of sodium
- 130 mg of potassium
- 7 g of carbs
- 3 g of sugar
- 12 g of protein

One downside to cottage cheese is that it can be high in sodium (e.g., 1/2 cup/125 mL can contain up to 16% of your daily recommended intake of sodium). Choose low-sodium options.

Enjoy once a week!

makes: 6 servings
preparation time: 20 min
cooking time: 1 hr 10 min
total time: 1 hr 40 min

per serving: calories 312, protein 20 g, total fat 8 g, saturated fat 3.5 g, carbohydrates 42 g, fibre 8.5 g, sodium 603 mg, cholesterol 17 mg

portobello mushroom stir-fry

You'll savour this low-fat but tasty recipe made with meaty Portobello mushrooms. Quick and easy to make, this is a light dinner option for any day of the week.

4	large Portobello mushrooms	4
1 tsp	olive oil	5 mL
1 tsp	minced garlic	5 mL
1 cup	finely chopped onion	250 mL
1 cup	finely chopped green onion tops	250 mL
1	large red pepper, sliced into thin strips	1
1 cup	low-sodium chicken broth	250 mL
1 tbsp	low-sodium soy sauce	15 mL
1 tbsp	hoisin sauce	15 mL
1 tsp	sesame oil	5 mL
1 cup	bean sprouts	250 mL
1 tbsp	cornstarch	15 mL

1. Remove stems from Portobello mushrooms and cut into 1/2-inch (1 cm) slices.
2. Heat olive oil in nonstick skillet over high heat.
3. Add garlic and mushroom slices.
4. Sauté for 2 minutes, turning mushroom slices once. Remove from skillet.
5. Add onion, green onion, and red pepper to skillet and cook over high heat for 4 minutes, stirring often.
6. For the sauce, combine chicken broth, soy sauce, hoisin sauce, and sesame oil in a bowl; whisk together.
7. Return mushroom to pan and pour in sauce.
8. Cook for 5 minutes.
9. Add bean sprouts, cover, and cook for 2 minutes.
10. Whisk cornstarch with 4 oz water in small bowl.
11. With stir-fry mixture at a boil, add cornstarch/water mixture. Stir until thickened.
12. Serve.

kitchen tip

Olive oil is ideal for cooking as it has the highest oxidation threshold. In other words, it remains stable at higher temperatures and does not easily become hydrogenated or saturated.

health tip

Keep in mind that the fat found in olive oil is monounsaturated, making it a "good" type of fat. In addition to containing a rich supply of disease-fighting antioxidants, monounsaturated fat is beneficial for weight loss and lowering cholesterol and the risk of heart disease.

🍓🍓🍓 Super skinny!

makes: 2 servings
preparation time: 15 min
cooking time: 15 min
total time: 30 min

per serving: calories 286, protein 12 g, total fat 12 g, saturated fat 2 g, carbohydrates 34 g, fibre 7.5 g, sodium 421 mg, cholesterol 3 mg

hearty cabbage rolls

Cabbage is one of the healthiest vegetables around and yet not commonly eaten by North Americans. After you try these delicious tomato and rice cabbage rolls, you'll be a cabbage lover too. This hearty and healthy entree—a savoury meal on a cold winter day—will not disappoint.

1	medium green cabbage	1
1 cup	wild rice	250 mL
1 cup	brown rice	250 mL
1 tsp	butter	5 mL
1 cup	diced white onion	250 mL
1 cup	sliced crimini mushrooms	250 mL
1/2 cup	diced red pepper	125 mL
12 oz	extra firm tofu	340 g
1 cup	finely chopped green onion tops	250 mL
1 tbsp	fresh basil	15 mL
1 1/2 tsp	minced garlic	7 mL
1/2 tsp	salt	2 mL
1 tsp	black pepper	5 mL
2	large omega-3 eggs	2
1	can (28 oz/796 mL) diced tomatoes	1
1	can (14 oz/398 mL) low-sodium tomato sauce	1
1	can (5 1/2 oz/156 mL) tomato paste	1

1. With a sharp knife, remove the core of the cabbage.
2. In a pot large enough to submerge the cabbage in water, bring water to a boil.
3. Place cabbage in the boiling water and with metal tongs, begin to remove layers of cabbage leaves as they begin to cook and soften (it should take about 2 minutes per layer). This recipe will yield 12 to 16 cabbage rolls, depending on the size of the leaves.
4. Once leaves are removed, place them in a separate bowl of cold water.
5. Cook wild rice and brown rice according to package directions. Allow to cool and combine. (Generally, 1 cup (250 mL) of rice will produce about 2 cups (500 mL) cooked.)

6. Melt butter in nonstick pan and sauté onion, mushrooms, and red pepper for 2 to 3 minutes.
7. Cut tofu into 1/4-inch (5 mm) cubes.
8. In a large mixing bowl, combine cooked rice, onion, mushrooms, red pepper, tofu, green onion, basil, garlic, salt, and pepper; mix thoroughly.
9. Crack eggs into a separate bowl and beat until fully mixed.
10. Pour egg mixture over rice mixture and stir well.
11. For each cabbage roll, portion 1/3 cup (75 mL) of the mixture onto the centre of each leaf. Roll up the cabbage leaf to wrap the filling.
12. Lightly oil a 10- x 13-inch (25 x 33 cm) baking dish and arrange the cabbage rolls with the seam side down.
13. In a mixing bowl, combine diced tomatoes, tomato sauce, and tomato paste; mix thoroughly.
14. Spoon mixture over top of cabbage rolls.
15. Cover with foil and bake at 375°F (190°C) for 45 minutes.
16. Allow to cool for a few minutes prior to serving.

Note: These hearty cabbage rolls are filling. One along with a side salad is usually enough to keep you satiated.

health tip
Cabbage contains high levels of vitamins A, C, E, B, and glutamine. It's also a terrific option for weight-loss seekers, as 1 cup (250 mL) of cabbage contains only 15 calories!

🍠🍠🍠 Super skinny! (with proper portion size in mind)

makes: 12 to 16 cabbage rolls
preparation time: 20 min
cooking time: 1 1/2 hours
total time: 1 hr 50 min

per serving (1 roll): calories 225, protein 10 g, total fat 3 g, saturated fat 0.5 g, carbohydrates 38 g, fibre 6 g, sodium 299 mg, cholesterol 36 mg

whole grain pad thai

Many people avoid making pad Thai because they think it's too difficult. After following this simple recipe, you'll be pleasantly surprised to find out that one of the most enjoyed Thai dishes is remarkably easy to make. Instead of using rice noodles, enjoy this healthier version of pad Thai by adding whole grain noodles.

8 oz	whole grain fettuccine noodles	240 mL
2	boneless, skinless chicken breasts (5 oz/142 g)	2
2 tbsp	olive oil	25 mL
1/2 cup	diced onion	125 mL
1/2 cup	thinly sliced red pepper	125 mL
1/3 cup	sweet Thai chili sauce	75 mL
1/4 cup	fish sauce	50 mL
3 tbsp	lime juice	50 mL
1 tbsp	cane sugar	15 mL
1	omega-3 egg	1
1/2 cup	finely chopped green onion tops	125 mL
4 tbsp	crushed peanuts	60 mL
1 cup	bean sprouts	250 mL

Note: If you are on a salt-restricted diet, please reduce the fish sauce by half.

1. Undercook fettuccine noodles by 2 to 3 minutes. Drain and wash in cold water in strainer; set aside.
2. Cut chicken into 1/2-inch (1 cm) cubes.
3. Heat 1 tbsp (15 mL) of the olive oil in a nonstick pan. Add chicken, onion, and red pepper; sauté over medium heat until chicken is thoroughly cooked.
4. In medium-sized bowl, combine chili sauce, fish sauce, lime juice, and sugar; mix thoroughly.
5. In small bowl, thoroughly beat egg.
6. Heat remaining 1 tbsp (15 mL) olive oil in a nonstick pan.
7. Empty cooked noodles into pan.

8. Pour fish sauce mixture over noodles and cook over medium-high heat until heated through.
9. Stir in egg, green onion, crushed peanuts, and bean sprouts.
10. Mix thoroughly and cook until heated. (Don't overcook or bean sprouts will lose their consistency.)
11. Serve.

kitchen tip

When cooking pasta, add 1 tsp (5 mL) of salt to reduce stickiness. Use about 2 quarts (2 L) of water for 2 cups (500 mL) of pasta. Ideally, whole grain pasta is served immediately, as it can dry out more quickly than regular pastas. Mixing it with some extra virgin olive oil will keep it fresh and tasty.

health tip

Whole grains contain all three parts of the original grain: the bran, the germ, and the endosperm. Whole grains are a rich source of fibre and are mostly low in fat. A diet rich in whole grains offers numerous health benefits and may reduce your risk of heart disease.

Save for an occasional treat!

makes: 4 servings
preparation time: 20 min
cooking time: 25 min
total time: 45 min

per serving: calories 505, protein 37 g, total fat 17 g, saturated fat 3 g, carbohydrates 54 g, fibre 7 g, sodium 1483 mg, cholesterol 116 mg

crustless mushroom and broccoli quiche

This easy-to-make crustless quiche offers a protein boost that will help you lose weight and rebuild muscle. And it makes for satisfying next-day leftovers.

6	large omega-3 eggs	6
6	egg whites	6
1/2 cup	1% milk	125 mL
1 tsp	butter	5 mL
1 cup	diced onion	250 mL
1 cup	diced red pepper	250 mL
1 cup	sliced mushrooms	250 mL
1 cup	broccoli florets	250 mL
2 tsp	minced garlic	10 mL
1/2 tsp	salt	2 mL
1/4 tsp	black pepper	1 mL
1 cup	chopped green onion tops	250 mL

1. Break eggs into medium-sized bowl; combine with egg whites and milk; mix thoroughly.
2. Melt butter in nonstick pan and sauté onion, red pepper, mushrooms, broccoli, garlic, salt, and pepper for 5 minutes. Turn off heat and sprinkle in green onion tops. Keep them raw.
3. Pour egg mixture into lightly greased 7- x 12-inch (18 x 27 cm) baking dish. Pour sautéed vegetables into egg mixture and distribute evenly.
4. Bake at 375°F (190°C) for 20 minutes.
5. Allow to cool for 5 minutes prior to cutting into serving sizes.

kitchen tip
You can generally use two egg whites for every whole egg required.

health tip
Eggs have received a bad rap over the last few decades. However, recent studies indicate that it's *not* dietary cholesterol that raises cholesterol levels, but rather

saturated fat found in the diet (red meat, full-fat cheeses, and so on). The fat found primarily in the egg yolk is a polyunsaturated fat while the white is pure protein. Thus, for individuals with normal cholesterol levels, it appears that eating 2 eggs a day is indeed a healthy choice.

Note: If you're looking to drop fat levels altogether, always mix one egg with egg whites.

Super skinny!

makes: 6 servings
preparation time: 15 min
cooking time: 25 min
total time: 40 min

per serving (1 slice): calories 135, protein 12 g, total fat 5.5 g, saturated fat 2 g, carbohydrates 9 g, fibre 2 g, sodium 335 mg, cholesterol 217 mg

vegetarian sweet potato pot pie

Rich in beta-carotene and protein and big on taste, you'll love this meatless, healthier version of pot pie.

6 cups	mashed sweet potatoes	1.5 L
1 tbsp	butter	15 mL
2 cups	diced onion	500 mL
2 cups	sliced mushrooms	500 mL
3/4 lb	veggie meat	375 g
2 tsp	minced garlic	10 mL
1 tbsp	cane sugar	15 mL
2 tsp	basil	10 mL
1 1/2 tsp	oregano	7 mL
1 tsp	salt	5 mL
1 tsp	black pepper	5 mL
1/2 tsp	cayenne pepper	2 mL
2 cups	frozen peas and carrots	500 mL
1	can (14 oz/398 mL) tomato sauce	1

1. Peel sweet potatoes and dice into 2-inch (5 cm) cubes.
2. Place in steamer and steam for 20 minutes or until very tender.
3. Empty sweet potatoes into a large mixing bowl and mash with a potato masher.
4. Melt butter in large nonstick skillet. Add onion and mushrooms. Sauté on high for 5 minutes.
5. Unwrap veggie meat and break into small pieces. Add to the skillet and stir.
6. Stir in garlic, sugar, basil, oregano, salt, pepper, and cayenne pepper.
7. Empty frozen peas and carrots into boiling water and cook until tender.
8. Add to veggie meat mixture. Stir in tomato sauce.
9. Continue to heat for 3 minutes.
10. Lightly grease 15- x 10-inch (38 x 25 cm) baking pan and distribute meat/veggie mixture evenly over the bottom
11. Spoon mashed sweet potatoes evenly on top.
12. Bake at 375°F (190°C) uncovered for 40 minutes.
13. Serve.

kitchen tip

Once the potato is peeled, use a French knife to dice it into smaller portions for steaming. Dicing the potato into smaller portions will reduce the time needed to steam and provide more even cooking.

health tip

When looking to be heart smart, it's always wise to lower the amount of saturated fat you're consuming. Switching from red meat to leaner options such as lean ground turkey, chicken, or vegetarian meat is a tasty and healthy step to take. According to government guidelines, total fat intake should be between 20 and 30 percent of total calories, with 10 percent or less coming from saturated fats. According to the American Heart Association, less than 7 percent of total calories should be derived from saturated fat.

🍓🍓🍓 Super skinny!

makes: 10 servings (8 oz/225 g each)
preparation time: 25 min
cooking time: 1 hr 20 min
total time: 1 hr 45 min

per serving: calories 260, protein 10 g, total fat 3.5 g, saturated fat 0.8 g, carbohydrates 50 g, fibre 9 g, sodium 749 mg, cholesterol 3 mg

Note: If on a salt-restricted diet, omit salt from recipe and opt for low-sodium tomato sauce.

smoked salmon fettuccine

Enjoy the taste of creamy whole grain fettuccine noodles without worrying about the excess calories usually found in heavy creams and sauces.

4 oz	whole grain fettuccine noodles	113 g
1 tbsp	butter	15 mL
1 tbsp	flour	15 mL
1 cup	1% milk	250 mL
4 oz	smoked salmon	113 g
2 tbsp	grated Parmesan cheese	25 mL
2 tbsp	chopped fresh dill	25 mL
2 tbsp	capers	25 mL

1. Cook fettuccine noodles al dente (about 9 minutes).
2. To make the sauce, in nonstick skillet, melt butter. Once it begins to bubble, sprinkle in the flour and whisk until cooked. (Don't allow it to brown.)
3. Slowly pour in the milk and continue to whisk.
4. Cut smoked salmon into 1-inch (2.5 cm) pieces.
5. Once the sauce begins to thicken, add the smoked salmon, Parmesan cheese, dill, and capers; mix thoroughly.
6. Add cooked fettuccine noodles to the sauce and continue to cook until heated through.
7. Mix thoroughly.
8. Serve.

health tip
For a bad case of the hiccups, natural health practitioners recommend 1 cup of dill leaf tea to relax the spasms of your diaphragm. Mix 1 tsp (5 mL) of dill leaf with 1 cup (250 mL) of boiled water, strain out the leaves, and drink slowly.

Save for an occasional treat!

makes: 2 servings
preparation time: 15 min
cooking time: 15 min
total time: 30 min

per serving: calories 419, protein 24 g, total fat 12 g, saturated fat 6 g, carbohydrates 52 g, fibre 5 g, sodium 944 mg, cholesterol 38 mg

buttery pesto chicken with brown rice

Don't let the name of this recipe fool you. While this dish does taste buttery and creamy, the entire dish (which makes 4 servings) contains just 1 tbsp (15 mL) of butter. Loaded with lean protein and rich in fibre from the brown rice, this is a perfect wintertime dinner to fill you up in a healthy way.

3/4 cup	brown rice	175 mL
1 lb	boneless chicken breast	500 g
1/2 tsp	poultry seasoning	2 mL
1/4 tsp	salt	1 mL
1/4 tsp	black pepper	1 mL
1 tsp	olive oil	5 mL
1 1/2 cups	sliced crimini mushrooms	375 mL
1 tbsp	butter	15 mL
1 tbsp	flour	15 mL
1 cup	1% milk	250 mL
5 tbsp	pesto sauce*	75 mL

*See recipe on page 256.

1. Measure rice into pot and add 1 3/4 cups (425 mL) water. Bring to a boil and cover pot with tight-fitting lid; reduce heat to simmer. Leave lid on and cook for 45 minutes. Remove the lid and fluff the rice with a fork.
2. Cut boneless chicken breast into 1-inch (2.5 cm) cubes.
3. Season with poultry seasoning, salt, and pepper.
4. Heat oil in nonstick pan and cook chicken, covered, over medium-high heat for 7 to 8 minutes or until cooked through.
5. For the last 3 to 4 minutes of cooking the chicken, add the sliced mushrooms.
6. Remove from the pan and set aside.
7. To make sauce, in nonstick skillet, melt butter. Once it begins to bubble, sprinkle in the flour and whisk until cooked. (Don't allow it to brown.)
8. Slowly pour in the milk, whisking constantly.
9. Add the pesto sauce and continue to whisk until sauce is fully mixed and has thickened.

10. Return the chicken and mushrooms to the sauce, cover, and simmer for 10 minutes.
11. Serve over rice.

kitchen tip
To bring out even more of the flavour of the rice, mix it with a little tamari and 2 tbsp (25 mL) of sesame seeds.

health tip
The difference between long-grain rice and short-grain rice is ... the shape. Examples of short-grain rice include Japanese rice, such as sushi rice. The outer layer of short-grain rice absorbs water very easily and, as a result, once it's cooked it ends up soft and a little sticky. Long-grain rice is more slender in shape and tends to cook up firmer.

🍓🍓 Enjoy once a week!

makes: 4 servings
preparation time: 15 min
cooking time: 1 hr 10 min
total time: 1 hr 35 min

per serving: calories 402, protein 35 g, total fat 12 g, saturated fat 4 g, carbohydrates 35 g, fibre 21 g, sodium 431 mg, cholesterol 81 mg

beef tenderloin stack

For those who love to enjoy an occasional piece of red meat, this dish will definitely be a hit at your summer barbecue. Stacked with asparagus, tasty Dijon, and beef tenderloin, this elegant-looking meal will wow any guest.

3/4 lb	beef tenderloin	375 g
1 1/2 tsp	minced garlic	7 mL
1/4 tsp	salt	1 mL
1/4 tsp	black pepper	1 mL
8	aparagus spears	8
2	medium Portobello mushrooms	2
1 tsp	butter	5 mL
2 tsp	Dijon mustard	10 mL
2 tsp	horseradish	10 mL

1. Cut tenderloin into 6 slices.
2. Rub with 1/2 tsp of the garlic, salt, and pepper.
3. Pre-heat barbecue to high heat.
4. Wash asparagus and break off bottom woody section.
5. Remove stems and cut Portobello mushrooms into 3/4-inch (2 cm) slices.
6. Melt butter in nonstick pan with remaining 1 tsp (5 mL) garlic.
7. Sauté mushrooms and asparagus in butter for 5 minutes.
8. Barbecue tenderloin over high heat for 2 to 3 minutes each side (longer if you prefer well done).
9. Plate tenderloin as follows. On each plate, place one slice of tenderloin. Spread 1/2 tsp (2 mL) Dijon mustard and top with 1/2 tsp (2 mL) horseradish.
10. Top with 2 asparagus spears and mushroom slices.
11. Repeat this step until you have a stack of 3 slices of tenderloin on each plate. If desired, the top slice of tenderloin may be spread with an additional 1/2 tsp (2 mL) horseradish.
12. Serve.

kitchen tip

For a grab-and-go cooking option, always keep minced garlic and minced ginger in your fridge. Both are available pre-minced at most grocery stores.

health tip

Horseradish is a perennial plant that comes from the same family as mustard and cabbage. In addition to its distinctive taste, horseradish can be used to help clear the sinuses and for treating hay fever.

Save for an occasional treat!

makes: 2 servings
preparation time: 15 min
cooking time: 10 min
total time: 25 min

per serving: calories 446, protein 50 g, total fat 21 g, saturated fat 8 g, carbohydrates 9 g, fibre 3 g, sodium 486 mg, cholesterol 148 mg

black-eyed peas and walnut lettuce wraps

Filled with omega-3-rich walnuts, creamy butternut squash, and crunchy red peppers and peas, this tasty alternative to wraps can be used as an appetizer or entree.

2 cups	frozen black-eyed peas	500 mL
3/4 cup	water	175 mL
1	onion, chopped	1
1	red pepper, seeded and chopped	1
6 oz	butternut squash, cut in 1/2 inch (1 cm) strips	170 g
1/2 cup	chopped California walnuts	125 mL
1/4 cup	wine vinegar	50 mL
1/4 cup	chopped parsley	50 mL
	Salt and pepper to taste	
16	leaves iceberg lettuce	16

1. In a medium saucepan, combine the black-eyed peas and water. Bring to a boil over high heat, then reduce the heat to low and simmer, covered, for about 30 minutes, until the peas are tender but not mushy. Discard any liquid remaining in the pan and transfer the peas to a large bowl.
2. Coat a large nonstick skillet with cooking spray and place over medium-high heat. Add the onion, pepper, and squash; cook, stirring occasionally, for 5 minutes. Turn the heat to low, cover the pan, and continue cooking until the squash is just tender, 5 to 7 minutes. Stir in the walnuts.
3. Add the walnut mixture to the peas along with the vinegar and parsley. Stir and toss to combine, then season with salt and pepper to taste. Let cool slightly.
4. Spoon approximately 1/4 cup (50 mL) of the pea and walnut mixture into each lettuce leaf. Fold the leaves in half and eat them "taco style."

kitchen tip
To slice an onion without crying, cut out the bottom of the onion (where the root comes out). The diameter of this cone should be about one-third the diameter of the onion—about one-third deep. This part of the onion contains the gland that makes you tear up.

health tip

Looking to cut down on carbohydrates but still enjoy a wrap-style meal? Use the leaves from iceberg or butter lettuce or endive leaves. Simply fill each leaf with any filling you desire and enjoy eating them taco style.

🍓🍓🍓 Super skinny!

makes: 4 servings (4 wraps each)
preparation time: 15 min
cooking time: 45 min
total time: 1 hr

per serving: calories 262, protein 11 g, total fat 11 g, saturated fat 1 g, carbohydrates 34 g, fibre 9 g, sodium 15 mg, cholesterol 0 mg

Source: www.walnutinfo.com

healthy sloppy joe

Loaded with taste, crunchy vegetables, and "meatless" ground beef, this healthier, lower-fat version of the classic sloppy joe sandwich will fool any meat lover.

1 tsp	butter	5 mL
1/2 cup	diced white onion	125 mL
1/4 cup	diced green pepper	50 mL
1 cup	sliced crimini mushrooms	250 mL
3/4 lb	veggie meat	375 g
1	can (8 oz/227 mL) low-sodium tomato sauce	1
1	can (5.5 oz/156 mL) tomato paste	1
2 tbsp	hot sauce (optional)	25 mL
1 tbsp	brown sugar	15 mL
1 tbsp	prepared mustard	15 mL
1 tsp	minced garlic	5 mL
1/4 tsp	black pepper	1 mL
2	slices whole grain bread per serving	2

1. Melt butter in nonstick pan.
2. Sauté onion, green pepper, and mushrooms over medium-high heat for 3 minutes.
3. Break up veggie meat and add to pan.
4. Stir in tomato sauce, tomato paste, hot sauce (if using), brown sugar, mustard, garlic, and pepper; mix thoroughly.
5. Continue to stir and cook over medium-high heat for 5 minutes.
6. Serve over whole grain bread.

kitchen tip

A moderate sodium level is 140 to 400 mg per serving. Boxed and canned goods tend to be very high in sodium. When doing your next grocery shop, purchase items that are low or light in sodium, such as the tomato sauce in this recipe. "Light in sodium" means the sodium is reduced by 50 percent.

health tip

For a healthier version of ground beef, opt for vegetarian ground beef made from soy or lean ground turkey or chicken. Please see the Product Resource Guide for vegetarian ground beef recommendations.

🍓🍓 Enjoy once a week!

makes: 4 cups (1 L); 3/4 cup (175 mL) per serving
preparation time: 10 min
cooking time: 10 min
total time: 20 min

per serving (1 slice of bread, 3/4 cup/175 mL of sloppy joe mixture): calories 303, protein 20 g, total fat 7 g, saturated fat 1 g, carbohydrates 43 g, fibre 9 g, sodium 59 mg, cholesterol 2 mg

desserts

banana walnut chocolate chip spelt muffins

There's nothing more decadent than the smell of fresh baked goods in your kitchen. Although these muffins are indeed a treat, they're a much healthier version—made with whole grain spelt flour and sweetened with applesauce and ripe bananas.

1 cup	spelt flour	250 mL
1 cup	organic unbleached all-purpose flour	250 mL
1/2 cup	sugar	125 mL
1 tsp	baking powder	5 mL
2	omega-3 eggs	2
1/4 cup	applesauce	50 mL
1	ripe banana, mashed	1
3/4 cup	soy milk	175 mL
1 tsp	vanilla extract	5 mL
1/2 cup	chocolate chips	125 mL
1/4 cup	chopped walnuts	50 mL

1. Mix spelt flour, all-purpose flour, sugar, and baking powder in a large bowl.
2. In a medium-sized bowl, mix the eggs and applesauce with the mashed banana; stir in soy milk and vanilla extract.
3. Add the liquid ingredients to the dry ingredients and gently stir without overmixing.
4. Fold the chocolate chips and walnuts into the batter.
5. Lightly grease a 12-cup muffin tin and fill muffin cups three-quarters full.
6. Bake at 375°F (190°C) for 25 minutes or until top is brown.

health tip
Spelt is significantly higher in protein than wheat. One of these tasty muffins offers 5.5 g of protein!

🍓🍓 Enjoy once a week!

makes: 12 muffins
preparation time: 10 min
cooking time: 25 min
total time: 35 min

per serving: calories 189, protein 5.5 g, total fat 6 g, saturated fat 2 g, carbohydrates 31.5 g, fibre 4 g, sodium 40 mg, cholesterol 32 mg

whole grain cinnamon mandelbrot

Mandelbrot, which translates as "almond bread," is similar in taste to Italian biscotti. This classic family recipe is given a nutritional boost with the addition of whole wheat flour.

3	omega-3 eggs	3
1 cup	brown sugar	250 mL
1 cup	canola oil	250 mL
1 tsp	vanilla	5 mL
2 cups	whole wheat flour	500 mL
1 1/2 tsp	baking powder	7 mL
1 cup	dark chocolate chips	250 mL
1 cup	ground almonds	250 mL
1 tsp	cinnamon	5 mL

1. Beat eggs until bubbly.
2. Add sugar, oil, and vanilla and continue to beat.
3. Sift in whole wheat flour and baking powder a bit at a time and beat.
4. Stir in chocolate chips, almonds, and cinnamon.
5. On a buttered or oiled baking sheet, spoon mixture into 3 long, skinny rows.
6. Bake at 325°F (160°C) for 20 to 30 minutes and remove.
7. Slice and separate into pieces and put back in oven at 250°F (120°C) for 15 to 20 minutes. Brown carefully (while watching!) under broiler.

kitchen tip

Bakers are often hesitant to switch to whole grain or whole wheat flour for fear the end results will taste too dense, dry, or bitter. To avoid this (it's happened a few times in my kitchen!), follow these few steps.

- When switching a recipe from all-purpose white flour to wheat flour, start by replacing half of the regular flour with whole wheat. If the recipe works out to your liking, you can increase the ratio.

- Because whole wheat flour tends to absorb more liquid than white flour, making baked goods dry, add more liquid to the recipe. The exception is the mandelbrot, as it's supposed to have a more dense texture (like Italian biscotti).

health tip

Research has shown dark chocolate to be beneficial for heart health, in lowering cholesterol and lowering blood pressure. Dark chocolate is rich in flavonoids, a natural compound found in the cocoa bean that gives dark chocolate its bittersweet taste. When determining the right type of chocolate or chocolate chip to add to your recipes, choose ones that are 70 percent cocoa solids (e.g., milk chocolate is 30 to 40 percent).

Save for an occasional treat!

makes: 50 pieces
preparation time: 10 min
cooking time: 45 min
total time: 55 min

per serving (one piece): calories 108, protein 1.7 g, total fat 7 g, saturated fat 1 g, carbohydrates 10 g, fibre 1 g, sodium 12 mg, cholesterol 11 mg

quinoa raisin pudding

Quinoa is a high-protein grain available in most health food and grocery stores. This sweet pudding—full of plump raisins and decadent vanilla and nutmeg—is easy to make. Served warm on a fall or winter's eve, this healthy dessert will satisfy your need for comfort food.

1 cup	quinoa	250 mL
1 1/2 cups	1% milk	375 mL
1/2 cup	raisins	125 mL
4 tsp	brown sugar	20 mL
1/2 tsp	nutmeg	2 mL
1/2 tsp	vanilla	2 mL

1. Place quinoa in 1 1/2 cups (375 mL) hot water and soak for 5 minutes. Drain and rinse to remove loose outer shells.
2. Put quinoa and 1 1/2 cups (375 mL) water in saucepan and bring to a boil.
3. Cover, reduce heat, and simmer until all water is absorbed (10 to 15 minutes).
4. Fluff with a fork and allow to cool.
5. Stir in milk, raisins, brown sugar, nutmeg, and vanilla.
6. Mix thoroughly and serve.

kitchen tip
Quinoa, a versatile grain, is suitable for a range of meals, from puddings to chilies to stir-fries. With a delicious, light nutty flavour, it goes well in salads mixed with vegetables. It can take the place of rice, couscous, or noodles. Alternatively, you can serve it as a breakfast cereal with honey, chopped apples, raisins, and cinnamon.

🍓🍓🍓 Super skinny!

makes: 4 cups (1 L), 8 servings
preparation time: 15 min
cooking time: 20 min
total time: 35 min

per serving (1/2 cup/125 mL): calories 139, protein 5 g, total fat 2 g, saturated fat 0.5 g, carbohydrates 26 g, fibre 2 g, sodium 23 mg, cholesterol 2 mg

chocolate berry pudding

Looking for a decadent dessert with a little antioxidant blast? This chocolaty pudding will please every age group and will also provide fibre, antioxidants, and essential fats found in the berries and walnuts.

1/2	medium banana	1/2
1/2 cup	low-fat chocolate pudding	125 mL
1/2 cup	fresh raspberries	125 mL
1/2 cup	blueberries	125 mL
2 tbsp	roughly chopped walnuts	25 mL

1. Slice banana into 1/2-inch (1 cm) slices.
2. Combine banana, chocolate pudding, raspberries, and blueberries in mixing bowl; mix thoroughly.
3. Distribute into serving bowls and top with chopped walnuts.
4. Serve.

kitchen tip
Do not wash any of your berries until ready to use. They will stay fresher longer and avoid the buildup of mould.

health tip
Impress your guests by layering this dessert with colourful berries in a martini glass. Top with a fresh mint leaf for an elegant look.

🍓🍓 Enjoy once a week!

makes: 4 servings (1/2 cup/125 mL each)
preparation time: 10 min
total time: 10 min

per serving (1/2 cup/125 mL): calories 118, protein 2 g, total fat 5 g, saturated fat 0.5 g, carbohydrates 18 g, fibre 2 g, sodium 42 mg, cholesterol 0 mg

homemade banana ice cream

Ice cream doesn't have to be filled with tons of saturated fat and calories. This homemade banana ice cream is lower in calories and will satisfy any sweet tooth naturally.

2	medium bananas	2
1/4 cup	soy milk	50 mL
2 tbsp	vanilla yogurt	25 mL
2 tbsp	crushed walnuts	25 mL
2 tbsp	chocolate sauce	25 mL

1. Cut bananas into 1-inch (2.5 cm) slices.
2. Place on plate and freeze for 1 1/2 hours.
3. Remove from freezer and empty into food processor or mixing bowl.
4. Add soy milk and vanilla yogurt.
5. In food processor or with an electric hand blender, blend until fully mixed (mixture will have the consistency of ice cream).
6. Distribute evenly between 2 serving bowls.
7. Top each bowl with 1 tbsp (15 mL) of crushed walnuts.
8. Drizzle with chocolate sauce and serve.

health tip
For an extra antioxidant boost, sprinkle cocoa powder over the ice cream. Cocoa powder contains a higher level of total antioxidant capacity (TAC) than any other chocolate product.

🍓🍓 Enjoy once a week!

makes: 2 servings
preparation time: 5 min
freezing time: 1 hr 30 min
total time: 1 hr 35 min

per serving (1/2 cup/125 mL): calories 234, protein 4 g, total fat 6 g, saturated fat 0.5 g, carbohydrates 44 g, fibre 3.5 g, sodium 36 mg, cholesterol 1 mg

baked stuffed apples

Looking for a healthy yet decadent dessert or snack to warm you up on a cool autumn evening? These hearty stuffed baked apples will give you the warmth and sweet taste you're craving without too many excess calories.

1/3 cup	brown rice	75 mL
1/3 cup	chopped walnuts	75 mL
1/4 cup	raisins	50 mL
2 tbsp	brown sugar	25 mL
1 tsp	cinnamon	5 mL
4	large McIntosh apples	4
1/2 cup	orange juice	125 mL

1. Combine brown rice with 3/4 cup (175 mL) water. Bring to a boil, cover with tight-fitting lid, and reduce heat to simmer. Cook for 45 minutes. Remove lid and fluff with a fork. It will yield 1 cup (250 mL) cooked.
2. Empty rice into mixing bowl.
3. Stir in walnuts, raisins, brown sugar, and cinnamon, mixing thoroughly.
4. Remove the core from each of the apples. Remove enough to leave a hole of approximately 1 1/4 inches (3 cm).
5. Place apples in nonstick baking dish.
6. Fill apples with mixture.
7. Pour orange juice over top of each apple filling, distributing evenly.
8. Place 1/2 cup (125 mL) of water in bottom of pan.
9. Cover tightly with foil.
10. Bake at 350°F (180°F) for 35 minutes.
11. Allow to cool slightly prior to serving.

kitchen tip
When coring an apple, you can use a knife or an apple corer to remove the seeds and inner core. If using a knife, choose one with a rounded edge rather than a pointed one.

health tip

A study published in the *Journal of Medicinal Food* reported that drinking 12 oz
(355 mL) of apple juice or eating 2 apples a day can benefit the heart. The study
showed that daily consumption of apples or apple juice over a period of six weeks
benefited cholesterol levels in a group of 25 healthy men and women.

🍓 Save for an occasional treat!

makes: 4 servings
preparation time: 15 min
cooking time: 1 hr 20 min
total time: 1 hr 35 min

per serving (1 stuffed apple): calories 303, protein 3.6 g, total fat 7 g, saturated fat 0.5 g, carbohydrates
61 g, fibre 7 g, sodium 8 mg, cholesterol 0 mg

healthy fruit sundae

As a dessert or a mid-afternoon treat for the kids, this creamy sundae always leaves people feeling as though they've indulged.

1	medium banana	1
6 tbsp	vanilla yogurt	90 mL
4 tbsp	sliced strawberries	60 mL
3 tbsp	finely chopped pineapple	50 mL
3 tbsp	fresh blueberries	50 mL
2 tbsp	finely chopped walnuts	25 mL
2 tbsp	chocolate sauce	25 mL

1. Slice banana in half.
2. Place banana slices in 2 separate serving dishes.
3. Top each banana slice with yogurt, strawberries, pineapple, blueberries, and walnuts.
4. Drizzle with chocolate sauce.

health tip
When selecting yogurt, ensure that it has no more than 200 calories per serving. Keep in mind that yogurt is made from milk (1 cup/250 mL of fat-free milk has 86 calories). Any additional ingredient in the yogurt should not add more than 100 calories or so. Do not purchase yogurts that contain high fructose corn syrup—they are a one-way ticket to weight gain!

Enjoy once a week!

makes: 2 servings
preparation time: 10 min
freezing time (if desired): 30 min
total time: 10 min

per serving: calories 221, protein 4.4 g, total fat 6 g, saturated fat 1 g, carbohydrates 40 g, fibre 3 g, sodium 39 mg, cholesterol 4 mg

whole wheat sesame, apple, and chocolate chip cookies

These are a huge hit with my four-year-old and are a healthier cookie option to keep on hand. As a special sweet treat, I add 1/4 cup (50 mL) of mini dark chocolate chips to the recipe.

1 1/4 cups	rolled oats	300 mL
3/4 cup	all-purpose flour	175 mL
3/4 cup	whole wheat flour	175 mL
1/4 cup	sesame seeds	50 mL
1/4 cup	cane sugar	50 mL
1 1/2 tsp	baking powder	7 mL
1 1/2 tsp	cinnamon	7 mL
1/4 tsp	salt	1 mL
1 cup	finely chopped McIntosh apples	250 mL
1/3 cup	skim or soy milk	75 mL
1/2 cup	honey	125 mL
1/2 cup	canola oil	125 mL
1	omega-3 egg	1

1. In a large bowl, combine oats, all-purpose flour, whole wheat flour, sesame seeds, cane sugar, baking powder, cinnamon, and salt.
2. Stir in apples.
3. In a medium-sized bowl, whisk together milk, honey, oil, and egg. Add to dry ingredients and stir thoroughly.
4. Drop by spoonfuls onto ungreased baking sheet.
5. Bake at 375°F (190°F) for 10 to 12 minutes or until lightly browned.
6. Allow to cool and enjoy.

baking tip
When baking, it's best to plan ahead and ensure that you have all ingredients. This will save having to run to the store halfway through the process to pick up that one missing ingredient.

health tip

Prior to packing the cookies as a healthy treat in your child's lunchbox, ensure that no children in the classroom have a sesame allergy.

🍓 Save for an occasional treat!

makes: 3 dozen cookies
preparation time: 10 min
baking time: 10 min
total time: 20 min

per serving (1 cookie): calories 86, protein 1.5 g, total fat 4 g, saturated fat 0.5 g, carbohydrates 12 g, fibre 1 g, sodium 40 mg, cholesterol 6 mg

chocolate raspberry brownie bites

Don't feel guilty about indulging in these bite-sized brownies because the applesauce keeps them moist without the added fat. The chocolaty taste is accented with a hint of raspberry. They freeze well and are great for take-along snacks or for a dessert tray.

1 tbsp	butter	15 mL
2 oz	bittersweet chocolate, chopped	56 g
1/2 cup	unsweetened applesauce	125 mL
1/2 cup	seedless raspberry jam	125 mL
1/2 cup	packed brown sugar	125 mL
1	egg	1
1	egg white	1
1 tsp	vanilla	5 mL
3/4 cup	all-purpose flour	175 mL
1/2 cup	chopped California walnuts	125 mL
24	California walnut halves	24

1. In a large glass bowl, melt butter and chocolate in microwave, stirring once, until melted and smooth, about 1 minute.
2. Stir in applesauce, jam, and sugar until well blended.
3. Lightly beat egg with egg white and vanilla. Stir into chocolate mixture. Gently stir in flour and chopped walnuts.
4. Use light cooking spray to grease 24-cup mini muffin pan. Spoon batter into cups, filling to top. Top each brownie with a walnut half.
5. Bake in 350°F (180°C) oven until tester comes out clean, about 10 to 12 minutes. Let cool in pan 5 minutes; transfer to rack and cool completely.

baking tip

Applesauce can be used as a substitute for oils in low-fat baking. However, baking with applesauce does require some experimentation. As a general rule, you need to use half as much applesauce as you would oil. In some cases, you need to retain some oil in the recipe or it won't work out.

health tip

Adding walnuts to your baked goods boosts your daily intake of omega-3 fats, the essential fats necessary for optimal health and wellness. In fact, 1/4 cup of walnuts contains approximately 2.3 g of omega-3—a substantial amount.

🍓 Save for an occasional treat!

makes: 24 servings (0.9 oz/25 g each)
preparation time: 10 min
baking time: 10 min
total time: 20 min

per serving (1 brownie): calories 81, protein 1.3 g, total fat 3 g, saturated fat 0.9 g, carbohydrates 13 g, fibre 0.5 g, sodium 14 mg, cholesterol 9 mg

Source: www.walnutinfo.com

frozen lemon berry torte

Made with high-antioxidant raspberries and whole grain bread, this summertime recipe is a light, delicious, and calorie-wise treat. Your guests will love the naturally sweet and decadent taste.

1	package (12 oz/300 g) frozen mixed berries	1
1/3 cup	Cointreau or berry juice	75 mL
2 tbsp	sugar	25 mL
8	slices of whole grain bread, crusts removed	8
2 cups	lemon (or vanilla) frozen yogurt, softened	500 mL
	Fresh berries for garnish	

1. Arrange plastic wrap in a 6-inch (15 cm) springform pan to cover bottom and sides. Set aside.
2. In bowl, toss frozen berries with Cointreau and sugar. Let sit at room temperature for 1 hour and up to 4 hours until thawed.
3. Pour berries into a colander or drain over a large measuring cup. Top up liquid with water to make 1 cup (250 mL).
4. Dip bread slices, one at a time, into berry liquid and arrange slices to fit into the bottom of springform pan, breaking pieces if necessary.
5. Top with half of the berries and half of the frozen yogurt. Repeat layers, smoothing top with a spatula.
6. Put into freezer until completely frozen, about 8 hours. Remove pan and plastic from torte and arrange on a cake stand. Garnish with fresh berries.

kitchen tip

To soften frozen yogurt, place in refrigerator for 30 minutes before using. If lemon-flavoured frozen yogurt isn't available, stir 2 tbsp (25 mL) lemon juice and 1 tbsp (15 mL) lemon zest into softened vanilla frozen yogurt.

health tip

Cointreau is a liqueur made of different types of orange skins that are soaked in alcohol. For an alcohol-free version of this recipe, use any type of berry juice, such as raspberry, blueberry, or strawberry.

🍓🍓🍓 Super skinny!

makes: 10 servings
preparation time: 10 min; however, frozen berries may need to thaw for up to 4 hr
freezer time: 8 hr (should be made the day before)

per serving: calories 62, protein 2.5 g, total fat 0.7 g, saturated fat 0.5 g, carbohydrates 10 g, fibre 1 g, sodium 46 mg, cholesterol 4 mg

Source: www.stonemillbakehouse.com

sweet baked pears

The waft of fresh baked pears will have your home smelling like a decadent bakery. Low in fat and rich in natural sweetness, these spice-scented baked pears are a guilt-free pleasure.

4	firm ripe pears (Bosc are best)	4
1/2 cup	orange juice	125 mL
2 tsp	brown sugar	10 mL
1/2 tsp	cinnamon	2 mL
4 tbsp	chopped walnuts	60 mL
2 tsp	chocolate sauce	10 mL

1. Peel pears and cut in half. Remove core and seeds.
2. Place in Pyrex baking dish, core side up, and baste with orange juice.
3. Sprinkle with brown sugar and cinnamon.
4. Cover and bake at 375°F (190°C) for 45 minutes.
5. Remove cover and baste pears with juices in baking dish .
6. Sprinkle chopped walnuts over top and continue to bake for 10 minutes.
7. Remove and place in serving dishes.
8. Drizzle with chocolate sauce.
9. Serve.

health tip

Did you know that pears actually have more pectin (fibre) than apples? This makes pears one of the best fruits when it comes to lowering cholesterol levels and keeping the digestive system in tip-top shape!

♡♡ Enjoy once a week!

makes: 4 servings
preparation time: 15 min
cooking time: 55 min
total time: 1 hr 10 min

per serving: calories 181, protein 2 g, total fat 5 g, saturated fat 0.5 g, carbohydrates 36 g, fibre 6 g, sodium 4 mg, cholesterol 0 mg

dairy-free chocolate banana mousse

For those who love the creamy taste of dairy but need to follow a dairy-free diet because of a sensitivity or allergy, this decadent dessert is for you.

3/4 cup	dairy-free semi-sweet chocolate chips	175 mL
1 1/2 cups	silken tofu	375 mL
2	medium bananas	2
2 tbsp	brown sugar	25 mL
1 tsp	vanilla	5 mL
1 tsp	raspberry vinegar	5 mL
1/4 tsp	salt	1 mL
1/4 cup	raspberries	50 mL

1. Melt chocolate chips in double broiler. Set aside.
2. Purée tofu and bananas in blender.
3. Add brown sugar, vanilla, raspberry vinegar, and salt; purée again.
4. Add melted chocolate; purée.
5. Chill for 2 hours or until set.
6. Garnish with raspberries and enjoy!

kitchen tip

Silken tofu (also called soft, silk, or Japanese-style tofu) has a softer consistency than regular tofu and will fall apart if not handled carefully. Silken tofu offers a creamy, custard-like texture and is suitable to use in desserts, shakes, salad dressings, sauces, and soups.

health tip

A 4-oz (113 g) serving of tofu contains just 6 g of fat and contains no cholesterol. As a general rule, the softer the tofu, the lower the fat content. Some nutritional highlights of tofu include:

NUTRIENTS IN 4 OZ (113 G) OF:	TOFU, FIRM	TOFU, SOFT
Calories	79	69
Protein (g)	9.25	7.4
Carbohydrate (g)	1.91	2.03
Fat (g)	4.71	4.17
Saturated Fat (g)	.975	.602
Cholesterol	0	0
Sodium (mg)	14	9
Fibre (g)	1	0.2
Calcium (mg)	227	125
Iron (mg)	1.82	1.25

Save for an occasional treat!

makes: 6 servings
preparation time: 15 min
setting time: 2 hr
total time: 2 hr 15 min

per serving: calories 208, protein 3 g, fat 8.5 g, saturated fat 5 g, carbohydrates 29 g, fibre 0.6 g, sodium 108 mg, cholesterol 0 mg

acknowledgments

Healthy Sin Foods was a project that involved the collaboration of a lot of different hands. To start, a big thank you to Andrea Magyar and the entire Penguin team for their dedicated efforts and ongoing support. A special thank you also goes to Heather Sangster for her terrific editing.

A heartfelt thank you to the best group ever at Shulman Weight Loss Clinic. A shout-out to Doris and Jamie—two rising stars in the nutritional world. To my office manager and right-hand woman, Linda Gallacher, a sincere thanks for all that you do. You make work and play feel like the same thing.

To Jill Hillhouse, for her diligent research and for being such a delight to work with. To the nutrition team who performed the recipe analysis for all the recipes in the book: Leonard A. Piché, PhD RD, full professor (project supervisor), and Kimberly L. Zammit, senior foods and nutrition student, Division of Food and Nutritional Sciences, Brescia University College, University of Western Ontario, London, Ontario. Recipe analysis was performed with the Food Processor SQL Version 10.3 (includes more than 5000 food items from the 2007b version of the Canadian Nutrient File), ESHA Research Inc., Salem, Oregon.

Of course, to my entire "clan" of family and friends—I am truly blessed to have all of you in my life. A special mention to my parents, for their ongoing love and support that is priceless.

This book would never have reached completion without the creative talent of my husband, Randy. As the best cook I know, his dedication to creating healthy and delicious recipes was tireless. As a husband, you are my one true *besheret*, whom I quietly say thank you for each and every day. To the moon and back again forever.

To the other man in my life, Jonah (the bear)—you show Daddy and me all the colours in the rainbow and have a joie de vivre I relish watching. We love you so much.

To the new addition to our family—Faith Ella. I am sure you must have met Bubbi Elsie on the way. We waited a long time to finally meet you, and now we can say she's here, she is finally here! And now … we are complete.

product resource guide

Foods

Stonemill Bakehouse

Stonemill Bakehouse offers a variety of top-quality breads and bagels with various health benefits. Visit www.stonemillbakehouse.com for more information.

Sprouted Grains
The sprouted grain family of breads contains all-natural ingredients and is free of artificial additives and preservatives. These delicious breads are also a source of fibre and iron without the added soy, dairy, sugar, or fat found in other breads.

- 12 Grain Rye Bread—made with freshly sprouted whole grain, added oat bran fibre, and ancient grains
- 3 Grain & Oatmeal Bread—low glycemic index tested!
- Milled Flax Bagel—a heart-healthy bagel made with freshly milled flax and low in sodium

Omega-3 Breads and Bagels
Omega-3 essential fats support heart health along with numerous other health benefits. Flaxseed and walnuts are both sources of omega-3 fats. These breads are also a source of fibre and iron and are free of artificial additives and preservatives and added soy, dairy, sugar, and fat.

- Golden Flax Bread—free of saturated fat and trans fats
- Sunflower & Walnut Bread—walnuts and sunflower seeds provide a rich source of omega-3 fat
- Swiss Muesli Bagel—made with whole and ground flaxseeds

Heart Health Breads and Bagel

These naturally delicious breads are sweetened with high-antioxidant raisin juice. They are both low in sodium and a source of fibre and iron.

- Flax & Fibre Bread—sprouted grains, freshly milled flax, and low sodium
- Milled Flax Bagel—all-natural ingredients and low in sodium

Yves Veggie Cuisine

Yves products range from barbecue items, such as skewers and dogs, to more home-style meals, such as meatless ground and deli slices. All of Yves products are meatless and boast fewer calories, lower cholesterol, less fat, and more protein than their meat counterparts. For more information, visit www.yvesveggie.com

Imagine Soups

Imagine Soups offers more than 20 varieties of packaged and resealable soups loaded with organic vegetables. For those following a heart-healthy diet, low-sodium broths are available. Visit www.imaginesoup.ca for more information.

California Walnut Commission

California walnuts taste great and add texture and essential nutrients to cooking. Walnuts are the only nut with a significant amount of omega-3 fatty acids. For more health information and walnut recipes, visit www.walnutinfo.com or call 1-800-743-6282.

Supplements and Protein Powders

Genuine Health

www.genuinehealth.com
Phone: (416) 977-8765
Toll Free: 1-877-500-7888

1. **Protein powder:** *proteins+* contains superior alpha+™ whey protein isolate, digestive enzymes, and no artificial ingredients. The protein powder is low in calories, fat, and carbohydrates and is available in natural vanilla or chocolate

flavour. Also available: *Vegan proteins+ and proteins+ Instant Smoothie a day* in a natural orange cream flavour.

2. **Multivitamins:** *multi+ complete* provides all of your daily vitamin and mineral requirements with no artificial fillers or ingredients. This food-based, high-potency multivitamin/mineral contains 50 mg of each of the B vitamins, 400 IU of vitamins D and E, and 500 mg of calcium and vitamin C.

3. **Fish oils:** *o3mega* offers a line of the highest-quality distilled fish oils according to your health desire (skin, heart, mood, general health and wellness, etc.). The cleanliness and quality of the *o3mega* line is put through rigorous testing to ensure that you are absorbing the highest-quality oil available. This wild, pure fish oil has a unique delivery system (idSystem™), which is enteric-coated soft gels, to ensure maximum absorption and no fishy repeat. Also available in liquid format.

4. **greens+:** A superfood formula that has a synergistic blend of more than 23 plant-based essential nutrients. Highly alkaline forming and rich in antioxidants, *greens+* helps to nourish and protect the body, increases energy, and promotes healthier bones. Available in original, mixed berry, tangerine, and watermelon flavour.

5. **healthy skin chocolate soft chews:** These delicious chews (only 90 calories each) combine the powerful skin-restoring ingredients of theobroma cacao and hydrolyzed collagen (marine-based) for gorgeous overall skin health. Benefits include increased skin hydration and moisture, improved elasticity, and decreased dryness. Overall, a visibly more radiant appearance!

Websites

www.gourmetsleuth.com
www.calorieking.com
www.nutritiondata.com

For Dr. Joey Shulman's free newsletter filled with recipes and articles, please visit www.drjoey.com.

references

chapter 1: back to the basics

Stein, C.J. and G.A. Colditz. "Modifiable risk factors for cancer." *British Journal of Cancer* January 26, 2004; 90(2):299–303.

Young, R.W. and J.S. Beregi Jr. "Use of chlorophyll in the care of geriatric patients." *Journal of the American Geriatrics Society* 1980; 28:46–47.

chapter 2: crazy for carbs

Rozin, P. "The ecology of eating: Smaller portion sizes in France than in the United States help explain the French Paradox." *Psychological Science* September 2003; 14(5):450.

http://lowcarbdiets.about.com/od/nutrition/a/oligosaccharide.htm

www.hc-sc.gc.ca/fn-an/nutrition/whole-grain-entiers-eng.php

chapter 3: powerful proteins

Johnston, Carol S., Sherrie L. Tjonn, and Pamela D. Swan. "High-protein, low-fat diets are effective for weight loss and favorably alter biomarkers in healthy adults." American Society for Nutritional Sciences *Journal of Nutrition* March 2004; 134:586–591.

chapter 4: fabulous fats

Alam, K., et al. "Cinnamon improves glucose and lipids of people with type 2 diabetes." *Diabetes Care* 2003; 26:3215–3218.

Institute of Medicine, National Academies of Sciences. *Dietary Reference Intakes for Energy, Carbohydrates, Fibre, Fat, Protein and Amino Acids.* Washington, D.C.: National Academies Press, 2002.

Leaf, A. "Prevention of sudden cardiac death by n-3 polyunsaturated fatty acids." *Journal of Cardiovascular Medicine* 2007; 8 Suppl 1:S27–29.

Purba, M., et al. "Skin wrinkling: Can food make a difference?" *Journal of the American College of Nutrition* 2001; 20(1):71–80.

101 *healthy sin foods* recipes

American Journal of Preventative Medicine 2007; 32:147–150 and 32:257–263.

Katcher, Heather I. et al. "The effects of a whole grain–enriched hypocaloric diet on cardiovascular disease risk factors in men and women with metabolic syndrome." *American Journal of Clinical Nutrition* January 2008; 87(1):79–90.

Piers, L.S., K.Z. Walker, R.M. Stoney, M.J. Soares, and K. O'Dea. "Substitution of saturated with monounsaturated fat in a 4-week diet affects body weight and composition of overweight and obese men." *British Journal of Nutrition* September 2003; 90(3):717–727.

www.stonemillbakehouse.com

www.walnutinfo.com

index

guacamole and pepper dip, 251

horseradish hummus, 252

sweet mango and pear salsa, 250

dressings and vinaigrettes (recipes)

    creamy dill salad dressing, 264

    ginger and mandarin orange salad
dressing, 261

    homemade raspberry vinaigrette, 260

    mixed-herb red wine vinaigrette, 262

    orange sesame salad dressing, 265

    spicy mango mint salad dressing, 263

E

edamame, 135–136

eggs, 64–65, 137–138

ellagic acid, 178

endosperm, 36

energy, 15–16

enriched white flour, 36

entrees (recipes)

    beef tenderloin stack, 347–348

    black-eyed peas and walnut lettuce wraps,
349–350

    blackened tilapia on greens, 320–321

    buttery pesto chicken with brown rice,
345–346

    Cajun blackened chicken breast, 329–330

    California walnut-stuffed salmon,
318–319

    chicken breast stuffed with asparagus,
325–326

    creamy lasagna, 331–333

    crustless mushroom and broccoli quiche,
340–341

    dill-crusted wild salmon fillets, 316–317

    healthy sloppy joe, 351–352

    hearty cabbage rolls, 336–337

    hearty turkey chili, 327–328

    orange and ginger chicken scallops,
323–324

    portobello mushroom stir-fry, 334–335

    sautéed chicken in creamy mushroom
sauce, 322

    smoked salmon fettuccine, 344

    vegetarian sweet potato pot pie, 342–343

    whole grain pad Thai, 338–339

EPA (eicosapentaenoic acid), 61, 67, 105, 202

essential fatty acids, 60, 61, 66–69

estimating portions, 87

excuses, 3–4

exercise, 18, 21

F

fat-free foods, 65

fat-soluble vitamins, 61

fats

    "bad" fats, 69–72

    cholesterol, 72–73

    daily requirements, 73–75

    fat myths, 62–65

    "good" fats, 65–69

    role of, 59–62

fibre, 17, 44–45, 126, 170, 189

fish oils, 18

flavonoids, 97, 107, 168, 191

flaxseed, 17, 139–140

folate, 102, 103, 184, 191

food journal, 80

food labels, 83–86

food substitutions, 83

free range chicken, 123–125

fruits, 39–40, 40

fuel for the body, 21–22

fungicides, 39–40